To:

From:

DAILY WISDOM
for Women

2026
DEVOTIONAL COLLECTION

BARBOUR
PUBLISHING

© 2025 by Barbour Publishing, Inc.

Print ISBN 979-8-89151-128-6

Adobe Digital Edition (.epub) 979-8-89151-129-3

All rights reserved. No part of this publication may be reproduced or transmitted for commercial purposes, except for brief quotations in printed reviews, without written permission of the publisher. Reproduced text may not be used on the World Wide Web. No Barbour Publishing content may be used as artificial intelligence training data for machine learning, or in any similar software development.

Churches and other noncommercial interests may reproduce portions of this book without the express written permission of Barbour Publishing, provided that the text does not exceed 500 words or 5 percent of the entire book, whichever is less, and that the text is not material quoted from another publisher. When reproducing text from this book, include the following credit line: "From *Daily Wisdom for Women 2026 Devotional Collection*, published by Barbour Publishing, Inc. Used by permission."

Scripture quotations marked skjv are taken from the Barbour Simplified KJV™ Bible, copyright © 2022, 2025 by Barbour Publishing, Inc., Uhrichsville, Ohio 44683. All rights reserved.

Scripture quotations marked niv are taken from THE HOLY BIBLE, NEW INTERNATIONAL VERSION®. NIV®. Copyright © 1973, 1978, 1984, 2011 by Biblica, Inc.® Used by permission. All rights reserved worldwide.

Scripture quotations marked msg are taken from *THE MESSAGE*, copyright © 1993, 2002, 2018 by Eugene H. Peterson. Used by permission of NavPress. All rights reserved. Represented by Tyndale House Publishers, Inc.

Scripture quotations marked nlt are taken from the *Holy Bible*, New Living Translation copyright © 1996, 2004, 2015 by Tyndale House Foundation. Used by permission of Tyndale House Publishers, Inc., Carol Stream, Illinois 60188. All rights reserved.

Scripture quotations marked ampc are taken from the Amplified® Bible, Classic Edition, Copyright © 1954, 1958, 1962, 1964, 1965, 1987 by The Lockman Foundation. Used by permission.

Scripture quotations marked voice are taken from The Voice™. Copyright © 2008 by Ecclesia Bible Society. Used by permission. All rights reserved.

Scripture quotations marked esv are from The ESV® Bible (The Holy Bible, English Standard Version®). ESV® Text Edition: 2016. Copyright © 2001 by Crossway, a publishing ministry of Good News Publishers. The ESV® text has been reproduced in cooperation with and by permission of Good News Publishers. Unauthorized reproduction of this publication is prohibited. All rights reserved.

Scripture quotations marked nlv are taken from the New Life™ Version, copyright © 1969 and 2003 by Barbour Publishing, Inc., Uhrichsville, Ohio 44683. All rights reserved.

Scripture quotations marked tlb are taken from The Living Bible copyright © 1971 by Tyndale House Foundation. Used by permission of Tyndale House Publishers Inc., Carol Stream, Illinois 60188. All rights reserved. The Living Bible, TLB, and the The Living Bible logo are registered trademarks of Tyndale House Publishers.

Scripture quotations marked nasb are taken from the New American Standard Bible®, Copyright © 1960, 1971, 1977, 1995, 2020 by The Lockman Foundation. All rights reserved.

Cover image © Greg Jackson, Thinkpen Design

Published by Barbour Publishing, Inc., 1810 Barbour Drive, Uhrichsville, Ohio 44683, www.barbourbooks.com

Our mission is to inspire the world with the life-changing message of the Bible.

Member of the
Evangelical Christian
Publishers Association

Printed in China.

Introduction

Our minds are often consumed with many cares and concerns of this life. But above them all, our faith in Jesus Christ is what matters most. Accepting Jesus as Savior and choosing to love and live for Him reveals our identity in Christ. In Him, we are accepted, forgiven, and redeemed through His work on the cross to save us from our sin. We are celebrated and deeply loved. We hold immeasurable value in our heavenly Father's eyes. And not only do we find our true identity in Christ, we also find our every need met in Him.

So, what role is faith playing in your life right now? Are you standing strong in your identity as a child of God, or are you letting the world define you? Are you deepening your relationship through time in the Word and in prayer, or are your priorities upside-down? What if you recommit your heart to Him today—and then watch how that blesses you? Make reading the Bible, *seeking God's wisdom daily*, part of your norm. Let Him guide you and keep you on His good paths and within His perfect plans for your life.

Trust in the Lord with all your heart; do not depend on your own understanding. Seek his will in all you do, and he will show you which path to take.
PROVERBS 3:5–6 NLT

JANUARY 2026

SUNDAY	MONDAY	TUESDAY	WEDNESDAY	THURSDAY	FRIDAY	SATURDAY
				1 New Year's Day	2	3
4	5	6	7	8	9	10
11	12	13	14	15	16	17
18	19 Martin Luther King Jr. Day	20	21	22	23	24
25	26	27	28	29	30	31

New Year's Day   THURSDAY, JANUARY 1

*Genesis 1–2 / Matthew 1 / Psalm 1

Creation Caretaker

At the time GOD made Earth and Heaven, before any grasses or shrubs had sprouted from the ground—GOD hadn't yet sent rain on Earth, nor was there anyone around to work the ground. . . GOD formed Man out of dirt from the ground and blew into his nostrils the breath of life. The Man came alive—a living soul!

GENESIS 2:5, 7 MSG

At first glance, Genesis 2:5, 7 explains that God created man from the dust of the earth. But if we look deeper, we notice something else: These verses are quite significant to our identity in Christ because they set the stage for humanity. They point—at least in part—to an element of our purpose.

At this moment in the creation story, God had yet to send rain. Plants and grass had not made their appearance. "Nor was there anyone around to work the ground." Something *very important* was missing—"a living soul!" Man had not set foot in the garden of Eden. . .there were no apple orchards or tomato plants or rows of corn. God knew He needed a creation caretaker first (verse 15).

If you ever have a day when you doubt your purpose, these words from Genesis will reassure your heart. You—along with every other person on the planet—were designed to care for all of God's creation.

Heavenly Creator, thank You for entrusting me with the care of Your creation. I will do my best to nurture it!

---

*This devotional follows a yearlong Bible reading plan that corresponds with each day. If you choose to complete these readings, at the end of the year, you will have read God's Word from cover to cover!

FRIDAY, JANUARY 2

Genesis 3–4 / Matthew 2 / Psalm 2

Sinner Saved by Grace

The Woman said to the serpent, ". . .We can eat from the trees in the garden. It's only about the tree in the middle of the garden that God said, 'Don't eat from it; don't even touch it or you'll die.'" The serpent told the Woman, "You won't die. God knows that the moment you eat from that tree, . . .you'll be just like God, knowing everything."

GENESIS 3:2–5 MSG

This is one suspenseful account from God's Word, isn't it?

Man and woman spend leisurely days in a perfect garden paradise. Enter deceitful serpent, who convinces woman to eat the forbidden fruit. She has a nibble, then shares it with man, who takes a big, juicy bite.

What happens to this couple? Do they gain the knowledge the serpent had promised? Not quite! Adam and Eve suffer tragic consequences for their disobedience to God—life becomes difficult, and eventually they both die.

But. . . Hope follows. God sends His Son, Jesus, to earth, where He pays the ultimate price for our sins: death on the cross. When we accept Jesus' sacrificial gift, we receive eternal life in heaven. Death is never permanent for those who say yes to Jesus (John 3:16).

How about you? Has hope followed the hardship in your life? Are you a sinner saved by grace?

Jesus, my Savior, thank You. Because of Your bold sacrifice, I will spend eternity in heaven.

SATURDAY, JANUARY 3

Genesis 5–7 / Matthew 3 / Psalm 3

Through-the-Roof Confidence

Right to my face [my adversaries] say, "God will not save you!"...
But You, Eternal One, wrap around me like an impenetrable shield.
You give me glory and lift my eyes up to the heavens. I lift my voice
to You, Eternal One, and You answer me from Your sacred heights.
PSALM 3:2–4 VOICE

On a scale of 1 to 10, how would you rate your confidence? Is it a measly 1—you're not feeling it? A 5—just so-so? A whopping 10—*nothing* and *no one* could cause you to doubt? If we're honest, it's probably hovering somewhere well below a 10 for most of us.

What would you give to have the confidence level of David here in Psalm 3? Talk about *through-the-roof* confidence!

David expresses his complaint to God: "Right to my face [my adversaries] say, 'God will not save you!'" David was likely battling voices in his own mind too—and the additional negativity coming from his enemies only made things worse. He was overwhelmed!

However, something changes—a shift takes place—and David springs from doubt to absolute certainty because he trusts the Eternal One. David knows he is protected, his prayers are answered, he is healthy and strong. . .he doesn't need to be afraid! The same goes for you, friend!

Eternal One, because I am Yours, my confidence
should be at an all-time high. Whenever I begin to doubt,
remind me of Your unfailing protection and provision.

SUNDAY, JANUARY 4

Genesis 8–10 / Matthew 4 / Psalm 4

Incredible Healing Power

Jesus traveled throughout the region of Galilee, teaching in the synagogues and announcing the Good News about the Kingdom. And he healed every kind of disease and illness. News about him spread as far as Syria, and people soon began bringing to him all who were sick. And whatever their sickness or disease, or if they were demon possessed or epileptic or paralyzed—he healed them all.

MATTHEW 4:23–24 NLT

Jesus traveled and taught the good news. In His travels, He frequently healed those who had physical and mental illness and disabilities: "Whatever their sickness or disease, or if they were demon possessed or epileptic or paralyzed—he healed them all." Can you imagine having a window into the past to see His healing miracles firsthand? Faith would just bubble up inside, wouldn't it?

We don't often think about it, but the King of kings and Lord of lords heals even today! And though He isn't physically present to do the healing, He is still here with us, wrapping us in His restorative embrace.

Do you need healing, dear one? If so, ask God to remind you of His power, His love, His ability to cure every illness. Ask Him for a miracle. Then leave your request in His healing hands. Trust Him to see you through. Believe that He will restore, refresh, repair. What a beautiful blessing to have access to the incredible healing power of our heavenly Father!

Father, pull me into Your restorative embrace.

MONDAY, JANUARY 5

Genesis 11–13 / Matthew 5:1–20 / Psalm 5

Yes = Blessed!

"God blesses those who are poor and realize their need for him, for the Kingdom of Heaven is theirs. God blesses those who mourn, for they will be comforted. God blesses those who are humble, for they will inherit the whole earth. God blesses those who hunger and thirst for justice, for they will be satisfied. . . . God blesses those who are persecuted for doing right, for the Kingdom of Heaven is theirs."

MATTHEW 5:3–6, 10 NLT

If you're a Christ follower, when did you first realize you needed Him? When did it occur to you that you didn't want to—just *couldn't*—live without Him?

When we choose to follow Jesus, we're often at our lowest low. . .and something stirs deep within our souls. That's when God nudges our hearts toward Him. And though we may come to Him from a place of hardship or desperation, He loves us without limits! His blessings are many, and they come in all forms:

When we grieve, He comforts.
When we hunger and thirst, He satisfies.
When we are persecuted for doing right, He promises us the kingdom of heaven.

Where and when have you experienced God's blessings in your life? Grab your journal and write it all down. Read it often. Praise the blessings giver!

> *Father God, I'm so glad I said yes to You. You are the leader of my life, and that comes with abundant benefits and blessings. Thank You for saving me!*

TUESDAY, JANUARY 6

Genesis 14–16 / Matthew 5:21–48 / Psalm 6

"Set-Right-with-God"

Abram said, "God. . .what use are your gifts as long as I'm childless and Eliezer of Damascus is going to inherit everything?" . . . Then God's Message came: "Don't worry. . . a son from your body will be your heir." Then he took him outside and said, "Look at the sky. Count the stars. . . . Count your descendants! You're going to have a big family, Abram!" And he believed! . . . God declared him "Set-Right-with-God."
GENESIS 15:2, 4–6 MSG

You believe God keeps His promises—*but* have you ever felt like He's forgotten about you? You've received many of His blessings, but there's that *one thing*. . . And it doesn't seem like God will come through. No matter how hard you pray, He doesn't seem to be listening.

This is how Abram must have felt when he expressed his discontent to God. His words were bold: "What good are all Your gifts, when I don't have a son to inherit it all?" Abram asked the hard question—and God answered! Not only did God assure Abram of His promise, but He went deeper, confirming it with an illustration: "Look at the stars. You'll have as many descendants!" Abram believed. And God declared him "Set-Right-with-God."

As a daughter of the Most High, you can be "Set-Right-with-God" too! Share the desires of your heart. . .*then* express your belief! Wait for God to move. He hasn't forgotten you!

Heavenly Father, I trust You to make good on Your promises.

WEDNESDAY, JANUARY 7

Genesis 17–18 / Matthew 6:1–18 / Psalm 7

Noticed

> *"When you give to the needy, do not announce it with trumpets...to be honored by others.... But when you give to the needy, do not let your left hand know what your right hand is doing, so that your giving may be in secret. Then your Father, who sees...will reward you."*
> MATTHEW 6:2–4 NIV

When we do good things for others, we often have a little voice in our heads (sidenote: That little voice is pride!) that tells us others will be impressed. So, when we give to the poor...or write a large check at church...or donate in abundance to the community food drive, we're secretly hoping *someone* will notice, that someone will be astounded by our generosity, that someone will ooh and aah over how charitable we are.

When we say it out loud, it feels pretty icky, doesn't it? But honestly, it's kind of a letdown if we complete some grand gesture of giving and no one notices...am I right?

Even if no human being ever acknowledges your generosity and kind heart, there is someone who does—it's Jesus (He doesn't miss a thing!). So do your giving and praying and serving in secret. The Lord sees, and His rewards are better than any earthly praise you could ever receive!

> *Lord, I'm sorry for seeking human recognition. Remind me that all the good I do in secret is noticed by You—and nothing else matters.*

THURSDAY, JANUARY 8

Genesis 19–20 / Matthew 6:19–34 / Psalm 8

Faithful Living

Do not consume yourselves with questions: What will we eat? What will we drink? What will we wear? Outsiders make themselves frantic over such questions; they don't realize that your heavenly Father knows exactly what you need. Seek first the kingdom of God and His righteousness, and then all these things will be given to you too. So do not worry about tomorrow. Let tomorrow worry about itself. Living faithfully is a large enough task for today.
MATTHEW 6:31–34 VOICE

Do you practice faithful living?
If you're not sure, ask yourself:

- Am I an insider in God's kingdom?
- Do I belong to Him? Is my identity in Him?
- Do I rely on the heavenly Father to supply all my needs?
- Do I trust that God will always come through for me?
- Is my eternal home in heaven?

If you answered yes to each of these questions, you're fully equipped to practice faithful living just as God intended. Your "insider" status in God's kingdom allows you to live worry-free 365 days a year. You name it, you can trust God to provide it! *That* is authentic, faithful living.

What a beautiful promise you can claim when your identity lies in Christ. . .when you "seek first the kingdom of God," His good promises—*all of them*—are yours for the taking!

Father God, it's my heart's desire to practice faithful living every day. Help me. . .guide me. . .to always seek You first.

FRIDAY, JANUARY 9

Genesis 21–23 / Matthew 7:1–11 / Psalm 9:1–8

Look Up

I can't bear to watch my child die. As [Hagar] sat there, she cried loudly. . . . A messenger of God [said,] . . . Don't be afraid. God has heard the voice of young Ishmael. Come now. . .take him by the hand. I have plans to make a great nation from his descendants! Then God opened Hagar's eyes. She looked up from her grief and saw a well of water not far away. She. . .gave the young man a drink. God watched over him for the rest of his life.
GENESIS 21:16–20 VOICE

It's difficult to see beyond our grief, isn't it? Whether we're mourning a broken marriage, a dashed dream, the loss of health, or the death of a loved one. . .we get stuck in our sorrow. It's hard to break free from it—without Jesus, that is.

That's where Hagar found herself, locked in grief's tight grip, as she prepared to watch her beloved son die from thirst. But when a heavenly messenger appeared to deliver a promise for her son's future, God opened Hagar's eyes: "She looked up from her grief." She saw a well of water! Her son's life was spared—and God's promise fulfilled!

Are you stuck in a season of grief, dear one? Remember the hope you have as a child of Almighty God. Ask Him to remind you of His enduring promises. He will open your eyes to the beautiful days ahead.

Father God, today I will look up and recognize Your good plans for my future.

SATURDAY, JANUARY 10

Genesis 24 / Matthew 7:12–29 / Psalm 9:9–20

A Safe House for Your Soul

*GOD's a safe-house for the battered, a sanctuary
during bad times. The moment you arrive,
you relax; you're never sorry you knocked.*
PSALM 9:9–10 MSG

If you've ever felt beat up—emotionally and spiritually—you're not alone. Life has a way of knocking us around from time to time, and it's difficult to find our way back to hope and healing. (Some friendly advice? That negative self-talk you default to only makes it worse.)

So, instead of beating yourself up over a past mistake, a failed relationship, an unmet goal, or *whatever* it is that has made you feel "less than," run into the arms of Jesus. Instead of steeping your mind in pessimism, focus on the goodness of your heavenly Father. Instead of listening to the misleading voices of the world, open your heart to the truth of God's Word. The Creator of heaven and earth has got you! You're His, after all: "Know this: GOD is God. . . . He made us. . . . We're his people, his well-tended sheep" (Psalm 100:3 MSG).

In your down-and-out moments, remember that God is your "safe-house," your "sanctuary." The second you enter His holy presence, your heavy burdens become lighter, and your stressed-out spirit can unwind and relax. Rest in Him today.

God, thank You for being my safe place—the one I can always run to for comfort and assurance. I am so thankful that I am Yours!

SUNDAY, JANUARY 11

Genesis 25–26 / Matthew 8:1–17 / Psalm 10:1–11

God Is with You

Isaac moved to Beersheba, where the LORD appeared to him on the night of his arrival. "I am the God of your father, Abraham," he said. "Do not be afraid, for I am with you and will bless you. I will multiply your descendants, and they will become a great nation. I will do this because of my promise to Abraham, my servant." Then Isaac built an altar there and worshiped the LORD.
GENESIS 26:23–25 NLT

What scares you? Spiders? Heights? Clowns? Storms? The dark? Everyone is afraid of something. Whatever it is that makes you quake in your sneakers, it nearly always stems from irrational thoughts and worries. Our fears are rarely rooted in reality or logic.

Fear is a strange emotion because it can get the best of us *even when we know better*. It can overpower our minds and bodies—causing us to freeze in fright. It can easily grow to epic proportions if we're not careful.

So how can you keep fear under control? Simply by remembering that God is with you, and He will bless you. If you trust that God has nothing but the best in mind for you, then what do you have to fear? Not a single thing!

Fear crusher, I am so thankful I get to do life with You as my guide and companion. When fear lurks in my mind, help me to overcome it with Your wonderful promises for my future!

MONDAY, JANUARY 12

> Genesis 27:1–28:9 / Matthew 8:18–34 / Psalm 10:12–18

The Hopes of the Helpless

Lord, you know the hopes of the helpless. Surely you will hear their cries and comfort them. You will bring justice to the orphans and the oppressed, so mere people can no longer terrify them.
PSALM 10:17–18 NLT

Helpless. Overlooked. Unwanted. Insignificant. Rejected. Unloved. These are only a few of the words we could use to describe poor Leah. (You can read her full story in Genesis 29:25, 28, 30–31.)

When Jacob said "I do" on his wedding day, he had no idea that Leah was standing in for her younger sister, Rachel. Rachel was the one Jacob truly loved—the woman Jacob had been promised in exchange for seven years of hard work. Laban, Jacob's father-in-law, had tricked him, and Jacob was furious! So, what did the devious Laban do? A week later, he allowed Jacob to marry Rachel.

As expected, Leah was treated as second best. She was undoubtedly embarrassed and humiliated, jealous and angry. And though she had been placed at the center of a grossly unfair situation, one thing made all the difference in the world: God "saw" Leah (Genesis 29:31). He knew her hopes. He understood her feelings. And, when no one else showed love to her, God did. He blessed Leah with children.

Do you identify with Leah? Call out to the one who knows your hopes.

*Father, thank You for seeing me,
for knowing my hopes, for loving me.*

TUESDAY, JANUARY 13

Genesis 28:10–29:35 / Matthew 9 / Psalm 11

Fully Known

The Eternal has not moved. . . . He sits squarely on His heavenly throne. He observes. . .examining us within and without, exploring every fiber of our beings. The Eternal searches the hearts of those who are good.
PSALM 11:4–5 VOICE

Coffee or tea?
Roses or daisies?
Movies or books?

Who knows *you* best? You probably have a sister, best friend, or mom who knows nearly everything about you. This person knows your likes and dislikes, hopes and dreams, fears and secrets, and everything in between. This kind of understanding and knowledge is built through years of togetherness—spending time talking and sharing. These close relationships are invaluable. But no matter how well another person knows you, she can't possibly know *everything* about you. (There may even be details about yourself that you've chosen to keep to yourself for fear of being rejected or abandoned. *"If you only knew this about me, you'd no longer love me."*)

There is one who will never stop loving you, who will never reject you. The Eternal One, the one who "has not moved" knows you better than any person on the planet ever has or will. Not only does He know and understand you, inside and out (every fiber of your being, in fact!), but He also searches your heart. He loves you today, tomorrow, for eternity.

Eternal One, search my heart and know me.
Thank You for saving me. I am Yours—always.

WEDNESDAY, JANUARY 14

Genesis 30:1–31:21 / Matthew 10:1–15 / Psalm 12

Remembered

God remembered Rachel. God listened to her and opened her womb. She became pregnant and had a son. She said, "God has taken away my humiliation."
GENESIS 30:22–23 MSG

When Rachel's father tricked Jacob into marrying her older sister first. . .*then* allowed him to marry Rachel, she was devastated. And, in the years that followed, her sister Leah gave birth to many children, while Rachel was unable to get pregnant. Rachel wanted nothing more than to be a mother. And, to make the situation even more painful, Jacob didn't even love Leah; he loved Rachel.

Rachel became extremely jealous of her sister. In her desperation, she said to Jacob: "Give me sons or I'll die!" . . . While none of us enjoys reliving our most painful experiences, we've all had our "Give me (fill in the blank) or I'll die" moments. We can certainly relate to Rachel's outburst. . .yes?

How did God handle Rachel's suffering? He didn't ignore her pain. He didn't turn His back on her. He didn't leave her alone. "God *remembered* Rachel" (emphasis added). After she had experienced immense sadness and humiliation, He enabled her to have children of her own (even though it wasn't in the time frame Rachel had hoped for).

The same is true for us. Even in our darkest times, God hears our cries. As He remembered Rachel, He will remember you and me.

Lord, thank You for remembering me. I trust that I am always wrapped in Your loving embrace.

THURSDAY, JANUARY 15

Genesis 31:22–32:21 / Matthew 10:16–36 / Psalm 13

In His Hands

*"Don't be bluffed into silence by the threats of bullies.
There's nothing they can do to your soul. . . . Save your fear
for God, who holds your entire life. . .in his hands."*
MATTHEW 10:28 MSG

Have you ever given another human being the power to influence your thoughts, words, or actions? Whether conscious or not, we've granted other people authority, for good or for bad, over us. A parent. A teacher. A friend. A bully. A boss. We've caved to someone else's wants and whims either to avoid conflict or to make them happy, when all the while, we're miserable.

More times than we realize, we allow someone to push or pull us in a direction *they'd* like us to go. So, we do things we don't want to—or shouldn't—do. We remain quiet instead of speaking up. We allow another's criticism to echo in our minds and chip away at our self-confidence. We make frivolous purchases when we should be saving for the future.

Whenever you feel yourself caving to the pressure. . .giving someone else that kind of power over you, call out to God. Have a heart-to-heart conversation with the one who holds you in His hands. When you let Him lead, you give Him *alone* the power of influence over your life. And unlike our human counterparts, our heavenly Father will never steer you in the wrong direction.

*From the moment I said yes to You, Father, You have held
me, guided me, loved me. In Your hands, I am safe.*

FRIDAY, JANUARY 16

Genesis 32:22–34:31 / Matthew 10:37–11:6 / Psalm 14

Turned-Around Lives

God takes the side of victims. Do you think you can mess with the dreams of the poor? You can't, for God makes their dreams come true. Is there anyone around to save Israel? Yes. God is around; God turns life around.

PSALM 14:5–7 MSG

On days when it feels like you're drowning in darkness and despair, turn to the certainties of God's Word. Remember these verses from Psalm 14. The biblical truths will bring you into the light:

God is on your side, dear one! He is for you, never against you.

No one can mess with your dreams. And God can make them come true!

When it feels like you're stuck in a dark pit (with no way out), God will reach in and pull you into the light.

And when it feels like no one has your back, God does—*always*! God can turn any situation—and any life—around.

Our God is so, so good. Where there seems to be no way, He makes a way. He is the dream maker and miracle worker—the one and only life changer.

Say a prayer of thanks to the heavenly Father right this minute, friend. Express your gratitude for the beautiful ways He works in you and through you—today and always.

Father God, You have changed my life and the lives of so many others. Thank You for adopting us into Your family and for calling us Yours.

SATURDAY, JANUARY 17

Genesis 35–36 / Matthew 11:7–24 / Psalm 15

You're a Perfect Fit

Who may worship in your sanctuary, LORD? Who may enter your presence on your holy hill? Those who lead blameless lives and do what is right, speaking the truth from sincere hearts.
PSALM 15:1–2 NLT

Have you ever been somewhere and felt like you didn't belong? Like you weren't accepted? Or you just didn't fit in? Perhaps you get that sense all the time: You rarely, if ever, feel like a piece of the puzzle that fits "just right."

Truth is, we've all experienced the pain of rejection at one time or another. That women's Bible study group? Awkward! The dinner party you were invited to? You couldn't wait for the evening to end! Human beings are fickle creatures, aren't they? And sometimes they don't treat us the way we'd like them to. . .leading us to feel like the odd woman out.

That's what makes being a Christ follower so special. The beautiful thing about belonging to Jesus is that you *always* fit perfectly into His plans. You *always* have a place in His kingdom. You never have to wonder if you belong, because you do—today and for all eternity! You are *always* welcome in His presence—you're invited to praise, to worship, to sit quietly. . .just as you are. When you say yes to Jesus, you're a perfect fit!

Father God, thank You for assuring me that I fit into Your plans. That You love me and have a place for me always!

SUNDAY, JANUARY 18

Genesis 37–38 / Matthew 11:25–30 / Psalm 16

Well Rested

Jesus said, "Come to me, all of you who are weary and carry heavy burdens, and I will give you rest. Take my yoke upon you. Let me teach you, because I am humble and gentle at heart, and you will find rest for your souls. For my yoke is easy to bear, and the burden I give you is light."

MATTHEW 11:28–30 NLT

We all need rest. We crave it. And most of us would probably agree that we never feel completely rested. Day-to-day living has too many of us in a perpetual, stressed-out, ever-drained state. And it's not just physical. . .it's mental and emotional too.

What about you, sister? Are you exhausted? Frazzled? Frustrated? Are you weary *and* burdened? *YES?* If so, then there's a promising remedy. And the wonderful thing is that it doesn't require a prescription, and it's proven to be supereffective. It will fill your energy tank to overflowing.

What's this miracle remedy, you may be wondering? It's Jesus! The scriptures tell us that He alone offers rest for our weary souls. When we walk with Him, we can truly be refreshed, because He removes the weight of our burdens.

If you're in need of some rest for your head, your heart, your body. . .don't accept your exhaustion as "just the way it is." Off-load your stresses and strains to Jesus today.

Rest giver, thank You for taking my heavy burdens so I can find respite for my weary soul.

Martin Luther King Jr. Day   MONDAY, JANUARY 19

Genesis 39–40 / Matthew 12:1–29 / Psalm 17

Nothing Against You

Listen, O Eternal One, to my cry for justice. . . . Announce that I am free of all the charges against me—only You can see into my heart to know that to be true. Treat me with fairness; look at me with justice. You have searched me. . . . You've found nothing against me. . . . Your ways and Your voice now guide my journey. I will press on—moving steadfastly forward along Your path. I will not look back.

PSALM 17:1–5 VOICE

Life isn't fair. For as long as we can remember we've dealt with injustice in one form or another. . . We've been judged by people who don't know the first thing about us. We've been labeled as "guilty" when we are innocent. We've been mistreated and misunderstood. And. . .it's frustrating, to say the least.

The world and life's circumstances—as unfair as they may be—don't have to dictate the direction of our moods and feelings. *Especially* when we know Jesus.

When we invite Him into our hearts, our chains are broken. We are set free. The one who saves us, loves us, forgives us, directs us. . .He treats us with fairness and looks upon us with justice. Let Him be your life guide. With Him in the lead, press on and don't ever look back.

Father God, with You as my guide, I am free. You hold nothing against me. You see directly into my heart. You know the real me.

TUESDAY, JANUARY 20

Genesis 41 / Matthew 12:30–50 / Psalm 18:1–15

Right Here, Right Now

Pharaoh removed the signet ring from his hand and put it on Joseph's. Then he dressed him in fine linens and put a gold chain around his neck. He had Joseph ride in the chariot reserved for his second-in-command, and servants ordered everyone, "Kneel!" as he rode by. So this was how Pharaoh appointed Joseph head over all of the land of Egypt.

GENESIS 41:42–43 VOICE

If you're familiar with the people of the Bible and their stories, you know that God chose to put each one at a special time and in a specific place to fulfill His good purpose for their lives:

Joseph—this boy who wore a coat of many colors was sold into slavery and later imprisoned, only to be appointed by Pharaoh as head over all of Egypt.

Esther—this orphan-turned-queen of the Persian empire heroically saved her people, the Jews, from genocide.

Moses—this baby in a basket grew up to become a stuttering fugitive who was chosen by God to lead the Egyptian people to freedom.

Saul (later renamed Paul)—this despiser and persecutor of Christians became a lover of Jesus and preacher of the good news.

God uses men and women today just as He did in ancient times. And God has chosen *you* right here, right now. Ask Him to walk alongside you as you work to fulfill your purpose for His kingdom.

Lord, thank You for choosing me. Use me as You see fit. I'm all Yours!

WEDNESDAY, JANUARY 21

Genesis 42–43 / Matthew 13:1–9 / Psalm 18:16–29

Complete

*God made my life complete
when I placed all the pieces before him.*
Psalm 18:20 msg

We often go through our lives in a perpetual search for that missing "thing" that will make us feel complete. . .

Certainly, that new career will make us happy.

Or finding a husband to share life with. . .*that's* the missing piece to our perfect life.

Or that gorgeous house—the one with the white picket fence and the kitchen of our dreams.

But what happens when we receive these things? We want *the next thing*, don't we? Because a person, a bank account, a "thing" (no matter how significant it seems) can never fill the empty places in our hearts. Psalm 18 says, "*God* made my life complete" (emphasis added). It's not "God *and*," but rather God *alone*. Only He can fill the missing pieces in our lives.

The beauty of this is that when we have our identity in Him, we can stop the mad search for that next thing that promises to fill our joy buckets. Ask the heavenly Father to fill the empty places in your heart right now. Ask Him to make your life complete. He can. . .He will!

Heavenly Father, I come to You today incomplete, with a void in my heart that I know only You can fill. Would You please help me stop searching and instead rest in Your wonderful promise? Make my life whole and complete as only You can.

THURSDAY, JANUARY 22

Genesis 44–45 / Matthew 13:10–23 / Psalm 18:30–50

Beauty in the Hard

God arms me with strength. . . . He trains my hands for battle; he strengthens my arm to draw a bronze bow. You have given me your shield of victory. Your right hand supports me; your help has made me great. You have made a wide path for my feet to keep them from slipping.
Psalm 18:32, 34–36 nlt

Life has a sneaky little way of catching us off guard. For a time, everything goes according to plan—the sun is shining, the birds are chirping, the cats are purring—and then. . .*bam!* The storm clouds move in and lightning strikes. We get pummeled by an unexpected hardship. In those moments, we feel weak, insecure, unsure, and unsteady on our feet. We feel utterly helpless!

It's tempting to give in to our human weakness, to throw up our hands in defeat. But when we know Christ as our Lord and Savior, there's beauty in the hard, friend—and it comes from knowing He will make a way when we can't see to take our next step. He will give us strength; He will protect and support us; He will make the rocky path smooth. Whatever it is that threatens to defeat us. . .when we call out to God for saving, victory awaits!

Calmer of the storms, please stop the rain and quiet the thunder. Make the sun shine again. I trust You will show me the beauty through this hardship.

FRIDAY, JANUARY 23

Genesis 46:1–47:26 / Matthew 13:24–43 / Psalm 19

Revived

The instructions of the Lord are perfect, reviving the soul. The decrees of the Lord are trustworthy, making wise the simple. The commandments of the Lord are right, bringing joy to the heart. The commands of the Lord are clear, giving insight for living. Reverence for the Lord is pure, lasting forever.
Psalm 19:7–9 nlt

Something that is "revived" has been brought back to life or health. . .it has been given fresh strength and energy. It's like brand-new again!

Is there anything in your life that needs revival today? Is your heart weak and weary? Is your faith drained and dried up? Is your trust in the heavenly Father's plan waning? Are your relationships growing stale? If your answer is yes, then you need some revival in your life. . .stat!

So, what's a woman of God who's in need of reviving to do? Get in the Word daily. Make a habit of continual prayer. Quiet your heart in the Lord's holy presence and wait for Him to speak. . .then wait for Him to move. He will provide exactly what your heart needs: wisdom, joy, assurance, insight, strength. . .revival for your soul.

Praise Him today!

Lord Jesus, reviver of my soul, I am forever grateful for Your movement in my life. Whatever I need, You provide it. You can—and will—bring my faith, my joy, my strength, and my soul back to life. I trust You with all I have.

SATURDAY, JANUARY 24

Genesis 47:27–49:28 / Matthew 13:44–58 / Psalm 20

Dreamer

*May He grant the dreams of your heart and
see your plans through to the end.*
PSALM 20:4 VOICE

We are born dreamers. When we were children, our larger-than-life imaginations had us taming lions, swimming with mermaids, walking on the moon, and riding unicorns. As grown women, our dreams look very different—marrying our Prince Charming, traveling to exotic locations, getting that much-desired promotion, or running a marathon.

While it's human nature to have big dreams for our futures, have you ever wondered where those dreams come from? Why does one woman dream of raising a large family in the country, while another desires to raise a small family in the city? Why does one woman set a goal of piloting a plane and another to drive a school bus full of children? Our unique dreams for the years ahead come from someplace, don't they?

No matter what we dream of being or doing, our yearnings were all placed in our hearts by the same God who created us—who knew us before we were born. And when we delight in the Lord and follow Him, He will become the granter of those hopes and dreams: "Take delight in the LORD, and he will give you your heart's desires" (Psalm 37:4 NLT).

Are you delighting in the Lord today?

> *Eternal God, thank You for my passions that come from You. You know me better than anyone in the world. I delight in You with all my heart and soul.*

SUNDAY, JANUARY 25

Genesis 49:29–Exodus 1:22 / Matthew 14 / Psalm 21

Wave Walker

Jesus [said,] "Courage, it's me. Don't be afraid." Peter. . .said, "Master, if it's really you, call me to come to you on the water." He said, "Come ahead." Jumping out of the boat, Peter walked on the water to Jesus. But when he looked down at the waves churning beneath his feet, he lost his nerve and started to sink. He cried, "Master, save me!" Jesus didn't hesitate. He reached down and grabbed his hand.
MATTHEW 14:27–31 MSG

You probably know some women in your circle whom you'd describe as strong, courageous, bold, and determined. But are they truly "fearless"?

Consider these Bible women: Mary, the mother of Jesus, who trusted God's plan; Queen Esther, who risked her own life to save the Jews; and Deborah, who helped lead the Israelites to defeat the army of Sisera. Did these ladies live and make decisions in the absence of fear? Likely not! But for what courage they lacked, they made up for in something much bigger: trust in their heavenly Father.

Just like these leading ladies of the Bible, you also have a heavenly Father who is bigger than your fears. Trust Him when He invites you to walk on the stormy seas, because if—and when—you begin to doubt and start to sink into the dark, watery depths, He will reach out and rescue you. Every. Single. Time.

Father, when You invite me to walk with You on crashing waves, I have nothing to fear. You are mightier than my doubt and bigger than my fear.

MONDAY, JANUARY 26

Exodus 2–3 / Matthew 15:1–28 / Psalm 22:1–21

Sent

Eternal One: I AM WHO I AM. This is what you should tell the people of Israel: "I AM has sent me to rescue you." This is what you are to tell Israel's people: "The Eternal, the God of your fathers, the God of Abraham, the God of Isaac, and the God of Jacob is the One who has sent me to you." This is My name forevermore, and this is the name by which all future generations shall remember Me.

EXODUS 3:14–15 VOICE

Did you know that we daughters of the Most High are "sent"? It's true!

And when we're sent. . .we have a purpose. We're on assignment, tasked with the heavenly Father's most vital mission: to share the good news of Jesus with the world.

Whatever your passion in life: to teach, to create, to serve, to entertain. . . *None* compares to your *true* purpose in life, the one given by your heavenly Father: helping men, women, and children come to know the Savior of the world, the one who died so we might live. . .*forever*. Nothing is more important than that!

If your eyes have been on your personal goals, ask the Lord to redirect your vision. To give you eyes to see as He wants you to see. . .your *heavenly* vision. Think bigger than yourself, friend. And don't forget to thank Him for sending you!

God, thank You for sending me, for giving me this high calling to serve You and to help others come to know You as I do.

TUESDAY, JANUARY 27

Exodus 4:1–5:21 / Matthew 15:29–16:12 / Psalm 22:22–31

No Excuses

But Moses pleaded..., "O Lord, I'm not very good with words. I never have been, and I'm not now.... I get tongue-tied, and my words get tangled." Then the LORD asked..., "Who makes a person's mouth? Who decides whether people speak or do not speak, hear or do not hear, see or do not see? Is it not I, the LORD? Now go! I will be with you...I will instruct you in what to say."

EXODUS 4:10–12 NLT

Moses pushed back when God chose him to speak. After all, when it came to speaking, Moses was kind of a mess. He wasn't good with words, he became easily tongue-tied, he stuttered... Of all the things God could have asked Moses to do, words weren't exactly his strong suit. Moses certainly *wasn't* the guy...or was he?

God didn't accept Moses' excuses. He reminded Moses that He was the one who supplied the words and gave the ability to speak (and to hear and to see!). God would be with Moses, and He would tell him exactly what to say. What could be more reassuring: When we don't have the words...God does!

Trust that whatever God asks you to do, He will provide the power, the wisdom, and the ability to do it. Now go!

God, thank You for equipping me. For providing the guidance, the words, the strength...even when it feels like I can't, I can because YOU can!

WEDNESDAY, JANUARY 28

Exodus 5:22–7:24 / Matthew 16:13–28 / Psalm 23

I Lack Nothing

The LORD is my shepherd, I lack nothing. He makes me lie down in green pastures, he leads me beside quiet waters, he refreshes my soul. He guides me along the right paths for his name's sake.

PSALM 23:1–3 NIV

Some days we wish for all the things we don't have. We look over the fence at the neighbor's bigger house, their in-ground pool, their new cars. . .and think, *Must be nice*. Meanwhile, we have other neighbors who would love to have what *we* have. . . It's a vicious cycle of envy.

While we could be focusing on all our blessings, we instead become fixated on the things we don't have. And we let it get to us, don't we? We turn into some very unhappy, discontented women. When we start playing the comparison game, it's difficult to appreciate our small but cozy home, our "average" but dependable car, our beautiful backyard where friends and family gather. . .

We need to set our sights elsewhere. Instead of looking over the fence, we should be looking up. In looking up, we will see the truth. And the truth is, when we are children of God, we lack *nothing*! Our contentment, our deep soul satisfaction, is in Him alone. He is our shepherd and our guide, our protector and provider. We need nothing else!

Lord, my shepherd, when I begin the comparison game, remind me to instead look to You!

THURSDAY, JANUARY 29

Exodus 7:25–9:35 / Matthew 17:1–9 / Psalm 24

All His!

The earth is the LORD's, and everything in it, the world, and all who live in it. . . . Who is he, this King of glory? The LORD Almighty.
PSALM 24:1, 10 NIV

A house. A car. A backyard overflowing with our favorite plants. A chicken coop full of hens. An antique piece of furniture. A handmade quilt. Our lives are full of things. And when the things we have are of value to us, we take care of them. We tidy up our homes, wash and wax our cars, feed our critters, weed and water our gardens, and make repairs to our possessions when needed—because when we're invested in something, we want it to last.

If we take such good care of the things we own, how much more will our heavenly Father take care of the things that are His? He owns the earth and everything in it—including you and me! What's more is that He places the highest value on us. . . He provides for us and has only good in mind for our futures (see Luke 12:6–7; Jeremiah 29:11). And He doesn't only care for us while we're here on earth—our God, who does not change, sent His only Son to die for us so that we might live forever (John 3:16–17)! His love and care have no end!

> *King of glory, my heavenly Father, I am Yours. I am so grateful for Your care today—and every day I have on earth. I look forward to eternity in heaven with You!*

FRIDAY, JANUARY 30

Exodus 10–11 / Matthew 17:10–27 / Psalm 25

Beautiful Work in Progress

Keep up your reputation, GOD; Forgive my bad life....
If I keep my eyes on GOD, I won't trip over my own feet.
Look at me and help me!... Then lift this ton of sin....
Keep watch over me.... Use all your skill to put me
together; I wait to see your finished product.
PSALM 25:11, 15–16, 18, 20–21 MSG

What if you were expected to be *everything* God created you to be right this very second? How would you rate yourself on a scale of 1 to 10?

If you'd give yourself a crummy rating because you're not where you need to be in your faith walk—you're not kind enough, not giving enough, not wise enough, not loving enough, not (fill in the blank) enough—you're not alone. But there's good news! You are a beautiful work in progress. God, who created you, is *still* putting you together. And He'll keep forgiving, leading, teaching, and loving you *as long as it takes*.

In the meantime, keep believing, trusting, and persevering. Stick close to your Creator and allow Him to mold you into the woman He made you to be. His plans for you are perfect after all, and He will *never* stop working in your life.

I'm a long way from where I should be in my faith, Father. I trust You to continue shaping me into the woman You made me to be.

SATURDAY, JANUARY 31

Exodus 12 / Matthew 18:1–20 / Psalm 26

Worthy Woman

"If someone has a hundred sheep and one of them wanders off, doesn't he leave the ninety-nine and go after the one? And if he finds it, doesn't he make far more over it than over the ninety-nine who stay put? Your Father in heaven feels the same way."

MATTHEW 18:12–14 MSG

Not worth the trouble.
Not worth loving.
Not worth saving.

Whether another person in our lives has made us feel unworthy or it's the deluge of negative self-talk we can't seem to control, we've all felt "less than" at one time or another. What's worse is that once we begin to believe the lies, it's difficult to overcome our feelings of shame and contempt that accompany them.

If you're battling these kinds of feelings right now, there's hope. You can find encouragement and healing in God's Word, where your heart will be reassured that your worth doesn't come from who you are, what you've said, or anything you've done. You don't have to be perfect or deserving of God's love, because Your worth comes from the one who has chosen you. He loves you so much that He'd chase after you. He loves you so much that He doesn't want to lose you—not ever!

God says, "You're worth the trouble. You're worth loving. You're worth saving." Nothing could change His mind! Yesterday, today, forever, our God is the same (Hebrews 13:8)!

Thank You for choosing me, for wanting me,
for loving me, Father. I am worthy. . .because of You!

FEBRUARY 2026

SUNDAY	MONDAY	TUESDAY	WEDNESDAY	THURSDAY	FRIDAY	SATURDAY
1	2	3	4	5	6	7
8	9	10	11	12	13	14 Valentine's Day
15	16 Presidents' Day	17	18 Ash Wednesday	19	20	21
22	23	24	25	26	27	28

SUNDAY, FEBRUARY 1

Exodus 13–14 / Matthew 18:21–35 / Psalm 27

Always Remember

Moses said to the people, "Always remember this day. This is the day when you came out of Egypt from a house of slavery. GOD brought you out of here with a powerful hand."
EXODUS 13:3 MSG

When Moses urged the Israelites to "always remember this day," some in the crowd probably chuckled to themselves. They would *never* forget the towering walls of water and the dry ground as they crossed the Red Sea to safety. And they'd certainly not forget the waves that crushed Pharaoh's chariots and army.

But it wasn't simply the events of the day that Moses was talking about. Instead, he asked them to always remember God's mighty power, His care and kindness, and His faithfulness to His chosen people. That day God saved the Israelites when there seemed to be no way of escape, and He would do it again. *Those* were the truths to always remember.

As God's beloved children, our Father is faithful to work all things together for our good, even when we don't see Him or feel Him. That's why it's so important to take note when we *do* notice His mighty acts, His answers to prayer, His gifts of peace and comfort. Those memories of what He's done can sustain us on hard days and assure us that He will come through for us every time.

Father, I live in memories of Your great faithfulness to me and look forward to an even greater future with You!

MONDAY, FEBRUARY 2

Exodus 15–16 / Matthew 19:1–15 / Psalm 28

Fickleness

> *So Moses brought Israel from the Red Sea, and they went out into the wilderness of Shur. And they went three days in the wilderness and found no water.*
> EXODUS 15:22 SKJV

Shortly after crossing the Red Sea, the Israelites worshipped God. "With your unfailing love you lead the people you have redeemed," they sang. "In your might, you guide them to your sacred home" (Exodus 15:13 NLT). The Israelites certainly trusted in God's plan.

But then they traveled for seventy-two hours without finding water, and when they arrived at the oasis of Marah, the water was too bitter to drink.

Their thirst seems to have affected their memories of God's recent miracles. "What are we going to drink?" they demanded. So Moses prayed, and God provided another miracle that made the bitter water fit to drink (15:24–25). There is no record of the Israelites' gratitude or worship this time.

It's tempting to judge the Israelites for their fickleness, but aren't we often guilty of the same? When life is smooth sailing, it's natural to trust in God and praise Him for His goodness. But when bad news knocks the wind out of our sails, too often our praise dries up and questions pop up. "God, what gives?"

Today, no matter what life brings, choose to believe God is working and His ways are good. Choose to be grateful.

> *Lord, I will sing of Your love and goodness!*
> *You are faithful even when I am fickle.*

TUESDAY, FEBRUARY 3

Exodus 17–19 / Matthew 19:16–30 / Psalm 29

Possible

Jesus answered, "If you want to be perfect, go, sell your possessions and give to the poor, and you will have treasure in heaven. Then come, follow me." . . . Jesus looked at them and said, "With man this is impossible, but with God all things are possible."

MATTHEW 19:21, 26 NIV

The rich young man in Matthew 19 seems confident that Jesus will punch his ticket to heaven. Imagine him, report card in hand, slapping a gold star sticker on each commandment as Jesus recited them. He'd never murdered or committed adultery. He wasn't a thief or a liar, and he did his best to love his neighbors. But Jesus' final requirement left him reeling. Even if he *wanted* to sell all his possessions, give to the poor, and follow Jesus, it just wasn't practical or possible. So he left, defeated.

The rich young man's error wasn't his righteousness. It wasn't his lack of doing good or even his wealth. His problem was he thought he could earn eternal life by being perfect, and humanly speaking, perfection is impossible. Only God's grace is perfect. That's the point of what Jesus taught His disciples in this passage. God's grace is the sole way to heaven, and it's a gift that we can only accept when we humble ourselves and acknowledge we can't be our own Savior—we need the salvation offered through Jesus' death, burial, and resurrection.

My eternity is safe in Your grace, God.
Thank You for making the impossible possible!

WEDNESDAY, FEBRUARY 4

Exodus 20–21 / Matthew 20:1–19 / Psalm 30

Clear Expectations

*Then God gave the people all these instructions:
"I am the Lord your God, who rescued you from
the land of Egypt, the place of your slavery."*
Exodus 20:1–2 nlt

After four hundred years of slavery, the Israelites were accustomed to oppression. From Pharaoh's increasing workload quotas to his death edict for newborn Hebrew boys, nearly every aspect of their lives was regulated and enforced.

So when Moses led his people to freedom in the wilderness, after the initial shock and awe wore off, the Israelites probably felt adrift. God was leading them to the Promised Land, but how were they to act every day? Left to their own devices, the Lord knew their human sinfulness would take over. So God gave them clear expectations—the Ten Commandments.

The world sees this set of laws as just another form of oppression like their Egyptian captivity, but the truth is that God's laws provide the framework for true freedom. Even for us today, following these rules doesn't earn us salvation, but it sets us up to receive God's blessings. When we put Him first and honor His name, idolatry won't sneak into our hearts. Prioritizing Sabbath rest boosts our physical, mental, and spiritual health. When we treat our family and friends, neighbors and strangers like we want to be treated, we shine God's light in a dark world.

*God, give me the correct perspective of Your commandments.
I want to learn to love Your laws and live righteously!*

THURSDAY, FEBRUARY 5

Exodus 22–23 / Matthew 20:20–34 / Psalm 31:1–8

The Law of Love

If you see the donkey of someone you know who hates you and it has fallen beneath its load, you must not leave it there. You must stop and help the donkey recover the load.

EXODUS 23:5 VOICE

In ancient civilizations, payback was an accepted form of justice, even among God's chosen people. "The punishment must match the injury," reads Exodus 21:23–24 (NLT), "a life for a life, an eye for an eye, a tooth for a tooth." Revenge-based law is simple to understand and is objectively fair.

But even in the Old Testament, we see glimpses of the coming shift to love-based law. Exodus 23:5 is a good example of kindness and mercy—not just to friends and family but to enemies. This idea would've been shocking to the Israelites!

Jesus, of course, took this command even further with stories of the Good Samaritan (Luke 10:30–37) where he challenged the listeners to think more broadly about who their neighbors are. And then in Matthew 5:43–45 (NIV), Jesus goes all in for love: "You have heard that it was said, 'Love your neighbor and hate your enemy.' But I tell you, love your enemies and pray for those who persecute you, that you may be children of your Father in heaven."

God, I'm thankful that You are a Father of mercy instead of retribution. Because even though my sins make me deserve death, Your grace provides me with love and life everlasting.

FRIDAY, FEBRUARY 6

Exodus 24–25 / Matthew 21:1–27 / Psalm 31:9–18

The Mountain

Then Moses climbed the mountain. . . . The Glory of GOD settled over Mount Sinai. The Cloud covered it for six days. On the seventh day he called out of the Cloud to Moses. In the view of the Israelites below, the Glory of GOD looked like a raging fire at the top of the mountain.

EXODUS 24:15–17 MSG

When Moses hiked up Mount Sinai, God's glory came down like a cloud and met him there. Moses might have expected God to immediately launch into His plans for the Israelites, but the Lord didn't talk for a week.

The Bible doesn't tell us what Moses did for the first six days. Maybe Moses talked and God listened. Maybe Moses rested in God's presence. What we do know is that Moses didn't give up and hike back down the mountain. He came expecting God to move, and on the seventh day God called out to Moses like a raging fire. For the next forty days, God gave Moses instructions for the Tabernacle and Ark of the Covenant.

Moses waited on God, and God was faithful to do what He said He'd do. "The LORD is good to those who wait for him," Lamentations 3:25 (ESV) says. If you're waiting on a mountain today, take courage. God is with you; God is for you. God is faithful to move as He did for Moses.

Almighty God, I'm ready for You to move.
While I wait, please give me peace in Your presence.

SATURDAY, FEBRUARY 7

Exodus 26–27 / Matthew 21:28–46 / Psalm 31:19–24

The Cornerstone

"The stone that the builders rejected has become the cornerstone; this was the Lord's doing, and it is marvelous in our eyes."

MATTHEW 21:42 ESV

In masonry construction, a cornerstone is the first block that's laid. It is the origin point from which all other stones are measured and set. A cornerstone determines the strength and integrity of the building. Using a crooked or weak cornerstone will someday end in disaster, but choosing a straight, solid cornerstone sets the foundation for a structure that can last thousands of years.

The Bible uses a cornerstone metaphor to describe Jesus, who is the origin of our faith and salvation. His life, teachings, and sacrifice on the cross make up the foundation of His church and every soul who has accepted His gift of grace and eternal life. He is faithful, reliable, solid, and plumb—yet there have been people throughout history who have rejected this truth, as we see in today's scripture where Jesus quotes Psalm 118:22–23.

Jesus' place as the cornerstone in your life is an essential part of who you are. You don't need special construction or masonry skills. If Jesus is the Lord of your heart, you can build your life on Him, ask Him to set the course for your choices, and know that no matter what happens, you are anchored to a rock that will not be moved.

Jesus, You are the perfect foundation for my life, my faith, and my salvation.

SUNDAY, FEBRUARY 8

Exodus 28 / Matthew 22 / Psalm 32

The Invitation

*Jesus also told them other parables. He said,
"The Kingdom of Heaven can be illustrated by the story
of a king who prepared a great wedding feast for his son."*
MATTHEW 22:1–2 NLT

If you've ever planned a big party, you may remember the excitement you felt when you sent out the invitations. Exceptional hosts will plan every detail of the event, including how to bless everyone in attendance.

So just imagine how you'd feel if every RSVP you receive sends regrets. Some invitees give excuses, but others simply say they won't come. Many others don't bother to send a response at all.

That's precisely the scenario in Jesus' parable of the wedding feast in Matthew 22. The father and king in the story is God, Jesus the son and groom. In the parable, the father invites his guests—God's chosen people—three times, and they reject each invitation. So the king widens the invitation list, welcoming everyone who would come. Here Jesus is telling His listeners that God's invitation for salvation is no longer limited to Jews but is for anyone who will accept the invitation to the feast and clothe themselves in the wedding garments of Jesus' grace and forgiveness.

Accepting the invitation to be a part of God's kingdom is the most important, life- and eternity-changing decision you can make. Today, show up and be counted among the saved!

*Father, You have prepared a glorious feast in Your
kingdom. I accept the invitation to attend!*

MONDAY, FEBRUARY 9

Exodus 29 / Matthew 23:1–36 / Psalm 33:1–12

What Others Think

"Everything they do, they do to be seen of men. They have words from the Holy Writings written in large letters on their left arm and forehead and they make wide trimming for their clothes. They like to have the important places at big suppers and the best seats in the Jewish places of worship. They like to have people show respect to them as they stand in the center of town where people gather. They like to be called teacher."

MATTHEW 23:5–7 NLV

Jesus didn't hold back when He described His disgust for the hypocrisy of the Jewish religious leaders. These men had Old Testament law memorized, but they didn't let the Word of God affect their hearts. They didn't want God to transform them; they just wanted to be admired and respected—to appear better than everyone else.

"The stuck-up fall flat on their faces," Proverbs 11:2 (MSG) says, "but down-to-earth people stand firm." We are wise to heed this warning, to let the Word of God transform us from the inside out with His love, and to not worry about what others think of us.

Today, and every day, do a heart check: Who are you trying to impress?

Jesus, today's reading is a bit of a punch to the gut. When I care too much about what other people think of me, remind me that what You think of me is the most important. You call me loved and accepted and worthy.

TUESDAY, FEBRUARY 10

Exodus 30–31 / Matthew 23:37–24:28 / Psalm 33:13–22

Trust and Hope

Our soul waits for the LORD; he is our help and our shield. For our heart is glad in him, because we trust in his holy name. Let your steadfast love, O LORD, be upon us, even as we hope in you.
PSALM 33:20–22 ESV

Here in Psalm 33, the author (likely David) talks about how our trust and hope in God are intertwined. Trust is built when we experience God's presence in our lives. As we get to know God better through reading His Word, of the great accounts of His power and care for His people, we learn we can trust that He is working on our behalf for His glory—even when we can't see it or feel it.

As your trust grows, your hope in His goodness and His future for you will grow too. He has good plans for you (Jeremiah 29:11), and He works all things together for your good (Romans 8:28). His love will never fail (Psalm 136; John 3:16), and He takes care of you (Psalm 23).

If you're feeling a lack of hope today, think about the times God was faithful to you in the past. Remember when He answered a prayer request, provided a needed blessing, or made a way through a hard situation. He is our faithful and trustworthy God yesterday, today, and forever!

Lord of all, I praise You for who You are. You don't forget me and You never go back on Your promises.

WEDNESDAY, FEBRUARY 11

Exodus 32–33 / Matthew 24:29–51 / Psalm 34:1–7

Impatience

When the people saw that Moses was staying a long time before coming down from the mountain, they gathered around Aaron, and said, "Come, make a god for us who will go in front of us. For we do not know what has become of Moses."
Exodus 32:1 NLV

Fewer than forty days prior to the events in Exodus 32, the Israelites agreed to "do everything the Lord has commanded" (Exodus 24:7 NLT). Yet here they are, abandoning the true God and demanding that Aaron make them a new and improved god.

It seems outrageous. After all, they've been able to *see* the presence of God as a cloud and a raging fire at the top of Mount Sinai. So why couldn't they wait for Moses to return with God's next instructions? Because they wanted control and took matters into their own hands.

But haven't we often done the same thing? We pray and ask God to move. We may pray again and again. Sooner or later questions start to pile up. *Why isn't He answering? How long do I have to wait?*

Sometimes God equips us to take action as an answer to our prayer, but often it's more important to rest in scripture's promises that He hears us (1 Peter 3:12), He cares about us (1 Peter 5:7), and He will answer our prayers (1 John 5:14–15).

You are always faithful, Lord. Help me to rest in Your presence and resist the urge to get ahead of You.

THURSDAY, FEBRUARY 12

Exodus 34:1–35:29 / Matthew 25:1–13 / Psalm 34:8–22

Taste. . .and See

Open your mouth and taste, open your eyes and see—how good God is. Blessed are you who run to him. Worship God if you want the best; worship opens doors to all his goodness.
Psalm 34:8–9 msg

Young children are often the pickiest of eaters. Presented with a bite of a food they've never tried, many will turn their noses up and say, "I don't like that," without even tasting a single morsel. They don't realize they're missing out on something delicious!

Our Father invites us, His children, to His table where we can taste course after course of His goodness. Once we understand that every good gift comes from Him as our loving Father (James 1:17, Matthew 7:11), our natural instinct is to return daily to the table, open to new blessings we haven't experienced yet.

If you've tasted and seen that the Lord is good, invite others to come and experience the same. For seekers and new believers, it may be a little scary to surrender and fully trust in God's goodness. So tell them about your own stories and the blessings you've received from God. Invite them to sit next to you at the Lord's table, where there's delicious fulfillment to be found in His presence.

Father, fill my plate with Your goodness, and I'll be back for seconds! I know I will always find complete satisfaction at Your table. Thank You for always providing exactly what I need—and more!

FRIDAY, FEBRUARY 13

Exodus 35:30–37:29 / Matthew 25:14–30 / Psalm 35:1–8

Attagirl!

"The master said, 'Well done, my good and faithful servant. You have been faithful in handling this small amount, so now I will give you many more responsibilities. Let's celebrate together!'"

MATTHEW 25:23 NLT

Doesn't it feel good to be celebrated? Personal satisfaction of hard work and pride of a job well done is good, but a sincere "Attagirl!" from someone else—especially someone who loves you—is a beautiful and encouraging blessing.

In Matthew 25, Jesus tells a story about a man who entrusts his three servants each with a portion of his money while he goes away on a trip. The servants who take initiative through hard work and investing are able to double their master's money. When the master returns, he praises them mightily, promotes them to higher positions within his household, and then celebrates with them.

This parable certainly teaches us the importance of being responsible with the blessings God gives us—talent, money, possession, time, and other resources—but it also illustrates that God celebrates with us in our successes. What are your current goals, and how can you invite God to be a part of them? What gifts has God blessed you with that you can multiply for His glory? Follow His lead, praising Him along the way, and He will lift you up as you celebrate your wins together!

Father, I'm so thankful to have You in my corner. Your "Attagirl" means everything to me.

SATURDAY, FEBRUARY 14
Valentine's Day

Exodus 38–39 / Matthew 25:31–46 / Psalm 35:9–17

Love in Action

"The King will reply, 'Truly I tell you, whatever you did for one of the least of these brothers and sisters of mine, you did for me.'"

MATTHEW 25:40 NIV

Every year in the middle of February, the world goes a little love crazy. Romance, Galentine's brunches, chalky conversation hearts, and of course. . .Valentine cards. While none of these things are bad, none give a full picture of what real love is.

First John 4:8 says it plainly: God *is* love, and so love should be the priority for every believer. Jesus said the first and second greatest commands are to love God and love others (Mark 12:30–31). First Corinthians 13 describes love as patient and kind. Love is not jealous or rude or selfish or irritable, and it keeps no record of wrongs. Love seeks out truth and never gives up. Jesus said that the world will know that we are God's children when we love others (John 13:34–35). Love is clearly much more than flowers and chocolate!

A life defined by love is one that seeks to serve others. Jesus set the perfect example by loving and serving everyone—including the poor, the sick, and the unwanted. When we choose to do the same, Jesus tells us in Matthew 25:40 that we are showing true love to our Savior and King.

Jesus, thank You for loving me so perfectly and completely. May I learn to do the same for others.

SUNDAY, FEBRUARY 15

Exodus 40 / Matthew 26:1–35 / Psalm 35:18–28

Obedience

[Moses did everything] just as the LORD had commanded [him].
EXODUS 40:16, 19, 21, 23, 27, 32 NLT

Exodus begins in a place of desperation. Enslaved in Egypt, the Israelites were forced to make bricks without straw and kill their newborn boys. Yet through God's display of miraculous power, His chosen people escaped Pharaoh's clutches. The conclusion of Exodus ends in glory as God's presence dwells with His people in the Tabernacle and He is leading them through the wilderness toward the Promised Land.

Throughout Exodus, we see Moses choosing to obey God. Was Moses perfect? No. When God called him from the burning bush, Moses resisted. He made excuses. But ultimately Moses did what the Lord required of Him. Here in Exodus chapter 40, we read six times where Moses followed the Lord's instructions for setting up the Tabernacle. This was no IKEA coffee table construction but a precise set of commandments and plans—spanning more than ten chapters of Exodus—that Moses worked hard to obey. His leadership and oversight in the construction and setup allowed God to have a home with His people.

Obedience matters to God. When we choose to follow His plans, He will lead us to places and experiences we could never achieve by ourselves. Will we be perfect at obeying? No. What's required is a willing heart and faith—even faith as tiny as a mustard seed (Matthew 17:20)!

God, I choose to obey You! Like Moses, I will be faithful to finish Your work (Exodus 40:33).

MONDAY, FEBRUARY 16

Presidents' Day

Leviticus 1–3 / Matthew 26:36–68 / Psalm 36:1–6

Emotions

Then [Jesus] said, "This sorrow is crushing my life out. Stay here and keep vigil with me."
MATTHEW 26:38 MSG

If you ever wonder if Jesus felt the same way you do, scripture records many emotions He experienced on earth. The soul-crushing dread He felt before His arrest in Matthew 26:38 is only the beginning. When His friend Lazarus died, He mourned and wept with Lazarus' sisters (John 11:35). He experienced thirst (John 4:7) and hunger (Mark 6:31). He demonstrated outrage at the hypocrisy of the Pharisees (Matthew 23:23), compassion and empathy for the sick (Matthew 9:20–22), concern and care for His mother (John 19:26), and a deep love for and joy in His disciples (John 15:9–11).

The Gospel accounts of Jesus' life show us that He experienced emotions in an authentic way. He didn't bottle up or push down His feelings, but He also didn't let emotions dictate His actions—He chose, instead, to follow God's plan to its completion. Today, as Jesus sits at the right hand of the Father, He understands every emotion and struggle you experience (Hebrews 4:14–16).

God created in you the ability to feel. When you struggle under the weight of your emotions, look to Jesus. He's ready, willing, and able to take away the burden of what you're feeling (1 Peter 5:7) and replace it with His peace (John 16:33).

Jesus, when my emotions feel too big, please help me to manage them in a way that brings You glory.

TUESDAY, FEBRUARY 17

Leviticus 4:1–5:13 / Matthew 26:69–27:26 / Psalm 36:7–12

God's Love

Your strong love, O True God, is precious. All people run for shelter under the shadow of Your wings. In Your house, they eat and are full at Your table. They drink from the river of Your overflowing kindness. You have the fountain of life that quenches our thirst. Your light has opened our eyes and awakened our souls.

Psalm 36:7–9 voice

The description of God's character in Psalm 36:5–9 reads like a beautiful, life-giving landscape. Gaze up at the countless points of light across a clear night sky and rest in the fact that God's love is even bigger than that. Envision billowy, snow-white clouds across a gorgeous, endless blue vista and trust that God's faithfulness stretches beyond the horizon, past where your eyes can see. His righteousness stands tall and rugged like a mountain that weathers the storms of evil, and His hand of justice reaches deeper than the lowest part of the ocean's floor. He provides shelter in a home large enough to accommodate everyone and a table with enough food to satisfy every belly. He kindly provides His living water that quenches the deepest thirst and shines His glorious light to illuminate the path of right.

God gives all this—and more—to every person who accepts His gift of grace, regardless of race, gender, age, wealth, health, intelligence, or anything else. His love always was, is, and will be.

I can spend my whole life learning about Your love, Father! To me, it is perfect.

WEDNESDAY, FEBRUARY 18 — *Ash Wednesday*

Leviticus 5:14–7:21 / Matthew 27:27–50 / Psalm 37:1–6

Your Heart's Desires

*Take delight in the Lord, and he will give you
your heart's desires. Commit everything you do
to the Lord. Trust him, and he will help you.*
Psalm 37:4–5 nlt

When you were a little girl, your heart's desire might've been an ice cream cone. . .with sprinkles. Or a new stuffed animal. Maybe you had your heart set on a purple bike with rainbow streamers or a glittery set of roller skates. As you grew and matured, perhaps your heart desired bigger, more expensive and grown-up delights. A car, a new wardrobe, a house. . .a husband. Any of these can certainly be wonderful blessings, but only a living relationship with God can provide lasting joy, fulfillment, and contentment.

What does it look like to "delight in the Lord"? By spending time in His presence, in prayer, and studying His Word, we will grow our relationship with our heavenly Father. When we prioritize thanking and praising Him for who He is and all He's done in the past, it makes us more aware of what He's doing now. Ask Him to align your heart with His and to guide your decisions—both big and small. That's when your heart will start wanting what *He* wants, and He'll use you in a special way in His kingdom. His desires and plans are the ones that will happen (Proverbs 19:21).

*Lord, give me a hunger for Your will. Mold me
and use me to do great things for You!*

THURSDAY, FEBRUARY 19

Leviticus 7:22–8:36 / Matthew 27:51–66 / Psalm 37:7–26

Joseph of Arimathea

Joseph took the body and put clean linen cloth around it. He laid it in his own new grave. This grave had been cut out in the side of a rock. He pushed a big stone over the door of the grave and went away.
MATTHEW 27:59–60 NLV

Joseph, a wealthy man from Arimathea, was a religious leader and honored member of the high council who also happened to be a secret follower of Jesus (Mark 15:43). After Jesus' death, he boldly asked Pilate for Jesus' body and buried Him in his personal tomb. By doing these things, Joseph essentially made a courageous, public statement: "Jesus is the Messiah." He risked his reputation and his life by doing so. His commitment to Jesus Christ seems even more impressive when you consider that the disciples—the men closest to Jesus—fled in fear after their leader was killed.

God is calling for more Josephs today—people who will do the right thing, the bold thing, the faithful thing, the loving thing— even when it's difficult or costs us a great deal. Josephs often work quietly behind the scenes, taking care of details that help further God's kingdom. Josephs know their battle is the Lord's and don't waste their energy shouting into the void of a dark world. Josephs lead by example and make an eternal impact. How can you be a Joseph today?

Lord, give me the boldness it takes to do the right thing even when it's not the easy thing.

FRIDAY, FEBRUARY 20

Leviticus 9–10 / Matthew 28 / Psalm 37:27–40

The Right Guide

The godly offer good counsel; they teach right from wrong. They have made God's law their own, so they will never slip from his path. . . . Look at those who are honest and good, for a wonderful future awaits those who love peace.

PSALM 37:30–31, 37 NLT

Mountain guides are highly trained professionals who have experience with terrain, equipment, conditions, and safety. A climbing newbie who wants to survive a treacherous mountain ascent should choose a guide who has years of experience and can navigate any scenario in the wilderness.

God's Word challenges us to think about our mentors—those we allow to influence and speak into our lives. Proverbs 37 says that a good role model will have a strong moral compass, know scripture, and follow what scripture says. That person will be trustworthy and wholesome and promote peace. In short, that person will reflect Jesus. The apostle Paul says it simply in 1 Corinthians 11:1 (NIV): "Follow my example, as I follow the example of Christ."

Who you follow is just as important as where you're headed. Whether you're in search of a seasoned Christian guide or you're blazing a trail for others to come after you, faith is a climb that takes endurance—one that Hebrews 12:2 (NLT) says we can conquer by "keeping our eyes on Jesus, the champion who initiates and perfects our faith."

Lord, please bring godly people my way who will speak Your truth to my heart.

SATURDAY, FEBRUARY 21

Leviticus 11–12 / Mark 1:1–28 / Psalm 38

A Simple Invite

"Come, follow me," Jesus said, "and I will send you out to fish for people." At once they left their nets and followed him.
MARK 1:17–18 NIV

Jesus' invitation to His first four disciples—Simon, Andrew, James, and John—couldn't have been simpler or more straightforward.

Jesus: "Come with me, and we'll find more people to come along as well."

Disciples: "We're right behind You."

Can you imagine a scenario where you'd ask *zero* questions about such an invitation? Yet from these four men we hear no whisper of "Where are we going?" "How long will we be gone?" "What should I bring?" or "What will it cost?" They simply dropped what they were doing and followed the man who would change the trajectory of all of God's creation.

The disciples were by no means perfect men. They did, however, make the perfect decision in this moment. What can you learn from their example? When you feel a tug from the Holy Spirit to show kindness to someone, when you think of sending a quick, encouraging text to a friend, when you have the resources to meet a need—see these as an invitation from Jesus. Don't overthink it. Don't talk yourself out of it. Drop what you're doing, follow the Lord, and do the loving thing—big or small—in the name of Jesus.

Jesus, I am listening for Your voice. When You call me to action, I won't make excuses. I will follow Your lead!

SUNDAY, FEBRUARY 22

Leviticus 13 / Mark 1:29–39 / Psalm 39

Life Is Short

*Hear my prayer, O LORD! Listen to my cries for help!
Don't ignore my tears. For I am your guest—a traveler
passing through, as my ancestors were before me.*
PSALM 39:12 NLT

For a child, the first twenty-four days of December feel like a year's worth of waiting for Christmas. A three-month summer break seems like a glorious stretch of forever, and becoming a grown-up is an eternity away. Then, before we know it, adulthood comes, and the older we get, the faster the months and years go by. A decade can slip past, and we look up and wonder, "Where did the time *go*?"

Life truly is short, and the psalm writer David points out that we are simply guests in this world. We are on a journey, passing through, because our forever home is with our Father. Our time here is short, but God calls each of us to use that time for good and His glory. Paul encourages us in Ephesians 5:16 and Colossians 4:5 to make the most of every opportunity to do what the Lord wants us to do: Love God, love others, talk about what Jesus has done in our lives, and work to support God's kingdom on earth. As we pass through, let's leave everyone we come in contact with closer to God because we were here.

*Father, You are my hope for today, tomorrow,
and forever! Help me to live wisely, as You want me to.*

MONDAY, FEBRUARY 23

Leviticus 14 / Mark 1:40–2:12 / Psalm 40:1–8

Compassionate Healing

A man with leprosy came and knelt in front of Jesus, begging to be healed. "If you are willing, you can heal me and make me clean," he said. Moved with compassion, Jesus reached out and touched him. "I am willing," he said. "Be healed!" Instantly the leprosy disappeared, and the man was healed.

MARK 1:40–42 NLT

Jesus felt the full struggle of the leper crawling before Him. The man was obviously suffering physically with numbness and the searing pain that accompanies leprosy. But Jesus also knew that the man ached spiritually and emotionally. Jewish law prohibited lepers from being a part of the community—touching a leper made a person ceremonially unclean—and others may have even thrown rocks at the man so he would steer clear of them.

Jesus saw past the disease to the man's heart; he was a child of God who needed help in a major way. So when the man displayed faith that Jesus had the power to heal him, Jesus honored his request.

Yes, Jesus is our healer, but His supernatural healing isn't limited to the physical realm. Jesus cares as much about our emotional pain as our physical pain. What are your struggles today? Who in your life needs healing? Approach the Lord humbly and authentically. In Him you will find healing and wholeness.

Jesus, I praise You for being my compassionate healer. Thank You for seeing all of me—especially when I'm struggling.

TUESDAY, FEBRUARY 24

Leviticus 15 / Mark 2:13–3:35 / Psalm 40:9–17

Holy Rest

The Sabbath was made for the needs of human beings, and not the other way around. So the Son of Man is Lord even over the Sabbath.

MARK 2:27–28 VOICE

The Jewish leaders were looking for any way to discredit Jesus' authority in religious matters. So when He and His disciples technically broke Sabbath law by snapping off heads of grain to eat, the Pharisees sounded the alarm, essentially calling Jesus a fraud and a hypocrite.

But Jesus took their legalistic approach to Old Testament law and infused it with His new covenant. He understood that the intent of the law is to love God and love others—and the loving thing to do that Sabbath was to encourage His disciples to feed their empty bellies.

Scripture tells us that after God created the heavens and the earth, He rested (Genesis 2:2–3). But God didn't take a nap because He needed a pick-me-up; Isaiah 40:28 tells us that God never gets tired. Instead, He rested as an example for us to follow. A Sabbath is intended to be a holy rest—a time to find refreshment in the act of worshipping God. Resting from gainful work also helps us admit that He is in control and that He will provide all we need. Sabbath is a gift from our loving Father.

God, I will honor You in my Sabbath rest. Give me a heart for the needs of others, and show me how to love them as You love me.

WEDNESDAY, FEBRUARY 25

Leviticus 16–17 / Mark 4:1–20 / Psalm 41:1–4

Scattered Seed

[Jesus] taught them by telling many stories in the form of parables, such as this one: "Listen! A farmer went out to plant some seed."

MARK 4:2–3 NLT

In this parable, the farmer's seed lands in four different places: on a footpath, in shallow soil, among thorns, and in fertile soil. The results of the seeds vary from place to place (see Mark 4:4–8), but only the seeds that end up in fertile soil yield a bountiful harvest.

Later in Mark 4, the disciples ask Jesus to explain the meaning of the story. The seed, He said, represents God's Word, and the different soils represent the way people respond to the gospel message.

The soils in this story are often assumed to be four different types of people, but this parable can also be interpreted as the soils representing the heart of one person at different times of their life. Consider this: Have you ever opened God's Word, returned to a passage you've read before, and received a completely fresh or deeper understanding? Your circumstances, attitudes, maturity, life experiences—any or all of these can have an impact on how you respond to and grow in God's Word.

Every time you open the Bible, ask God to reveal His truth to you. His Word is living and has the power to change you to be more and more like Jesus!

God, please use Your Word to grow my faith in You!

THURSDAY, FEBRUARY 26

Leviticus 18–19 / Mark 4:21–41 / Psalm 41:5–13

Dad Voice

When Jesus woke up, he rebuked the wind and said to the waves, "Silence! Be still!" Suddenly the wind stopped, and there was a great calm.

MARK 4:39 NLT

Even the best-behaved kids have their out-of-control moments, going berserk after too much sugar or overstimulation or excitement. Whether you're a parent or you remember what it was like to be a kid in that chaotic state, there's one (nearly) surefire way to stop kids in their tracks: Dad voice.

Dad voice isn't reserved solely for the male parent. Dad voice is a resource in the parenting toolbox that is best used sparingly (lest it lose its effectiveness). It's a clear, simple, loud pronouncement to *STOP AND LISTEN*. Done correctly, it's a display of parental authority that (most) kids will immediately obey.

It can be said that Jesus uses "Dad voice" here in Mark 4:39 when He calls out to the wind and waves. His clear, simple statement of "Silence! Be still!" resulted in sudden and immediate calm. He stopped the storm in its tracks—the chaos that threatened the life of His closest friends—in three simple words. Doing so, He demonstrated His authority over nature, His claim to be the Son of God, and His power, unmatched in creation.

You serve a Savior who is stronger than anything the world can throw at you. Today, rest in His great might and great love for you.

Jesus, thank You for being my powerful Savior and friend.

FRIDAY, FEBRUARY 27

Leviticus 20 / Mark 5 / Psalm 42–43

A Caring Savior

*"Daughter, your faith has healed you.
Go in peace and be free from your sickness."*

MARK 5:34 NLV

The woman who had been bleeding for twelve long years had heard stories about the carpenter from Nazareth. People said He had the power to heal the sick—and what's more is that He seemed to *care* about the people He was helping. No one—not even the lowest of the low—was beyond His compassionate care.

But she knew others found her condition shameful and disgusting and unforgivable. She could imagine no scenario where He would willingly touch her and risk becoming unclean under Jewish law. He was too good, too holy, to lower Himself to her level, but in her heart, she knew His power was so great that if she could just touch His robe, she would be healed. And that's just what happened.

The woman's relief turned to fear as Jesus asked who touched His robe. She'd been found out, but instead of ridicule and shame, in the Messiah she found healing and affirmation of her faith.

If you've ever felt like your struggles and problems are keeping you from God, take hope in this woman's story. His love reaches out to you no matter how impossible, painful, or hopeless a situation feels. You can *always* approach Him and find a sympathetic Savior and friend.

*Jesus, thank You for being so kind to the woman in this story.
I find the same comfort and hope in Your embrace, Lord.*

SATURDAY, FEBRUARY 28

Leviticus 21–22 / Mark 6:1–13 / Psalm 44

The Law

> "You must faithfully keep all my commands by
> putting them into practice, for I am the Lord."
> LEVITICUS 22:31 NLT

Bible scholars have tallied up 613 commandments in the Old Testament books of Exodus, Leviticus, Numbers, and Deuteronomy. Most Christians are familiar with the Ten Commandments (Exodus 20:1–17) but less familiar with the remaining 603. These rules, collectively and commonly known as "the Law," were God's clear expectations for the descendants of Abraham. If the people followed the Law, God would protect them and bless them (Deuteronomy 30:15–18).

God, by His very nature, is perfect, holy, and blameless—and He required His people to be the same. Breaking just one of the 613 laws broke their promise to God. The Law required elaborate and specific offerings to wipe away their sins. It must've been an exhausting cycle of breaking and fixing, breaking and fixing.

But Jesus rewrote the script and offered a new way to fellowship with God by sacrificing Himself on the cross—a sacrifice that created a way for grace and salvation through faith in Him. Our Savior and friend established a new covenant in the upper room with the Last Supper and through His teachings simplified all 613 commandments for us into the two most essential: Love God and love others.

God, the Law reminds me how sinful I truly am. You have every right to cut me out of Your life, but instead You sacrificed Your Son so I can stand blameless before You. Thank You!

MARCH 2026

SUNDAY	MONDAY	TUESDAY	WEDNESDAY	THURSDAY	FRIDAY	SATURDAY
1	2	3	4	5	6	7
8 Daylight Saving Time Begins	9	10	11	12	13	14
15	16	17 St. Patrick's Day	18	19	20 First Day of Spring	21
22	23	24	25	26	27	28
29 Palm Sunday	30	31				

SUNDAY, MARCH 1

Leviticus 23–24 / Mark 6:14–29 / Psalm 45:1–5

Praying for Our Leadership

You are fairer than the children of men; graciousness is poured upon Your lips; therefore God has blessed You forever. Gird Your sword upon Your thigh, O mighty One, in Your glory and Your majesty! And in Your majesty ride on triumphantly for the cause of truth, humility, and righteousness (uprightness and right standing with God); and let Your right hand guide You to tremendous things.

PSALM 45:2–4 AMPC

This psalm, written as a love song, unpacks the power and influence of God's chosen king who pursues truth and justice. It's a beautiful picture of what power can look like for those who seek the Lord's guidance. The reality is that those in authority affect the welfare of those they govern. There is a direct connection between our leaders and our health and safety. Their choices can bring either security or suffering.

Because we are believers who understand God's sovereignty, we're told to pray for them. It's our calling and purpose. It's our privilege and burden. And each day, we should ask God to work in the hearts of our leadership so they're steadfast to bring goodness and prosperity. It's a courageous request that may help shape leadership in significant ways. And as children of God, we have the right to petition Him for it.

Lord, capture the hearts of our leaders and let them seek Your face for wisdom and strength to do Your will with those they oversee!

MONDAY, MARCH 2

Leviticus 25 / Mark 6:30–56 / Psalm 45:6–12

Because You Are His

So follow My directives and live by My rules; as you do, you and your people will most certainly be secure in the land I will give you. The land will produce an abundance of food, and you will have all you need to eat and live safely in the land.

LEVITICUS 25:18–19 VOICE

Throughout the book of Leviticus, God is preparing Israel to become a nation finally settled in the land He promised. It unpacks rules and regulations about how to live as holy people of the holy God. It provides details on rituals, ceremonies, sacrifices, and priesthood. This is because they have been divinely chosen, and the Lord wants to equip them to live wholeheartedly in devotion to Him. He wants the Israelites to follow His directives and live by His rules for His glory and their good.

You too have been chosen as God's beloved. And He has given His holy Word as a guide to live in ways that please and delight His heart. There are commands in its pages designed to keep you secure in the Lord's arms and bring encouragement to stand in courage. Let the Bible be your guide as you walk through each day and every circumstance, and watch as you find unmatched comfort and peace from the Father who loves you fully.

Lord, thank You for providing the Bible and revealing Yourself and Your commands to me through its pages.

TUESDAY, MARCH 3

Leviticus 26 / Mark 7 / Psalm 45:13–17

Blessings from Obedience

I will make my home among you and never turn away from you. I will walk among you and be your God, and you will be My people. I am the Eternal One, your God, who led you out of the land of Egypt so that you would no longer be their slaves. I have shattered the yokes that broke your backs and helped you walk straight and upright.

LEVITICUS 26:11–13 VOICE

Throughout the Bible, there are countless reminders that God blesses our obedience. This chapter in Leviticus is one of those times. He clearly states that if the Israelites walk in His statutes and observe His commands, the Lord's goodness and provision will be given in abundance. One might wonder how anyone—after learning of the blessings that follow compliance and remembering the ways God has shown up—could choose otherwise, but they did. And sometimes we do too.

As believers, living in ways that honor the Lord should be our highest priority. Our obedience shouldn't be based solely on what He'll do for us, but He does incentivize us to live righteously, and it's a motivation we cannot ignore. God recognizes every decision we make to stand fully in our identity as His child, and He celebrates each one.

Today, choose to obey the Lord's ways in love and reverence.

*Lord, I am Yours, and my desire is to follow
Your will and ways every day. Strengthen me.
Impart Your wisdom. And give me courage.*

WEDNESDAY, MARCH 4

Leviticus 27 / Mark 8 / Psalm 46

Speaking Up

"If any of you are embarrassed over me and the way I'm leading you when you get around your fickle and unfocused friends, know that you'll be an even greater embarrassment to the Son of Man when he arrives in all the splendor of God, his Father, with an army of the holy angels."

MARK 8:38 MSG

Let Mark 8:38 encourage you to be loud and proud of your faith in Jesus. Because you have been accepted, forgiven, and redeemed, let nothing keep you silent. You are valued and celebrated by God, so be ready to share your testimony when the opportunity presents itself. You were created on purpose and for a purpose, and that is something to share! And you are forever protected and secure in the Father's arms, something that brings peace to every believer. Be quick to let others know that.

Since your identity is solid in Christ, there is every reason to share that good news with others. The world needs to know about Jesus and the saving faith His death on the cross provides. Make certain you are walking through the open doors that God places before you, confidently sharing His goodness!

Lord, I am not embarrassed of You or my steadfast faith.
Help me be vocal at the right times and in the right ways,
always willing to talk about Your grace in my life.
The world needs Jesus, and I want to help that happen!

THURSDAY, MARCH 5

Numbers 1–2 / Mark 9:1–13 / Psalm 47

Intricately and Intimately Involved

*The LORD spoke to Moses and Aaron, saying,
"The people of Israel shall camp each by his own standard,
with the banners of their fathers' houses. They shall
camp facing the tent of meeting on every side."*

NUMBERS 2:1–2 ESV

Have you considered how very intricately and intimately God is involved in the lives of those He loves? Not only did He facilitate their extraordinary exodus from Egypt, but He also fed the Israelites, clothed them, led them by a pillar of cloud by day and fire by night, provided His presence through the tent of meeting, and helped organize them into tribes. God was preparing them to enter the Promised Land.

This is why we can confidently trust that He is also deeply involved in our lives here and now. The Lord is always preparing us for the next step of His plan. And just as God was involved in every detail surrounding His chosen people back then, the same is true for today's believers. There is nothing about you that disinterests God. From the smallest situation to the biggest battle, He is already working all things for your good and His glory. Why? Because you are fully loved and known by the Father. Nothing can change that.

*Lord, what an unexpected blessing to understand
Your unwavering interest in the details of my life.
I may feel worthless from time to time, but this truth
speaks to my everlasting value in Your eyes.*

FRIDAY, MARCH 6

Numbers 3 / Mark 9:14–50 / Psalm 48:1–8

The Struggle of Unbelief

"And it has often cast him into fire and into water, to destroy him. But if you can do anything, have compassion on us and help us." And Jesus said to him, "'If you can'! All things are possible for one who believes." Immediately the father of the child cried out and said, "I believe; help my unbelief!"

MARK 9:22–24 ESV

This father was desperate for Jesus to heal his son plagued by demons. The situation was serious and dangerous, and he was worried for his son's well-being. In his worry, he asked for compassion. He asked for help. This distraught father asked Jesus to heal his son fully and completely. While he had faith that He could, Dad needed an extra dose of hope that a miracle of restoration was possible. And so, he asked for it.

Part of having a personal relationship with God is having the freedom to be honest with Him through prayer. The reality is there are times we need an extra measure of faith as we patiently wait for Him to act. We need a boost of confidence and courage as we navigate difficult times with the Lord. And because your identity rests in Christ, you can boldly ask the Father to help your struggle with unbelief.

Lord, thank You that I can be honest about my lacking and confident of Your abundance. I'm grateful for the freedom to tell You of my needs.

SATURDAY, MARCH 7

Numbers 4 / Mark 10:1–34 / Psalm 48:9–14

Trusting the Eternal Above the Earthly

And Jesus, looking at him, loved him, and said to him, "You lack one thing: go, sell all that you have and give to the poor, and you will have treasure in heaven; and come, follow me." Disheartened by the saying, he went away sorrowful, for he had great possessions. And Jesus looked around and said to his disciples, "How difficult it will be for those who have wealth to enter the kingdom of God!"

MARK 10:21–23 ESV

The rich young man did not want to do what was required to enter the kingdom, which was choosing to trust in the eternal God rather than any earthly riches. He worshipped worldly treasures more, unwilling to focus his life on the Lord above all else. This was a matter of the heart, and it kept him from a heavenly home.

There is nothing wrong with decorating our homes, wearing nice clothes, taking vacations, or maxing out a 401(k). The problem is when we rely on them for self-sufficiency. Sometimes money encourages us to be independent, and we stop relying on God for provision and protection. As children of God, we must fight the urge to find our identity in anything other than Him. Our security is in the Lord first and foremost.

Lord, there is nothing the world can offer that comes anywhere close to Your goodness. Keep my eyes on You to meet every need, every time. Help me trust in You alone.

Daylight Saving Time Begins SUNDAY, MARCH 8

Numbers 5:1–6:21 / Mark 10:35–52 / Psalm 49:1–9

Your Voice Is Heard in the Heavens

And they came to Jericho. And as he was leaving Jericho with his disciples and a great crowd, Bartimaeus, a blind beggar, the son of Timaeus, was sitting by the roadside. And when he heard that it was Jesus of Nazareth, he began to cry out and say, "Jesus, Son of David, have mercy on me!"

MARK 10:46–47 ESV

Bartimaeus called out for Jesus, and he was heard. Not only heard but healed. Jesus showed kindness and mercy, and this blind man recovered his sight. What if he hadn't cried out?

As a believer, your voice reaches God's ears each time you call on Him. Maybe you're struggling in a relationship. Maybe your child has chosen the wrong path forward. Maybe your finances are in the tank or you're grieving the loss of someone special. Or maybe you are desperate for physical healing like Bartimaeus. Regardless of your reasons, you can rest knowing your voice is heard in the heavens.

Don't let anything or anyone shut you up or shut you down, especially when your heart is aching for what only the Lord can provide. Call out to Him in prayer. Cry out His name through the tears. Tell God everything weighing you down and believe for His presence to bring peace and comfort. Let the Lord meet you in your mess and remind you that you are perfectly loved, every day and in every way.

Lord, thank You for hearing my voice.

MONDAY, MARCH 9

Numbers 6:22–7:47 / Mark 11 / Psalm 49:10–20

God's Will to Bless

The LORD spoke to Moses, saying, "Speak to Aaron and his sons, saying, Thus you shall bless the people of Israel: you shall say to them, The LORD bless you and keep you; the LORD make his face to shine upon you and be gracious to you; the LORD lift up his countenance upon you and give you peace. So shall they put my name upon the people of Israel, and I will bless them."
NUMBERS 6:22–27 ESV

This beloved passage of scripture is a priestly blessing demonstrating God's will to bless the entire Israelite community. He promises to extend His goodness to His chosen people through children, crops, and complete well-being. He promises to protect them from enemies. God promises to shine His favor on this nation, keeping His face turned toward them always. These verses show us the Lord's everlasting commitment to those He loves.

We can claim this for ourselves today. In the same ways God expressed His love to the Israelites then, He does the same for us now. Accepting Jesus as your personal Savior and choosing to live a righteous life that pleases Him reveals your identity in Christ. That means you are His, and His promises are yours. So, stand strong in confidence, knowing you are deeply and perfectly loved and His face shines upon you every day.

Lord, what a gift to realize that I am fully Yours and completely protected. Let me live worthy of your blessings.

TUESDAY, MARCH 10

Numbers 7:48–8:4 / Mark 12:1–27 / Psalm 50:1–15

Call to God When in Trouble

"Set out a sacrifice I can accept: your thankfulness. Be true to your word to the Most High. When you are in trouble, call for Me. I will come and rescue you, and you will honor Me."
PSALM 50:14–15 VOICE

Because you are His, you have the right and privilege to cry out to God for help. You can call for Him when the weight of stress feels too heavy. When your marriage is in trouble and you don't know what to do next, you can go directly to the Lord for wisdom. He will comfort you when parenting feels too big or your finances are in a tangle. He will rescue you from enemy traps you didn't see coming. God will intervene in those messy moments of grief when you can't seem to find your footing. Every time you pray for help, the Lord will meet you in significant and meaningful ways.

Never forget that as a believer, your identity is anchored in Christ, and with that comes countless blessings no one or nothing can match. But also remember to be thankful for God's demonstrated love, and honor Him through your words and actions. You hold great value to the one who created you, and His presence is your constant companion.

Lord, thank You for being but a prayer away when I need You. Thanks for hearing and protecting me when trouble comes. I love You.

WEDNESDAY, MARCH 11

Numbers 8:5–9:23 / Mark 12:28–44 / Psalm 50:16–23

The Call to Love

Jesus replied, "The most important commandment is this: 'Listen, O Israel! The LORD our God is the one and only LORD. And you must love the LORD your God with all your heart, all your soul, all your mind, and all your strength.' The second is equally important: 'Love your neighbor as yourself.' No other commandment is greater than these."

MARK 12:29–31 NLT

The greatest and most important command is rooted in love. It matters greatly to God! Scripture talks a lot about love and how it's foundational to living according to His plan, even saying others will know we are Christians because of how we love one another (John 13:35). It's not only loving God above all else but also loving our neighbors. When we fully embrace this command and walk it out each day, our obedience will reveal who we are and whose we are.

Why is this difficult for you at times? Are there people who make it almost impossible to do? Is there genuine trauma or past pain keeping you from opening your heart again? Are you filled with bitterness or unforgiveness?

The truth is that you can love because God loved you first. You are fully capable of extraordinary compassion. Ask the Lord to heal and unlock it in you so you can obey the most important command with passion and purpose.

Lord, help me be a woman who shows love and compassion well to You and those around me!

THURSDAY, MARCH 12

Numbers 10–11 / Mark 13:1–8 / Psalm 51:1–9

How to Withstand Deception

And as he sat on the Mount of Olives opposite the temple, Peter and James and John and Andrew asked him privately, "Tell us, when will these things be, and what will be the sign when all these things are about to be accomplished?" And Jesus began to say to them, "See that no one leads you astray. Many will come in my name, saying, 'I am he!' and they will lead many astray."

MARK 13:3–6 ESV

As believers, we can be confident that we hear God's voice. We spend time in the Word, learning what He has for us in its pages. We listen to sermons that remind us of His goodness. We spend time in godly community, journeying through life together and bringing encouragement as needed. And the Holy Spirit lives in us, growing our faith and activating it into action. We belong to the Lord, and He speaks to us every day.

Understanding this, Jesus tells us to be on guard, so we're not deceived. There will be false teachers with doctrine that's just a bit off from truth so it's hard to discern. And the best thing we can do in preparation is know God's Word, listen to the Spirit, and be in community with other believers. These will help us withstand deception, keeping us protected and secure.

> **Lord, honor my efforts to know the truth, and give me discernment to recognize deception and turn from it.**

FRIDAY, MARCH 13

Numbers 12–13 / Mark 13:9–37 / Psalm 51:10–19

Even When We Mess Up

Create in me a clean heart, O God; restore within me a sense of being brand new. Do not throw me far away from Your presence, and do not remove Your Holy Spirit from me. Give back to me the deep delight of being saved by You; let Your willing Spirit sustain me.
PSALM 51:10–12 VOICE

This psalm—written by King David—unpacks the emotions he felt after the prophet Nathan called him out regarding his affair with Bathsheba and murder of her husband. Can't you hear the desperation in his words? The lament? No doubt, he was a broken man.

The reality is that we must all face the natural consequences of our sin. We've been forgiven by God, but He doesn't always save us from the fallout. While there is no condemnation for those in Christ, many times He allows us to navigate the difficult outcomes because there are life-giving and life-changing lessons in them that we need. And the result is a clean heart that God has restored and made brand-new.

As we cry out for God's presence and goodness to come even closer, we will be refreshed. He will restore our joy and bring comfort and peace. And He will strengthen our spirit. We can trust the Lord to love us fully, even when we mess up completely.

Lord, thank You for the blessing of restoration for those whose identity rests in You alone.

SATURDAY, MARCH 14

Numbers 14 / Mark 14:1–31 / Psalm 52

The Lord's Supper

And as they were eating, he took bread, and after blessing it broke it and gave it to them, and said, "Take; this is my body." And he took a cup, and when he had given thanks he gave it to them, and they all drank of it. And he said to them, "This is my blood of the covenant, which is poured out for many."

MARK 14:22–24 ESV

As believers whose identity is anchored in Christ, we partake in the Lord's Supper as an act of remembrance. It's a sacred opportunity to reflect on what He did on the cross that allowed us to become daughters of the King. Jesus' death paid the debt for the sins of the world—for every sin we have committed or will commit—bridging the gap it left between us and the Father. Now when God looks at us, He does so through Christ's blood, which has cleansed us fully and completely. We are accepted, forgiven, and redeemed. There is nothing that can reverse it.

Every chance you have to participate in the Lord's Supper, do so with reverence. Eat the bread and drink the wine with a heart of gratitude for all He's done. Reflect on the weight of that sacrifice with humility. And remember that You were bought with a price because you hold immeasurable value to the God who created you, the Son who died for you, and the Holy Spirit who lives inside you.

Lord, thank You.

SUNDAY, MARCH 15

Numbers 15 / Mark 14:32–72 / Psalm 53

Colossal Mistakes

The girl spotted him and began telling the people standing around, "He's one of them." He denied it again. After a little while, the bystanders brought it up again. "You've got to be one of them. You've got 'Galilean' written all over you." Now Peter got really nervous and swore, "I never laid eyes on this man you're talking about." Just then the rooster crowed a second time. Peter remembered how Jesus had said, "Before a rooster crows twice, you'll deny me three times." He collapsed in tears.
MARK 14:69–72 MSG

Peter loved Jesus. He was one of His first followers and in the inner circle of trust. Peter was outspoken, a natural-born leader, and often the spokesperson for the disciples. He was also the first who confessed that Jesus was indeed the Son of God. And He told Peter he would be instrumental in building the church. For all intents and purposes, he was a big deal. He loved and served Jesus with passion and purpose. And while Peter's identity was secured in Jesus as Lord, he still denied Him.

Let this story bring encouragement that even when we make colossal mistakes that seem irreparable, we're forgiven. We can't lose our salvation. And the best thing we can do is go right to God and confess our mistake and let Him comfort our anxious heart.

Lord, what a relief to know I can't be stripped of salvation for making big mistakes. I'm Yours forever.

MONDAY, MARCH 16

Numbers 16 / Mark 15:1–32 / Psalm 54

The God of Again

God has pulled me out from every one of the troubles that encompass me, and I have seen what it means to stand over my enemies in triumph.

PSALM 54:7 VOICE

David wrote this psalm—this song of lament—when his so-called friends betrayed him to Saul. It was a song of hope and remembrance that God's promises are a sure thing, something we can also cling to when facing our own storms of life. In this verse, David recalls that the Lord faithfully pulled him out of every trouble, and he was certain He'd do it again.

We can be certain too. Think of the perfect track record God has in your life. Remember how He brought financial help at the right time. Has He restored broken relationships or helped you navigate a health challenge? Maybe the Lord's favor was evident in a court proceeding. Maybe you got pregnant when all hope was lost. Maybe he finally proposed, or God gave you peace and confidence to be single. Were you finally able to have the hard conversation and then watched goodness come from it? God has worked mightily in your life before, and like David, you can boldly trust that He will...again.

You are safe and secure in His hands. Forever and always.

Lord, I've seen Your mighty hand move in my life, and I am confident You will intervene in significant ways again. I trust You as my provider and protector.

TUESDAY, MARCH 17 — *St. Patrick's Day*

Numbers 17–18 / Mark 15:33–47 / Psalm 55

The Torn Curtain

But Jesus, with a loud cry, gave his last breath. At that moment the Temple curtain ripped right down the middle. When the Roman captain standing guard in front of him saw that he had quit breathing, he said, "This has to be the Son of God!"
MARK 15:37–39 MSG

The temple consisted of two sections, and the curtain served as the divider between the holy place and the most holy place. The latter is where God's presence manifested, and only a high priest could enter once a year. When Jesus *willingly* gave His last breath, the curtain ripped down the middle, from top to bottom, which signified what His death on the cross accomplished for believers. Now, we all have access to God. We can be in His presence because Jesus paid the price for the sin that kept us separated from our Father.

When you accept this gift, your new identity is in Christ alone. You are accepted as you are, no need to clean up your act first. Every sin—past, present, and future—is forgiven and forgotten. And the Holy Spirit comes into your heart to help grow and mature your faith into something beautiful.

Stand tall, friend. You are loved and valued by the one who created you on purpose and for a purpose. And you are celebrated, even in your imperfections.

Lord, thank You for making a way for me to commune directly with You. I love You!

WEDNESDAY, MARCH 18

Numbers 19–20 / Mark 16 / Psalm 56:1–7

God's Ways Are Higher

And Moses lifted up his hand and struck the rock with his staff twice, and water came out abundantly, and the congregation drank, and their livestock. And the LORD said to Moses and Aaron, "Because you did not believe in me, to uphold me as holy in the eyes of the people of Israel, therefore you shall not bring this assembly into the land that I have given them."

NUMBERS 20:11–12 ESV

Moses didn't follow God's command. Just a few verses earlier in the chapter, he was told to *speak* to the rock and water would come forth, but instead He *struck* it. And while the Israelites did get the water they grumbled for, Moses and Aaron paid a hefty price for their disobedience. They would not be permitted to enter the Promised Land.

This may seem like overkill, especially for two men who courageously approached Pharaoh and led God's people out of their slavery in Egypt. But part of faith means we trust God's will and ways. We aren't owed any explanation. The Bible tells us that His ways are higher than ours, as are His thoughts (Isaiah 55:8–9). We may never know why the Lord does what He does, but we can know and believe that love is His motivator. And we are deeply and perfectly loved by God.

Lord, help me trust You even when I don't understand. You are stronger and smarter and forever faithful. That's all I need to know.

THURSDAY, MARCH 19

Numbers 21:1–22:20 / Luke 1:1–25 / Psalm 56:8–13

God Collects Every Tear

You have taken note of my journey through life, caught each of my tears in Your bottle. But God, are they not also blots on Your book? Then my enemies shall turn back and scatter on the day I call out to You. This I know for certain: God is on my side.

Psalm 56:8–9 voice

What a sweet reminder that we are deeply and fully loved by God. Not only does He see our tears fall and understand every detail as to why, the Lord also collects them. He keeps an account of each one, never ignoring what concerns those who trust Him. God is for us. He is on our side. And you can know with certainty that He will always be faithful.

So when you suffer heartbreak in parenting or are grieving the discovered betrayal, He sees you. When your best efforts fail or your dreams aren't realized, God knows. When your finances are a mess or your health falters, He recognizes it. And when you're overwhelmed and unsteady in the moment, He sympathizes.

How does this truth encourage you today? In what current circumstances did you need this powerful reminder? As a believer, you can rest knowing you're immeasurably valuable to the Lord and nothing can change that. God is fully present in every mountaintop and valley of your life.

> *Lord, thank You for being so intimately involved in my every moment. I know I am loved by You.*

First Day of Spring   FRIDAY, MARCH 20

Numbers 22:21–23:30 / Luke 1:26–56 / Psalm 57

In the Shade of His Wings

Mercy. May Your mercy come to me, O God, for my soul is safe within You, the guardian of my life. I will seek protection in the shade of Your wings until the destruction has passed. I cry out to God, the Most High, to God who always does what is good for me. Out of heaven my rescue comes. He dispatches His mercy and truth and goes after whoever tries to run over me.

PSALM 57:1–3 VOICE

This is another psalm of lament written by David as he reflects on having to flee from Saul's pursuit and hide in caves for protection. As a man after God's own heart, he comes to realize that his safety wasn't truly found in the depths of those caves but in the shade of the Lord's wings. He survived because it was God's will, and nothing trumps that.

This is vital for us to know too. We must understand, like David, that our protection is in God's hands. He has plans for us that were determined long ago, and He will help us see them through.

Let's recognize that because our identity is in Christ, we've no need to look other places for security. We can confidently pray for guidance, wisdom, and strength, believing for them by faith. And we can trust God to do what is good for us, whether it be a rescue from the situation or His presence through it.

Lord, I trust You.

SATURDAY, MARCH 21

Numbers 24–25 / Luke 1:57–2:20 / Psalm 58

Jesus

There were shepherds camping in the neighborhood. They had set night watches over their sheep. Suddenly, God's angel stood among them and God's glory blazed around them. They were terrified. The angel said, "Don't be afraid. I'm here to announce a great and joyful event that is meant for everybody, worldwide: A Savior has just been born in David's town, a Savior who is Messiah and Master. This is what you're to look for: a baby wrapped in a blanket and lying in a manger."

LUKE 2:8–12 MSG

Because sin had separated us from the holiness of God, He made a way to bridge the gap back to His creation. There was nothing we could do to reconnect with the Lord ourselves, especially being limited and flawed in our humanity. So Jesus stepped off the throne, put on skin, and came into the world with a mission.

Every detail was planned. When on the kingdom calendar He'd be born and to whom. Where He'd make an entrance onto the world stage and how He'd be revealed. The life Jesus would live, who would follow Him, as well as the details of His death. And it was all done for. . .us.

Have you accepted Jesus as your Savior? Is your identity secured in Him?

Lord, I believe You are God's only Son who died on the cross and rose three days later, ensuring my salvation when I put my trust in You. I know it's through You alone that I am saved.

SUNDAY, MARCH 22

Numbers 26:1–27:11 / Luke 2:21–38 / Psalm 59:1–8

The Right and Privilege to Pray

They have staked out my life; they are going to ambush me! Those brutes are aligned, ready to attack me for no good cause, my Eternal One. I have not crossed them. I've done nothing wrong, yet they rush ahead to start the assault. I beg You to help me; come and see for Yourself! I plead with You, Eternal One, Commander of heavenly armies, True God of Israel, to get up and punish these people; do not let any betrayer off the hook; show no mercy to malicious evildoers!

PSALM 59:3–5 VOICE

As a believer, you have a powerful Daddy up in heaven who doesn't take kindly to others threatening or roughing up His children. He is a fierce protector, which means you're secure in His arms. Your mistreatment never goes unnoticed, and God will defend you because He loves you.

The reality is that you have the right and privilege to pray this kind of prayer, just as David did. The best thing you can do is take every fear and worry directly to the Lord and let Him guide you forward. Let Him handle the details of the situation. Be it keen wisdom, enduring strength, or divine intervention, God will meet you in the mess. He promises to equip believers for whatever comes their way, and He always keeps His word.

Lord, I know others are working against me.
Comfort my heart and help me trust Your plans.

MONDAY, MARCH 23

> Numbers 27:12–29:11 / Luke 2:39–52 / Psalm 59:9–17

A Heart of Thanksgiving

But me? I will sing of Your strength. I will awake with the sun to sing of Your loving mercy because in my most troubled hour, You defended me. You were my shelter. I will lift my voice to sing Your praise, O my Strength—for You came to my defense. O God, You have shown me Your loving mercy.

PSALM 59:16–17 VOICE

Let's not forget to show our gratitude to God when He works on our behalf. He deserves passionate praise for being our defender. We should thank Him for the mercy shown toward us. And His sheltering warrants our appreciation. For God is good to those whose identity is in Him.

What has the Lord done in your life? Where has He strengthened you for the battle or opened your eyes to truth? Where has He imparted discernment and wisdom, clearing out any confusion? When did God shelter you from the storm or calm the waves lapping at your ankles? When did He straighten the crooked path before you?

Just as the Lord celebrates you, be quick to celebrate Him too. Tell God about your joy. Tell Him how He brought peace into your heart. Pray with a glad spirit for the ways He's blessed you.

Lord, what would I do without You? My heart is relieved and satisfied once again, and the credit belongs only to You. Thanks for being my shelter, defender, and strength. I love You!

TUESDAY, MARCH 24

Numbers 29:12–30:16 / Luke 3 / Psalm 60:1–5

A Purposeful God

Now when all the people were baptized, and when Jesus also had been baptized and was praying, the heavens were opened, and the Holy Spirit descended on him in bodily form, like a dove; and a voice came from heaven, "You are my beloved Son; with you I am well pleased."

LUKE 3:21–22 ESV

Did you notice that when Jesus prayed, the heavens opened? Let this be evidence to believers that God hears prayers. The Spirit descending demonstrates that He is active. This also offers proof that God speaks to us. And we learn that it's possible to please the Lord. He is a purposeful Father who's intimately involved in our lives.

What is the Spirit speaking into your heart right now? Which of these insights encourages you most, based on the circumstances you're having to navigate? Do they bring you peace? Do they offer comfort?

Because you are chosen and loved, you can always count on God to be present in your life. It's not only in the valleys where you'll feel Him but in the daily choices of obedience. Your faith in His sovereignty is what brings delight to His heart. And you are fully loved by a God who will part the heavens to hear your voice rising to the heavens.

Lord, I'm encouraged by knowing that You are alive and active in my life. I am in awe of Your endless strength and compassion. And I want to please You.

WEDNESDAY, MARCH 25

Numbers 31 / Luke 4 / Psalm 60:6–12

The Sword of the Spirit

Now Jesus, full of the Holy Spirit, left the Jordan and was led by the Spirit into the wild. For forty wilderness days and nights he was tested by the Devil. He ate nothing during those days, and when the time was up he was hungry. The Devil, playing on his hunger, gave the first test: "Since you're God's Son, command this stone to turn into a loaf of bread." Jesus answered by quoting Deuteronomy: "It takes more than bread to really live."

LUKE 4:1–4 MSG

When temptation threatens, let's remember to use the sword of the Spirit—that is, God's Word—to fight back, just like Jesus did in today's verses. It's sharper than any two-edged sword (Hebrews 4:12) and is our best defense against what the enemy brings our way. It's part of the armor of God (Ephesians 6:10–17) and is available to anyone whose identity is anchored in Christ. Because you're His, God has made a way to withstand anything designed to entice you to live in unrighteous ways.

This is why time in the Word is essential. It's why we listen to theologically sound sermons and attend Bible-preaching churches. Knowing what's at stake, this is why we surround ourselves with godly friends who seek the Lord with fervor. It's also why we rely on the Holy Spirit's leading in every circumstance. Dig into scripture daily so you'll be ready when temptation tries to slither in.

Lord, I love Your Word!

THURSDAY, MARCH 26

Numbers 32–33 / Luke 5:1–16 / Psalm 61

When Pushed to the Edge

Hear me, O God, when I cry; listen to my prayer. You are the One I will call when pushed to the edge, when my heart is faint. Shoulder me to the rock above me. For You are my protection, an impenetrable fortress from my enemies. Let me live in Your sanctuary forever; let me find safety in the shadow of Your wings.
PSALM 61:1–4 VOICE

Where are you being pushed to the edge right now? Is the medical treatment not working as planned and you're scared? Did the financing fall through and you're stuck? Is your heart aching for a baby or to be married and it seems unlikely to happen? Are you struggling to navigate the intense grief, unable to find your footing? Did you just discover the betrayal? Are you lacking meaningful friendships? Is your child involved with the wrong crowd and not listening to your concerns? These are the times you cry out to your Father in heaven, trusting He hears you and will meet you right where you are.

As believers, we can know that God is with us and for us. He alone is our protection and provider—not anything worldly can even come close. And when we're in trouble and trying to manage a weary heart, we have the privilege as God's daughters to pray with passion for His help.

*Lord, see my struggles and hear my cries.
I cannot do this without You. Please come quick.*

FRIDAY, MARCH 27

Numbers 34–36 / Luke 5:17–32 / Psalm 62:1–6

Quietly Waiting

My soul quietly waits for the True God alone; my salvation comes from Him. He alone is my rock and my deliverance, my citadel high on the hill; I will not be shaken.

PSALM 62:1–2 VOICE

Would you agree that it's difficult to *quietly wait* for God to act or answer? Most of us would wholeheartedly agree! Yet that's exactly what we're to do as His chosen. As believers, we have assurance that the Lord hears us and will respond, but His timing rarely matches ours. We're to be steadfast, waiting with expectation for the Father to reveal His will and ways. We are to put our hope in Him alone rather than looking to the world for help. How are you doing with this, friend?

In what circumstances are you seeking God right now? Is your heart pestered or peaceful? Are you watching with faith or fear? Are you feeling secure or shaken?

Don't let anything take your peace—the peace Jesus came to give. Protect your mind from running too far down the path of *what if*. Stand in confidence that God sees you and knows what's on your heart. He hears your prayers. And let the Lord strengthen you for the quiet waiting until His goodness is revealed.

Lord, help me be the kind of woman who waits well. Let my faith in You steady my soul and settle my spirit in significant ways.

SATURDAY, MARCH 28

Deuteronomy 1:1–2:25 / Luke 5:33–6:11 / Psalm 62:7–12

God Knows

Once God has spoken; twice have I heard this: that power belongs to God, and that to you, O Lord, belongs steadfast love. For you will render to a man according to his work.
PSALM 62:11–12 ESV

When today's Bible passage says *once* and *twice*, take note. This signifies what is being said is certain. The truth that God holds all the power is being confirmed, and our best efforts without His help will fall flat. Our humanity is limited and imperfect. And we need the Lord to infuse our faith so that as we walk out the calling on our life, we do so through Him.

But beware because God knows if our belief is real or fake. He knows when someone talks the talk but fails to walk the walk. With clarity, He can see into the heart to determine intentions. The Lord knows when we do things to make ourselves look good versus when we do things with humility. The genuineness of our faith is determined by the combination of our attitude and actions.

For the believer who places their identity in Christ and tries to live in ways that please Him (even flawed and imperfectly), let this breed confidence. But for those faking their faith for an ulterior motive, this should raise all sorts of red flags and set off warning bells. God knows.

Lord, search my heart and create in me a real faith that will hold up under any testing.

SUNDAY, MARCH 29 — *Palm Sunday*

Deuteronomy 2:26–4:14 / Luke 6:12–35 / Psalm 63:1–5

Our Calling to Be His Hands and Feet

Listen, what's the big deal if you love people who already love you? Even scoundrels do that much! So what if you do good to those who do good to you? Even scoundrels do that much! So what if you lend to people who are likely to repay you? Even scoundrels lend to scoundrels if they think they'll be fully repaid.

LUKE 6:32–34 VOICE

In today's verses, Jesus is calling us to love in extraordinary ways. We're told to love even more than we feel is necessary. We're to have the kind of love for one another that sets us apart from others. This is what believers are commanded to do.

It's easy to love the lovable and be kind to those who are already kind. We can show generosity to those who are generous in return. But we're to go above and beyond that. And it's only something we can do through God's help.

When we think of all the ways the Lord has been compassionate to us, we're encouraged to pay it forward. He loved us in our sin and offered forgiveness in our wretchedness. Now that our identity is in Christ, our calling is to be His hands and feet to the world. And it's a privilege to do so.

> *Lord, it's hard to love so extraordinarily, and I'm asking for Your help. Teach me to show kindness and generosity when it's easy and when it's hard.*

MONDAY, MARCH 30

Deuteronomy 4:15–5:22 / Luke 6:36–49 / Psalm 63:6–11

What Does Your Life Preach?

You can know a tree by the fruit it bears. You don't find figs on a thorn bush, and you can't pick grapes from a briar bush. It's the same with people. A person full of goodness in his heart produces good things; a person with an evil reservoir in his heart pours out evil things. The heart overflows in the words a person speaks; your words reveal what's within your heart.

LUKE 6:44–45 VOICE

Let today's passage of scripture serve as a measuring stick for our faith. The things we do and the words we speak reveal what's in our heart, and it matters to God. Is our love for Him evident? Does our life point to the Father in heaven? Are we living as ambassadors for the Lord? Today, ask Him to open your eyes to truth as you take inventory of what your life is preaching to those around you.

Do you speak in ways that bless others and glorify the Lord? Are you compassionate toward those around you? Do you affirm and inspire? Are you willing to help those in need? Are your words encouraging? Do you give God the glory?

Because you are forgiven and redeemed, let your life shine. You were created on purpose and for a purpose, so live that way! Let your life bear holy fruit.

Lord, help my words and actions bring You glory. I want my life to honor You above all else.

TUESDAY, MARCH 31

Deuteronomy 5:23–7:26 / Luke 7:1–17 / Psalm 64:1–5

Chosen and Special

Remember: you're a people set apart for the Eternal your God; He is your God and has chosen you to be His own possession—His special people—out of all the peoples on the earth. The Eternal didn't become devoted to you and choose you because you were the most numerous of all the peoples—in fact, you were the least! Instead, He brought you out of Egypt with overwhelming power and liberated you from slavery to Pharaoh the king because He loved you and was keeping the oath He swore to your ancestors.

Deuteronomy 7:6–8 voice

Moses spoke this powerful truth over the Israelites, reminding them of who they were and who God is. Imagine how this must have encouraged their hearts. He declared them as chosen and special to Himself, more than any other people on earth. And it wasn't because of anything they'd done. It was God's unending love for them and His unshakable promise to their forefathers.

If you have asked Jesus into your heart and confessed your sins, you are chosen and special too! You've been accepted into God's family, fully forgiven, and redeemed. You're valued and deeply loved. And it's not because of anything you've done. You are saved by faith alone. So let the goodness of His compassion and faithfulness settle in your heart today and bolster your confidence.

Lord, I commit my life to You today and forever. Thank You for loving me. I love You!

APRIL 2026

SUNDAY	MONDAY	TUESDAY	WEDNESDAY	THURSDAY	FRIDAY	SATURDAY
			1 Passover Begins at Sundown	2	3 Good Friday	4
5 Easter	6	7	8	9	10	11
12	13	14	15	16	17	18
19	20	21	22	23	24	25
26	27	28	29	30		

WEDNESDAY, APRIL 1

Passover Begins at Sundown

Deuteronomy 8–9 / Luke 7:18–35 / Psalm 64:6–10

To Humble and Test You

Remember how the LORD your God led you all the way in the wilderness these forty years, to humble and test you in order to know what was in your heart, whether or not you would keep his commands. He humbled you, causing you to hunger and then feeding you with manna, which neither you nor your ancestors had known, to teach you that man does not live on bread alone but on every word that comes from the mouth of the LORD. Your clothes did not wear out and your feet did not swell during these forty years. Know then in your heart that as a man disciplines his son, so the LORD your God disciplines you.

DEUTERONOMY 8:2–5 NIV

God's Word answers the common question "Why?" we often ask when we're going through difficulty, challenges, and pain in this life. Our Father wants us to prove our faith and love for Him. We don't like to be told that we need to be humbled, but the reality is that self-pride flares and even flames at times in all of us. We don't like to be tested, but tests judge and verify what is true in our minds and hearts. And so we need to welcome tests and trials as opportunities for worship and testimony. They are a sign of endless love and care from our first and best Father who wants to know that we sincerely follow Him and that we truly love Him back.

Lord, help me to welcome tests and trials as opportunities for love and loyalty, devotion and worship—all for and to You, my perfect heavenly Father.

THURSDAY, APRIL 2

Deuteronomy 10–11 / Luke 7:36–8:3 / Psalm 65:1–8

For Your Own Good

And now, Israel, what does the Lord your God ask of you but to fear the Lord your God, to walk in obedience to him, to love him, to serve the Lord your God with all your heart and with all your soul, and to observe the Lord's commands and decrees that I am giving you today for your own good?

DEUTERONOMY 10:12–13 NIV

For your own good is a phrase that should be on repeat in our minds and hearts. God's commands and decrees were never meant to ruin our fun. He is not a killjoy. Those are the kinds of lies that the world controlled by Satan loves to spread to continue the depravity and decay of society as it rebels and runs farther away from our one true Creator God and His perfect designs. When temptation to believe any of those lies creeps in, we can focus on the phrase *for your own good* to remember what a privilege and honor it is to fear the Lord, to walk in the ways of the one who can guide us best, to love and serve and obey our perfect Father who only wants goodness and eternal life and blessing for His children.

Heavenly Father, remind me that every time I follow You rather than the sinful ways of the world, it is always for my good and leads me toward eternal life and blessing.

FRIDAY, APRIL 3 — *Good Friday*

Deuteronomy 12–13 / Luke 8:4–21 / Psalm 65:9–13

Seeds and Soils

"And the seeds that fell on the good soil represent honest, good-hearted people who hear God's word, cling to it, and patiently produce a huge harvest."

LUKE 8:15 NLT

Jesus' parable about the seeds and soils explains so much about society and Christian ministry. There are those who hear God's Word who are apathetic and unaffected. There are those who are receptive and excited about God's Word at first but then fall away shortly because there are no deep roots to keep their faith thriving or protected from temptation to sin. There are those who receive God's Word but then let it be pushed out by worldly cares and pleasures so that they never grow and mature. And finally there are those who hold on tight to the seed of God's Word in good soil; they nurture it and produce bushels of wonderful fruit.

As we ponder the parable, we all can probably think of examples of ones we know who fit each category. As much as we'd like to, we can't ever control how the seed is received; we can only keep spreading it wisely, hoping more and more people will find their true identity in Christ. And we must constantly cultivate the good soil in our own hearts and minds so that we'll produce an abundant harvest plus many blessings on top!

Jesus, help me to love and grow Your Word in my life. Help me to share it well and wisely to hopefully help more seed fall into good soil.

SATURDAY, APRIL 4

Deuteronomy 14:1–16:8 / Luke 8:22–39 / Psalm 66:1–7

Remember Your Red Seas

Say to God, "How awesome are your deeds! Your enemies cringe before your mighty power. Everything on earth will worship you; they will sing your praises, shouting your name in glorious songs." Come and see what our God has done, what awesome miracles he performs for people! He made a dry path through the Red Sea, and his people went across on foot. There we rejoiced in him. For by his great power he rules forever.

Psalm 66:3–7 nlt

Sometimes we just want to forget the horrible and hard times we've walked through. And certainly we shouldn't want to linger on them in an endless, "poor me" pity party kind of way. But we do need to remember the avenues God opened up and the miracles He worked inside and outside of ourselves during those hard times to help us endure and overcome. Reflecting on our personal Red Sea experiences—times when everything seemed hopeless but God made a miraculous way—should cause us to praise and worship Him in awe for all His mighty works in the past, plus give us confidence and peace that He continues to work miracles on our behalf both today and in the future, no matter what Red Sea we're running into.

Almighty God, help me to look back regularly and say, "How awesome are Your deeds that You have done in my life!" I am grateful beyond words, and I trust both today and my future to You.

SUNDAY, APRIL 5　　　　　　　　　　　　　　　　　　　*Easter*

Deuteronomy 16:9–18:22 / Luke 8:40–56 / Psalm 66:8–15

She Began to Tremble

*As Jesus went with him, he was surrounded by the crowds.
A woman in the crowd had suffered for twelve years with
constant bleeding, and she could find no cure. Coming
up behind Jesus, she touched the fringe of his robe.*

LUKE 8:42–44 NLT

Just one touch and she was immediately healed! As fellow women, many of us can imagine how desperate she must have felt in her plight. We can certainly empathize with her to some degree—but *constant* bleeding for twelve *years*? Most of us, gratefully, can't fully understand that. The poor thing!

"She began to tremble and fell to her knees" in front of Jesus, verse 47 (NLT) tells us. That was after she was healed. Was she shaking in relief or fear? Both? Was she worried that Jesus was angry that she chose to be sneaky rather than respectfully ask for His touch? Did she expect Him to retract her healing? Go back to never-ending blood? No wonder she trembled. It would be wonderful to chat with the dear woman right now and hear of her experience firsthand. Whatever the case, Jesus' response was total compassion and praise for her great faith. "'Daughter,' he said to her, 'your faith has made you well. Go in peace'" (Luke 8:48 NLT). What a precious example she is to us, and what a loving and merciful Savior we follow and find our identity in.

*Dear Jesus, my Savior and healer,
thank You for Your compassion for women.*

MONDAY, APRIL 6

Deuteronomy 19:1–21:9 / Luke 9:1–22 / Psalm 66:16–20

Only Five Loaves and Two Fish

Jesus said, "You feed them." "But we have only five loaves of bread and two fish," they answered. "Or are you expecting us to go and buy enough food for this whole crowd?" For there were about 5,000 men there.

LUKE 9:13–14 NLT

The Gospel of John tells us it was a young boy who provided the five loaves and two fish. Think about that boy for a minute. Did he have any idea what an impact his small act of generosity would have? Did his tummy rumble as he handed his food over and wondered when he might eat next? Surely his eyes grew big as Jesus took his loaves and fish and did something astounding—feeding thousands of people, with many baskets left over. Think about how many of those people must have believed in Jesus as the Son of God that day after seeing such a stunning miracle!

One boy's lunch is a reminder to us to be faithful and generous even in the small things we feel inspired to do—because that inspiration just might be God calling us to obey so that He can then show something amazing. Who knows what kind of showstopping miracles and blessings He wants to bestow because of our faithful giving and humble obedience?

Heavenly Father, I want to be humble, faithful, and generous to You even in the little things You ask of me. Show me how You want to amaze and bless and reward me for doing so.

TUESDAY, APRIL 7

Deuteronomy 21:10–23:8 / Luke 9:23–42 / Psalm 67

Daily Devotion

[Jesus] said to all, "If anyone would come after me, let him deny himself and take up his cross daily and follow me. For whoever would save his life will lose it, but whoever loses his life for my sake will save it. For what does it profit a man if he gains the whole world and loses or forfeits himself?"

LUKE 9:23–25 ESV

To follow Jesus, to truly find your identity in Him, is an all-in kind of loyalty and devotion. He is not interested in casual commitment or lukewarm people. In Revelation 3:15–16 (ESV) Jesus says, "I know your works: you are neither cold nor hot. Would that you were either cold or hot! So, because you are lukewarm, and neither hot nor cold, I will spit you out of my mouth." That's a *really serious* warning that we better be *really serious* about loving and following Jesus.

We have a *daily decision* to make to show our loyalty, devotion, and commitment to Jesus and deny ourselves and follow Him—choosing His will, obeying His Word, and following His paths instead of our own, with our heads held high because of our confidence that He is the one true Savior.

Dear Jesus, I'm serious about my love and commitment to You, and I want to show you that I choose You every day of my life through my thoughts and words and actions.

WEDNESDAY, APRIL 8

Deuteronomy 23:9–25:19 / Luke 9:43–62 / Psalm 68:1–6

The Greatest

Then his disciples began arguing about which of them was the greatest. But Jesus knew their thoughts, so he brought a little child to his side. Then he said to them, "Anyone who welcomes a little child like this on my behalf welcomes me, and anyone who welcomes me also welcomes my Father who sent me. Whoever is the least among you is the greatest."
LUKE 9:46–48 NLT

It's clear that comparison and competition among friends is nothing new. Even Jesus' disciples were guilty as they argued over which of them was the greatest. Did they mean greatest of all, like *ever*? Or the greatest friend of Jesus? Greatest at fishing? Greatest at grilling over the fire? Or any/all of the above? It's amusing and relatable to think about their rivalry.

Jesus stopped their bickering and set them straight with a little child as an example. He admonished them that those who welcome the little ones and the most humble ones, those who care the least about being the best—those people are truly the greatest. The point is, we're not supposed to care who is greatest among us. Jesus is greatest of all, and He loves us. That's what we really need to know!

Dear Jesus, help me not to compare; help me not to care who is greatest at anything. You are the greatest, and my identity is in You. That's all that matters, and I want to bring glory to You as I love and serve You and those around me who also need Your love.

THURSDAY, APRIL 9

> Deuteronomy 26:1–28:14 / Luke 10:1–20 / Psalm 68:7–14

The Real Reason to Rejoice

When the seventy-two disciples returned, they joyfully reported to him, "Lord, even the demons obey us when we use your name!" "Yes," he told them, "I saw Satan fall from heaven like lightning! Look, I have given you authority over all the power of the enemy, and you can walk among snakes and scorpions and crush them. Nothing will injure you. But don't rejoice because evil spirits obey you; rejoice because your names are registered in heaven."
LUKE 10:17–20 NLT

It was amazing to the disciples that they were given authority by Jesus over the power of Satan. Even demons obeyed them in the name of Jesus, and they were basically invincible. Who wouldn't think that incredible? But Jesus didn't want their heads to get too big. He reminded them what was really important—that their names were registered in heaven, and no one could ever cancel that. When we trust in Jesus and find our identity in Him, that's where our true reason for joy and our real invincibility lie too—in the facts that our futures are secure and our lives will last forever in perfect paradise.

Dear Jesus, I believe in You as the one and only Savior, and I'm so grateful my name is registered in heaven; my reservation is secure in perfect paradise for eternity.

FRIDAY, APRIL 10

Deuteronomy 28:15–68 / Luke 10:21–37 / Psalm 68:15–19

Go and Do the Same

"A despised Samaritan came along, and when he saw the man, he felt compassion for him. Going over to him, the Samaritan soothed his wounds with olive oil and wine and bandaged them. Then he put the man on his own donkey and took him to an inn, where he took care of him. The next day he handed the innkeeper two silver coins, telling him, 'Take care of this man. If his bill runs higher than this, I'll pay you the next time I'm here.' Now which of these three would you say was a neighbor to the man who was attacked by bandits?" Jesus asked. The man replied, "The one who showed him mercy." Then Jesus said, "Yes, now go and do the same."
Luke 10:33–37 NLT

Two people just walked on by the poor man who had been robbed and beaten. That kind of thing is all too common today too, isn't it? But then a Samaritan man chose compassion and helped a stranger, going above and beyond to make sure he was well cared for. Jesus gave us this story as an example of what it means to show true compassion and love for others and to teach us that our neighbor is anyone in need.

Jesus, help me to choose compassion for my neighbors in need. Show me the best ways to care for others in Your name, with Your love flowing through me.

SATURDAY, APRIL 11

Deuteronomy 29–30 / Luke 10:38–11:23 / Psalm 68:20–27

Love Him and Never Let Go

For I command you today to love the LORD your God, to walk in obedience to him, and to keep his commands, decrees and laws; then you will live and increase, and the LORD your God will bless you in the land you are entering to possess. But if your heart turns away and you are not obedient, and if you are drawn away to bow down to other gods and worship them, I declare to you this day that you will certainly be destroyed. . . . Now choose life, so that you and your children may live and that you may love the LORD your God, listen to his voice, and hold fast to him.

DEUTERONOMY 30:15–20 NIV

God's warnings of consequences and promises of blessings for His nation of Israel are for us to learn from today as well. Mercy and grace and eternal life are ours if we've accepted Jesus as Savior—because of His work on the cross. But if we turn away and disobey our Lord's leading in life, we will face the sad results and painful penalties of that rebellion. On the contrary, when we choose to listen and hold fast to the Lord with great love for Him, not only do we receive blessing but so do our children.

*Lord, I love You. I'm listening to You.
I want to hold fast to You and never let go.*

SUNDAY, APRIL 12

Deuteronomy 31:1–32:22 / Luke 11:24–36 / Psalm 68:28–35

Show Us Your Strength, God!

Summon your power, God; show us your strength, our God, as you have done before. Because of your temple at Jerusalem kings will bring you gifts. Rebuke the beast among the reeds, the herd of bulls among the calves of the nations. . . . Sing to God, you kingdoms of the earth, sing praise to the Lord, to him who rides across the highest heavens, the ancient heavens, who thunders with mighty voice. Proclaim the power of God, whose majesty is over Israel, whose power is in the heavens. You, God, are awesome in your sanctuary; the God of Israel gives power and strength to his people. Praise be to God!

PSALM 68:28–30, 32–35 NIV

There is nothing and no one more powerful than Almighty God, the Creator and sustainer of all things in all the universe. And so as we find ourselves in situations that seem impossible, we need to remember His power and sovereignty and ask Him to make Himself evident in the midst of our circumstances. Will He answer exactly the way we hope? Maybe, maybe not. But as we pray for His perfect will to be done and we focus on His glory and greatness, we will find peace and every reason to praise Him!

Almighty God, please show Your strength and sovereignty to all involved in this situation. We desperately need You. We need Your mercy, Your greatness, and Your perfect guidance to help and lead us.

MONDAY, APRIL 13

Deuteronomy 32:23–33:29 / Luke 11:37–54 / Psalm 69:1–9

Woe to the Pharisees

Then the Lord said to him, "Now then, you Pharisees clean the outside of the cup and dish, but inside you are full of greed and wickedness. You foolish people! Did not the one who made the outside make the inside also? But now as for what is inside you—be generous to the poor, and everything will be clean for you. Woe to you Pharisees, because you give God a tenth of your mint, rue and all other kinds of garden herbs, but you neglect justice and the love of God. You should have practiced the latter without leaving the former undone. Woe to you Pharisees."

LUKE 11:39–43 NIV

Jesus goes on in this passage with more "woes" as warnings to the Pharisees and anyone like them today. Our insides need to sincerely match what we portray on the outside about loving and serving the Lord! He will call out and give consequences for any greed or wickedness or hypocrisy in us, any unwillingness to care for the poor or work toward spreading God's true justice and love. May we constantly seek Him with humility, asking Him to help us never have the heart of a hypocritical Pharisee.

Lord, call out hypocrisy in me and forgive me, please. Help me to sincerely live and love like You!

TUESDAY, APRIL 14

Deuteronomy 34–Joshua 2 / Luke 12:1–15 / Psalm 69:10–17

Courageous and Careful to Obey

"Be strong and very courageous. Be careful to obey all the instructions Moses gave you. Do not deviate from them, turning either to the right or to the left. Then you will be successful in everything you do. Study this Book of Instruction continually. Meditate on it day and night so you will be sure to obey everything written in it. Only then will you prosper and succeed in all you do. This is my command—be strong and courageous! Do not be afraid or discouraged. For the LORD your God is with you wherever you go."

JOSHUA 1:7–9 NLT

With a bolstering call to action, God handed the reins of leadership to Joshua. In our roles and circles of influence, we have to ask ourselves daily if we are leading like God wanted Joshua to. Within our families and friendships. Within our teams at work. Within our churches and ministries we're involved in. Within our neighborhoods and communities. May we be strong and courageous. May we carefully obey God's Word and meditate on it day and night. May we remember God is with us in everything we do, everywhere we go. And may we find great success and prosperity because we joyfully obey God's commands and trust His promises!

Father God, thank You for Your call to action and courage. Thank You for never leaving me. Keep me so close to You, so careful to love and obey Your Word as I live and lead boldly for You!

WEDNESDAY, APRIL 15

> Joshua 3:1–5:12 / Luke 12:16–40 / Psalm 69:18–28

What Good Is Worrying?

"Can all your worries add a single moment to your life?... Don't be concerned about what to eat and what to drink. Don't worry about such things.... Your Father already knows your needs. Seek the Kingdom of God above all else, and he will give you everything you need. So don't be afraid, little flock. For it gives your Father great happiness to give you the Kingdom."
LUKE 12:25, 29–32 NLT

Finances. Groceries. Family. Career. Health. Home. Marriage. Children. Education. Friendships. Hobbies. Goals. Future. Whew! Sometimes we worry too much about any and all of these things. We want to know we will have everything we need for *all the things* to be taken care of, of course! But fretting gets us nowhere, and our faith is what matters—especially that the one our faith rests on is Jesus Christ! Not only do we find our true identity in Him, we also find our every need met in Him. As we seek Him and His kingdom above all else, living and giving generously to share His love, we can take deep, calming breaths and settle in to trusting His promises and watching Him provide.

Lord, I don't want to be dominated by worries like the world is. You know my needs, and You meet them perfectly. Remind me moment by moment of that precious truth. I want to keep seeking after You and finding real and lasting peace and provision.

THURSDAY, APRIL 16

Joshua 5:13–7:26 / Luke 12:41–48 / Psalm 69:29–36

Walls Come Tumbling Down

Now the gates of Jericho were tightly shut because the people were afraid of the Israelites. No one was allowed to go out or in. But the LORD said to Joshua, "I have given you Jericho, its king, and all its strong warriors. You and your fighting men should march around the town once a day for six days. Seven priests will walk ahead of the Ark, each carrying a ram's horn. On the seventh day you are to march around the town seven times, with the priests blowing the horns. When you hear the priests give one long blast on the rams' horns, have all the people shout as loud as they can. Then the walls of the town will collapse, and the people can charge straight into the town."

JOSHUA 6:1–5 NLT

Joshua fought the battle of Jericho, Jericho, Jericho. . . And the walls came tumbling down! Sing it! Lyrics and tunes from old Sunday school songs can emerge from dusty back corners of our minds to encourage us, reminding us of God's goals for His people—and His power to accomplish them. No matter the massive walls, overwhelming obstacles, intimidating enemies, debilitating anxieties, etc. we need to get past and destroy, God's will always prevails. We can follow Him closely, obeying Him right down to the details, and let Him give us ultimate victory—now and forever!

Lord, show me how to trust and obey You more specifically each day. Please break down the walls that are between me and Your perfect plans for my life.

FRIDAY, APRIL 17

Joshua 8–9 / Luke 12:49–59 / Psalm 70

Quickly, Please!

Please, God, rescue me! Come quickly, LORD, and help me. May those who try to kill me be humiliated and put to shame. May those who take delight in my trouble be turned back in disgrace. Let them be horrified by their shame, for they said, "Aha! We've got him now!" But may all who search for you be filled with joy and gladness in you. May those who love your salvation repeatedly shout, "God is great!" But as for me, I am poor and needy; please hurry to my aid, O God. You are my helper and my savior; O LORD, do not delay.

PSALM 70 NLT

There are times we need God's help *stat*. We all struggle with needing more patience, of course, but sometimes we truly need answers to prayer *immediately*. And so we ask God to hurry, and we can pray this psalm, pleading with Him to guide and protect and provide as soon as possible. And as He does, we can praise Him and be full of joy that at any time of day or night, we can call on our heavenly Father who is King of kings and Lord of lords and sovereign over all things—including every one of our pressing troubles.

Lord, it's urgent! With total respect and love and gratitude for You, I'm asking You to please, please hurry to help in this situation. I need to see Your powerful hand ASAP! I thank and praise You that I can pray to You!

SATURDAY, APRIL 18

Joshua 10:1–11:15 / Luke 13:1–21 / Psalm 71:1–6

All the Wonderful Things

On a Sabbath Jesus was teaching in one of the synagogues, and a woman was there who had been crippled by a spirit for eighteen years. . . . When Jesus saw her, he called her forward and said to her, "Woman, you are set free from your infirmity." Then he put his hands on her, and immediately she straightened up and praised God. Indignant because Jesus had healed on the Sabbath, the synagogue leader said to the people, "There are six days for work. So come and be healed on those days, not on the Sabbath." The Lord answered him, "You hypocrites! Doesn't each of you on the Sabbath untie your ox or donkey from the stall and lead it out to give it water? Then should not this woman, a daughter of Abraham, whom Satan has kept bound for eighteen long years, be set free on the Sabbath day from what bound her?"
LUKE 13:10–16 NIV

If we're not careful, sometimes we too can get too critical and judgy like those Pharisees. Rather than marvel and rejoice over the miracles of Jesus, they wanted to nitpick and accuse Him. Let's learn from them what *not* to do, and let's be super intentional to look for and celebrate all the wonderful things Jesus is doing in our own lives and all around us.

Jesus, open my eyes to truly see all the wonderful things You are doing, and then let me praise and worship You for them!

SUNDAY, APRIL 19

Joshua 11:16–13:33 / Luke 13:22–35 / Psalm 71:7–16

No Matter What

But I will keep on hoping for your help; I will praise you more and more. I will tell everyone about your righteousness. All day long I will proclaim your saving power, though I am not skilled with words. I will praise your mighty deeds, O Sovereign LORD. I will tell everyone that you alone are just.
PSALM 71:14–16 NLT

Life is hard. It's full of joy and blessings too, but it's a whole lot of hard. And we have an enemy named Satan who wants to defeat and destroy us and do anything to stop us from hoping in God and following Jesus. So we can hold fast to scriptures from the psalms as solemn, steadfast vows in our lives. No matter what, we will keep on hoping for God's help. We will praise Him even in the middle of the troubles and trials and pain. We will remember and celebrate His mighty deeds in the past. We will never stop proclaiming His saving power to ourselves and to others. We will worship the one true God, for He alone is just and worthy of all honor and praise!

Lord, I promise to keep on hoping in You alone for help and salvation. I promise to worship you and share you with others. Remind me to keep my promises, and thank You for never breaking Yours.

MONDAY, APRIL 20

Joshua 14–16 / Luke 14:1–15 / Psalm 71:17–21

Those Who Humble Themselves

When Jesus noticed that all who had come to the dinner were trying to sit in the seats of honor near the head of the table, he gave them this advice: "When you are invited to a wedding feast, don't sit in the seat of honor. . . . Instead, take the lowest place at the foot of the table. Then when your host sees you, he will come and say, 'Friend, we have a better place for you!' Then you will be honored in front of all the other guests. For those who exalt themselves will be humbled, and those who humble themselves will be exalted." Then he turned to his host. "When you put on a luncheon or a banquet. . .invite the poor, the crippled, the lame, and the blind. Then at the resurrection of the righteous, God will reward you for inviting those who could not repay you."

Luke 14:7–8, 10–14 nlt

Humility sure isn't popular in our society so driven by selfies, social media, celebrities, and the like today, yet Jesus taught us to be humble and to seek out the people and places in low positions. When we find our identity in Jesus, we shouldn't want to elevate and exalt ourselves; we should want to be pointing people to Him and lifting Him up for praise and honor. That's when we'll be truly blessed.

Dear Jesus, please teach me about real humility. Help me to rejoice in persistently pointing others to You and not myself.

TUESDAY, APRIL 21

Joshua 17:1–19:16 / Luke 14:16–35 / Psalm 71:22–24

Music Matters

I will praise you with the harp for your faithfulness, my God;
I will sing praise to you with the lyre, Holy One of Israel. My lips
will shout for joy when I sing praise to you—I whom you have
delivered. My tongue will tell of your righteous acts all day long.
PSALM 71:22–24 NIV

The music we love matters. We need to evaluate what the lyrics of our favorite artists make our minds focus on. Mostly, the music we love should help us praise and worship the one who created us with the ability to make and enjoy music in the first place! Sure, even music that is not specifically Christian worship music can help us appreciate and praise God simply for the awesome creativity He's blessed humankind with. But there's no denying that some types of music draw us away from God and His goodness for us. Bottom line is, our choices in music should help us focus on "whatever is true, whatever is noble, whatever is right, whatever is pure, whatever is lovely, whatever is admirable. . .excellent or praiseworthy" (Philippians 4:8 NIV)—and we should regularly sing and make music to bring honor and glory to our one true God who loves us and has saved us through His Son, Jesus Christ.

Lord, I'm so grateful for You in my life, and I want to honor
You even with the choices I make in music to listen to.
Please give me wisdom and discernment and joy as I seek
to worship and honor You more and more each day.

WEDNESDAY, APRIL 22

Joshua 19:17–21:42 / Luke 15:1–10 / Psalm 72:1–11

Seeking the Lost

Tax collectors and other notorious sinners often came to listen to Jesus teach. This made the Pharisees and teachers of religious law complain that he was associating with such sinful people—even eating with them! So Jesus told them this story: "If a man has a hundred sheep and one of them gets lost, what will he do? Won't he leave the ninety-nine others in the wilderness and go to search for the one that is lost until he finds it? And when he has found it, he will joyfully carry it home on his shoulders. When he arrives, he will call together his friends and neighbors, saying, 'Rejoice with me because I have found my lost sheep.' In the same way, there is more joy in heaven over one lost sinner who repents and returns to God than over ninety-nine others who are righteous and haven't strayed away!"

LUKE 15:1–7 NLT

Jesus cares about every single person. He wants each individual to trust in Him as Savior. He will seek after the souls who are lost, carry them home to Him, and greatly rejoice in their salvation. Jesus set the example that we should follow. We too must seek out individuals around us who need Jesus' love—and do our best to help those lost souls become found in Him.

Jesus, thank You for setting the example in caring about every single precious person on this earth. Thank You for wanting the lost to be found.

THURSDAY, APRIL 23

Joshua 21:43–22:34 / Luke 15:11–32 / Psalm 72:12–20

He Will Rescue and Redeem

He will rescue the poor when they cry to him; he will help the oppressed, who have no one to defend them. He feels pity for the weak and the needy, and he will rescue them. He will redeem them from oppression and violence, for their lives are precious to him.
Psalm 72:12–14 nlt

Do you look around the world and grow so weary sometimes, thinking of all the desperate needs? There is just so much hardship at every turn, it seems. We can't let discouragement and despair defeat us though. We can't be overcome by evil; we must overcome evil with good (Romans 12:21). And we're never alone in that ambition. It's not our job to somehow fix everything on our own. No, the one true Almighty God promises to rescue and redeem because every life is precious to Him. We only need to sincerely ask Him (and then follow through) how He'd like us to serve Him and help and be part of His perfect plans.

Sovereign Lord, help me to trust that You see and care about every human hurt and need. You are working out Your perfect rescue plans, and You have already provided rescue from sin through Your Son, Jesus. Help me to point others to Him for eternal salvation as I serve and help with immediate needs as You direct me. Help me to inspire others to join in practical helping too!

FRIDAY, APRIL 24

Joshua 23–24 / Luke 16:1–18 / Psalm 73:1–9

Surely God Is Good to Us

Surely God is good to Israel, to those who are pure in heart. But as for me, my feet had almost slipped; I had nearly lost my foothold. For I envied the arrogant when I saw the prosperity of the wicked. They have no struggles; their bodies are healthy and strong. They are free from common human burdens; they are not plagued by human ills. Therefore pride is their necklace.

PSALM 73:1–6 NIV

The psalmist openly admits what we all struggle with sometimes: It's so easy to feel jealous when we see all the worldly prosperity and arrogance of those who don't follow Jesus and who are often outright wicked. It's discouraging enough to make us nearly slip away from following Jesus ourselves. So we have to commit to actively protecting our hearts and minds from becoming comparative, envious, and bitter. We have to intentionally focus our eyes on Jesus and His leading and not look around to compare our lives and ideas of success with that of others who don't know and love Him. When we are sadly relating to the words of this psalm, we have to keep looping back to verse 1 to joyfully remind ourselves that surely God is good to us, His people, those who are pure in heart and truly seeking Him.

Heavenly Father, I want real, eternal success and prosperity— the kind that come from You and not this broken world. Help me to protect my mind and heart from comparison and envy of those entrenched in the wicked world around me.

SATURDAY, APRIL 25

Judges 1–2 / Luke 16:19–17:10 / Psalm 73:10–20

They Need to Repent and Turn to God

Jesus said, "There was a certain rich man who was splendidly clothed in purple and fine linen and who lived each day in luxury. At his gate lay a poor man named Lazarus who was covered with sores. . . . Finally, the poor man died and was carried by the angels to sit beside Abraham at the heavenly banquet. The rich man also died and was buried, and he went to the place of the dead. There, in torment, he saw Abraham in the far distance with Lazarus at his side. The rich man shouted, 'Father Abraham, have some pity! Send Lazarus over here to dip the tip of his finger in water and cool my tongue. I am in anguish in these flames.' But Abraham said to him, 'Son, remember that during your lifetime you had everything you wanted, and Lazarus had nothing. So now he is here being comforted, and you are in anguish. And besides, there is a great chasm separating us. No one can cross over to you from here, and no one can cross over to us from there.'"

LUKE 16:19–20, 22–26 NLT

Luke 16 is full of sobering scriptures. May they urge us to pray for all the precious lost souls who have not accepted Jesus Christ as Savior.

Lord Jesus, You know the dear people who are heavy on my heart and mind. They need to repent of their sins and accept You as their one and only Savior. Soften their hearts and open their eyes. Show me how to help them love and follow You.

SUNDAY, APRIL 26

Judges 3–4 / Luke 17:11–37 / Psalm 73:21–28

Yet I Still Belong to You

I was so foolish and ignorant—I must have seemed like a senseless animal to you. Yet I still belong to you; you hold my right hand. You guide me with your counsel, leading me to a glorious destiny. Whom have I in heaven but you? I desire you more than anything on earth. My health may fail, and my spirit may grow weak, but God remains the strength of my heart; he is mine forever. Those who desert him will perish, for you destroy those who abandon you. But as for me, how good it is to be near God! I have made the Sovereign LORD my shelter, and I will tell everyone about the wonderful things you do.

PSALM 73:22–28 NLT

Thankfully our heavenly Father does not hold our foolishness and ignorance against us! We always belong to Him despite it all (even when we seem like "senseless animals"), through the grace of His Son, Jesus! And He continues to guide us, holding our hands down every path of this life and then into perfect life with Him in paradise forever. Isn't it *so, so* good and merciful to be near Almighty God and make Him our shelter? Let's praise Him for that!

Sovereign Lord, I praise and worship You with more gratitude than I know how to fully express. I'm so thankful that You don't hold my sins against me. I'm so thankful that You guide, protect, and love me so well.

MONDAY, APRIL 27

> Judges 5:1–6:24 / Luke 18:1–17 / Psalm 74:1–3

Always Pray, Never Give Up

One day Jesus told his disciples a story to show that they should always pray and never give up. "There was a judge in a certain city," he said, "who neither feared God nor cared about people. A widow of that city came to him repeatedly, saying, 'Give me justice in this dispute with my enemy.' The judge ignored her for a while, but finally he said to himself, 'I don't fear God or care about people, but this woman is driving me crazy. I'm going to see that she gets justice, because she is wearing me out with her constant requests!'" Then the Lord said, "Learn a lesson from this unjust judge. Even he rendered a just decision in the end. So don't you think God will surely give justice to his chosen people who cry out to him day and night? Will he keep putting them off? I tell you, he will grant justice to them quickly!"

LUKE 18:1–8 NLT

Jesus clearly wants us to be persistent in prayer. The point of His story here was that if a judge in the worldly courts who did not even respect God was finally willing to help the woman who kept asking and asking, how much more will God help His dearly loved people who persistently request His help and justice? The answer is this: *so much more!*

> *Heavenly Father, I'm so incredibly grateful that You grant justice and that You never get tired of my prayers.*

TUESDAY, APRIL 28

Judges 6:25–7:25 / Luke 18:18–43 / Psalm 74:4–11

God's Victory with Gideon

The Lord told Gideon, "With these 300 men I will rescue you and give you victory over the Midianites. Send all the others home." So Gideon collected the provisions and rams' horns of the other warriors and sent them home. But he kept the 300 men with him.

Judges 7:7–8 nlt

At first Gideon was skeptical and scared, but eventually he was filled with powerful faith—and the Lord kept speaking to him to show him how to defeat Israel's enemy, the Midianites.

Gideon started with an army of 32,000 men, but then 22,000 gave up. They were too scared to fight. Then God told Gideon He wanted only 300 men to fight against the intimidating Midianites, to prove that all the real power comes from God alone. So, with God's power, Gideon and that very small army of men rescued Israel from Midian.

At first, Gideon was just an ordinary man doing ordinary things. But by trusting God and growing in faith, Gideon went on to do extraordinary, courageous things. The same God can empower us for amazing plans and purposes too!

Almighty God, even when I see lots of people giving up all around me, please help me bravely remember that You can use anyone and anything, no matter how big or small, to accomplish Your perfect, incredible plans. All good victory and power come from You!

WEDNESDAY, APRIL 29

> Judges 8:1–9:23 / Luke 19:1–28 / Psalm 74:12–17

There Was a Man Named Zacchaeus

[Jesus] entered Jericho and was passing through. And behold, there was a man named Zacchaeus. He was a chief tax collector and was rich. And he was seeking to see who Jesus was, but on account of the crowd he could not, because he was small in stature.

LUKE 19:1–3 ESV

Tax-collecting men like Zacchaeus were wealthy and known for cheating and taking too much of other people's money. So most people in Jericho hated and avoided Zacchaeus. But he was drawn to Jesus and wanted to do whatever it took to see Him as He traveled through Jericho.

So Zacchaeus ran ahead of where Jesus would walk, and he climbed a sycamore tree. With a good view from high in the branches, he waited and watched for Jesus. When Jesus passed by, He stopped and spotted Zacchaeus. He called him by name and said, "Come down right away. I am going to your house today" (Luke 19:5).

Zacchaeus was thrilled as he climbed down and welcomed Jesus to his home. As Zacchaeus spent time with Jesus, he repented of his sins and wanted to make all his wrongs right. He wanted to help the poor and give back to people all the money he had cheated them out of—plus four times more.

> *Dear Jesus, I want to learn from Zacchaeus, who was so eager to see You and welcome You—and so brave and humble as he was willing to admit his mistakes and then do everything to correct them.*

THURSDAY, APRIL 30

Judges 9:24–10:18 / Luke 19:29–48 / Psalm 74:18–23

Shout and Sing to Jesus

As he rode along, the crowds spread out their garments on the road ahead of him. When he reached the place where the road started down the Mount of Olives, all of his followers began to shout and sing as they walked along, praising God for all the wonderful miracles they had seen. "Blessings on the King who comes in the name of the Lord! Peace in heaven, and glory in highest heaven!" But some of the Pharisees among the crowd said, "Teacher, rebuke your followers for saying things like that!" He replied, "If they kept quiet, the stones along the road would burst into cheers!"

Luke 19:36–40 nlt

As Jesus entered Jerusalem, all His followers shouted and sang, giving Him the highest praise. They'd seen so many of His wonderful miracles, and they believed in and loved Him. And the Pharisees couldn't stand it. Jesus' reply to them reminds us today to not grow discouraged by scoffers and haters. There will always be people who truly love and worship Jesus who will encourage us as we worship too. And even if somehow all people kept quiet, even the rocks would cry out with praise to our one true Savior!

Lord Jesus, You are truly the King, the Son of God. You alone deserve all glory and praise. I will worship You no matter who tries to discourage me, and I know that all of Your creation worships You—and no power of man can ever stop the honor and glory You deserve!

MAY 2026

SUNDAY	MONDAY	TUESDAY	WEDNESDAY	THURSDAY	FRIDAY	SATURDAY
					1	2
3	4	5	6	7 National Day of Prayer	8	9
10 Mother's Day	11	12	13	14	15	16
17	18	19	20	21	22	23
24 / 31	25 Memorial Day	26	27	28	29	30

FRIDAY, MAY 1

Judges 11:1–12:7 / Luke 20:1–26 / Psalm 75:1–7

Stop and Trust

We praise you, God. . .people tell of your wonderful deeds. You say, "I choose the appointed time; it is I who judge with equity."
PSALM 75:1–2 NIV

Just deserts. . .the consequences that people deserve. We humans weigh the actions of others and then match appropriate rewards and punishments to their behavior:

Bad behavior = punishment
Good behavior = reward

Simple, right? But when we're waiting for evil to receive its comeuppance, our patience wears thin. Because the truth is, we want to see justice served *now*. And then we wait. . .and wait. . .and nothing. It's so unfair!

True, it often appears that those "just deserts" might never happen—a little too frequently for our liking. We might even begin to doubt and wonder if God sees or cares. This is where we can stop our worries and trust the heavenly Father's timeline. While we watch and wait, we know that God, in His wisdom, judges at the right time. He's never a minute too soon or a minute too late.

Whenever you begin to question God's justice and timing, remember this:

The Lord is not slow in keeping his promise, as some understand slowness. Instead he is patient with you, not wanting anyone to perish, but everyone to come to repentance. (2 Peter 3:9 NIV)

What a fair and righteous Father we serve!

> *Father God, I am thankful that the judging is up to You and no one else. I trust You and Your timing.*

SATURDAY, MAY 2

> Judges 12:8–14:20 / Luke 20:27–47 / Psalm 75:8–10

"Even Though" Promises

In those days a man named Manoah from the tribe of Dan lived in the town of Zorah. His wife was unable to become pregnant, and they had no children. The angel of the LORD appeared to Manoah's wife and said, "Even though you have been unable to have children, you will soon become pregnant and give birth to a son."

JUDGES 13:2–3 NLT

Manoah and his wife were unable to have children. In ancient times, barren women were humiliated and blamed. Imagine the guilt Manoah's wife must have felt over her perceived failure as a woman. Now imagine that layered on top of the sadness and depression she already felt over her personal desire to be a mother. The beliefs of her culture no doubt magnified the intensity of her shame.

But then. . .God showed up with His "even though" promise. What bewilderment and joy Manoah's wife must have experienced when she was promised a son!

Did you know that as God's daughter, you too are a receiver of His "even though" promises? And while He doesn't always give you what you want or expect, He *will* come through at just the right time and provide what you *need*—and it's always for your good. Trust Him today!

Lord, sometimes I want something so badly, and yet You take my life in another direction and provide something else instead. Remind me that You know what's best for me—and that's exactly what You'll give.

SUNDAY, MAY 3

Judges 15–16 / Luke 21:1–19 / Psalm 76:1–7

Your Marvelous Opportunity

"You will be dragged into synagogues and prisons. . .because you are my followers. But this will be your opportunity to tell them about me. . . . Even those closest to you. . .will betray you. They will even kill some of you. And everyone will hate you because you are my followers. But not a hair of your head will perish! By standing firm, you will win your souls."
LUKE 21:12–13, 16–19 NLT

What if you were presented with an amazing opportunity that came with a promise. Sounds great, doesn't it? But what if to get to that promise, you were required to experience some awful things: You'd encounter a time of great persecution. . . You'd be betrayed by your friends and loved ones. . . Your life would be put in harm's way. . .

You'd probably say, "Hard pass. That's not the kind of 'opportunity' I'd ever sign up for!" And yet, this is exactly what these Christ followers were presented with: a wonderful opportunity. . .wrapped in hardship. . .wrapped in a *beautiful* promise! Although hardship would come, they wouldn't be harmed—in fact, "not a hair of [their heads would] perish!" By enduring and obeying, by persisting through adversity, they would ultimately win—because souls would be saved! There's no better outcome or promise than that!

Won't you say yes to God's marvelous opportunity?

Lord Jesus, any adversity I face because I choose You. . .it's all worth it. Help me to stand firm and win many souls for You.

MONDAY, MAY 4

> Judges 17–18 / Luke 21:20–22:6 / Psalm 76:8–12

Liberated

There will be earth-shattering events. . . . Outsider nations will feel powerless and terrified in the face of a roaring flood of fear and foreboding. . . . "What's happening to the world?" people will wonder. . . . They will see the Son of Man coming in a cloud with power and blazing glory. So when the troubles begin, don't be afraid. Look up—raise your head high, because the truth is that your liberation is fast approaching.
LUKE 21:25–28 VOICE

Chaos surrounds us—in our neighborhoods, schools, workplaces, cities, and beyond. In real time, we learn of school shootings, natural disasters, political scandal, and more. It's enough to make the toughest soul tremble. In this calamitous climate, it's easy to become withdrawn and depressed. And it's difficult to see the good beyond all the bad. You might even begin to wonder if good even exists anymore.

When you find yourself quaking at the state of the world, take heart. You have every reason to be fearless, because you are a child of Almighty God! So, even in the middle of "earth-shattering events," you can chase away your fears with the courage given by your Creator. Repeat this truth: *Jesus is coming; He will return in glory; and all will be made right.*

Today, "raise your head high, because the truth is that your liberation is fast approaching."

Fear quencher, freedom giver, I look forward to Jesus' return when all will be made right!

TUESDAY, MAY 5

Judges 19:1–20:23 / Luke 22:7–30 / Psalm 77:1–11

Faithful

*I cry up to heaven, "My God, True God," and He hears.
In my darkest days, I seek the Lord. Through the night,
my hands are raised up, stretched out, waiting;
and though they do not grow tired, my soul is uneasy.*

PSALM 77:1–2 VOICE

Think back to a time that was your "darkest." What was going on? An illness, a severed relationship, a loss? "Darkest" days are no doubt our very worst. We are distraught, we wrestle with a roller coaster of emotions, we wonder if we can keep going. . . And this is right where we find our writer of Psalm 77. He is struggling—his troubles are deep and difficult and distressing. His soul is uneasy.

And yet, he knows he still has access to the light. So, he raises his hands, outstretched toward heaven, and waits for the Lord to act on his behalf. No matter how dark his days have been, still he hopes and trusts in his heavenly Father for rescue and comfort.

Friend, if you're in the middle of your darkest day, hold on to hope. Raise your hands to heaven and seek the Lord with all your might. He will comfort you and provide the strength you need. He will be faithful today, just as He was yesterday and will again be tomorrow. He will never, ever let you down.

*Father, just as You have always made a way for Your
people, You will lead me through the darkness and
into the light. You hear, and You will save.*

WEDNESDAY, MAY 6

Judges 20:24–21:25 / Luke 22:31–54 / Psalm 77:12–20

Our Big God

Your way is holy! No god is great like God! You're the God who makes things happen; you showed everyone what you can do—You pulled your people out of the worst kind of trouble, rescued the children of Jacob and Joseph.

PSALM 77:13–15 MSG

When you were a child, you probably did something wrong and got caught. You blamed your sibling for eating the last cookie when it was really you. You broke the neighbor's window after you were told not to play kickball in the front yard. You skipped school to hang out with friends. Later in life, we often recall our childhood troubles and laugh. Because we're all grown up, right?

But as adults, our troubles tend to be more serious—we battle bad habits and addictions, we get tangled up in unhealthy relationships, we break rules and sometimes laws. And the consequences of our bad decisions can be dire, the outcomes disastrous to ourselves and to others. Adult troubles are no laughing matter. Isn't it comforting to know that our God is bigger than any kind of trouble we could manage to get into? He is holy. . .He is great! And He shows up—every time we call on Him, He's there.

When it feels like you're in the worst kind of trouble, call out to the rescuer. The "God who makes things happen" will save you. That's a promise!

Rescue me from this trouble, Lord. I can't get out of this on my own strength. I need You!

National Day of Prayer — THURSDAY, MAY 7

Ruth 1–2 / Luke 22:55–23:25 / Psalm 78:1–4

Lovely Connection

Ruth said, "Don't force me to leave you. . . . Where you go, I go; and where you live, I'll live. Your people are my people, your God is my god; where you die, I'll die, and that's where I'll be buried, so help me GOD—not even death itself is going to come between us!"
RUTH 1:16–17 MSG

Human beings crave connection. There's nothing like having a circle of women to do life with, is there? You laugh together, cry together, sit in silence together. You offer advice, a helping hand, a listening ear.

When we're truly connected to one another, we're never alone in our happiness or hardship. We show up and cheer each other on. Ruth and Naomi shared this kind of connection. When their husbands passed away, Naomi told her daughter-in-law Ruth to go back to her family. . .and Naomi planned to return to her hometown. But Ruth refused. Her response? "I'm going where you go. We're doing this together. Nothing is going to pull us apart."

When we accept Jesus as our Lord and Savior, we become part of a new family—we gain our sisters in Christ. What a beautiful gift! Say a prayer of thanks today for the "sisters" in your life. Thank God for providing you with the connection your soul craves.

Lord, as part of Your family, I am gifted with a lovely connection to other women who also know You as Lord and leader of their lives. Thank You for this much-needed blessing!

FRIDAY, MAY 8

Ruth 3–4 / Luke 23:26–24:12 / Psalm 78:5–8

Truth Keeper

He planted a witness in Jacob, set his Word firmly in Israel, then commanded our parents to teach it to their children so the next generation would know, and all the generations to come—know the truth and tell the stories so their children can trust in God, never forget the works of God.

PSALM 78:5–7 MSG

How often do you talk about God in your home? Do you regularly discuss His creation, His mercy, His love, His miracles, His provision, His saving grace? Or is He all but forgotten except on Sundays when you head to church—or when the bottom falls out and you're in dire need of a miracle that only He can provide?

Sister, we are called to be keepers of God's truth. It's our responsibility to teach our children and grandchildren—to "set His Word firmly"—so they, in turn, can teach future generations. To be truth keepers, we must know and understand God's Word, and we must learn the lessons and stories from the pages of the Bible. We must stay in daily prayer. We must faithfully walk with God. Then, and only then, will we be successful in our mission to keep and share His truth.

Today, ask the heavenly Father to send you daily little nudges to keep Him front and center in your conversations at home. Don't let God and His Word become an afterthought.

Father God, thank You for appointing me to be a keeper of Your truth.

SATURDAY, MAY 9

1 Samuel 1:1–2:21 / Luke 24:13–53 / Psalm 78:9–16

Receiver of Miracles

The people of Ephraim, though fully armed, turned their backs and fled when the day of battle came because they didn't obey his laws.... They forgot about the wonderful miracles God had done for them and for their fathers in Egypt.

Psalm 78:9–12 tlb

What kind of miracles have you witnessed or experienced for yourself? Maybe you haven't seen any that you'd categorize as Bible-sized miracles: sight restored, seas parted, water turned to wine... But, surely, you've encountered some modern-day miracles: a clear scan before cancer treatment begins, a friend walking away from what should have been a deadly accident... These miracles certainly are attention-getters. They have us singing God's praises—until time passes and it seems the miracles are all but forgotten. This is just what happened to the people of Ephraim: They forgot God's miracles.

It's easy to get so wrapped up in our to-dos that we miss life's everyday miracles—the frozen dead of winter morphing into the warm awakening of spring, the way our lungs take in fresh air with each breath, a baby's first cry... But if we're awake to them, we'll see them for the marvels they are.

May we be women who look for the miraculous in the ordinary, everyday moments of life. Let's recognize them, celebrate them, share them.

Let's expect a miracle today!

Miracle giver, open my eyes. I want to recognize the miraculous in everyday moments. I thank You and praise You, Lord!

SUNDAY, MAY 10
Mother's Day

1 Samuel 2:22–4:22 / John 1:1–28 / Psalm 78:17–24

Perfectly Loved

He entered our world, a world He made; yet the world did not recognize Him. Even though He came to His own people, they refused to listen and receive Him. But for all who did receive and trust in Him, He gave them the right to be reborn as children of God; He bestowed this birthright. . .by God's will.
JOHN 1:10–13 VOICE

When we were born into our families, we did nothing to deserve what our parents provided. And yet, most of us were welcomed into loving homes where we were snuggled, rocked, fed, clothed, taught, and trained up to adulthood.

Good parents work hard to provide for their children—and most will happily sacrifice so they can give their kids a good life. This desire is wholly independent from what children bring to the relationship. After all, children are needy, self-centered, rebellious creatures. But despite a child's behavior, parents keep on loving, keep providing, keep instructing. . . They don't hold good things back because their children aren't perfect.

Doesn't this look a lot like our relationship with God? He freely gives what we don't deserve. We can be needy, demanding, and self-centered, and yet He loves us perfectly. He blesses and provides for us. How utterly amazing that the Creator of the universe claims us as His children. He's our heavenly Daddy. And we can trust Him for all good things!

God, calling You "Father" fills my heart with joy! Thank You for Your generous grace and love.

MONDAY, MAY 11

1 Samuel 5–7 / John 1:29–51 / Psalm 78:25–33

"Ebenezer" Moments

While Samuel was offering the sacrifice, the Philistines came within range to fight Israel. Just then GOD thundered, a huge thunderclap exploding among the Philistines. They panicked. . .and scattered. . . . Samuel took a single rock and set it upright. . . . He named it "Ebenezer" (Rock of Help), saying, "This marks the place where GOD helped us."

1 SAMUEL 7:10, 12 MSG

This is the place where. . .

>   *I grew up.*
>   *My child was born.*
>   *I got engaged.*

Many events or periods of time in our lives are so meaningful that we can recall them with absolute clarity. There are impactful moments in our faith too, when God steps in and helps us through a struggle—these are imprinted on our hearts as well. Often, later in life, we share these special memories and places with younger generations.

In today's scripture passage, Samuel had prayed fervently for God to save his people. In response, the Lord caused a loud thunderclap that confused and panicked the Philistines on the battlefield. Because the Philistines scattered, the Israelites were able to defeat them. What a significant event—God acting on behalf of His people! It was so meaningful that Samuel marked the place with a rock and named it "Rock of Help."

Do you have an "Ebenezer" memory that holds a special place in your heart?

> *Father, because I'm Yours, You'll always step in when I need rescuing. Thank You for all the "Ebenezer" memories I can share because of Your goodness.*

TUESDAY, MAY 12

1 Samuel 8:1–9:26 / John 2 / Psalm 78:34–41

Your Heart Is Known

No one needed to tell [Jesus] about human nature, for he knew what was in each person's heart.
JOHN 2:25 NLT

If you were handed a list of people—friends, family, and acquaintances—and then asked what you would find in each person's heart, could you offer solid, reliable answers? What sort of evidence would you use to draw your conclusions?

Certainly, you'd carefully consider how they treat other people. You'd look at their priorities—what they seem to care about more than anything else in the world. You'd also take a good, hard look at their character. But you wouldn't give one second of thought to their looks or their fashion sense or their bank account balances, would you? After all, a person's *heart* is key to who they are and what they hold most dear.

Thankfully, we serve a heavenly Father who knows (and works!) in our hearts:

> *The LORD weighs the heart. (Proverbs 21:2 NIV)*
>
> *"People look at the outward appearance but the LORD looks at the heart." (1 Samuel 16:7 NIV)*
>
> *"The LORD searches every heart and understands every desire and every thought." (1 Chronicles 28:9 NIV)*

Repeatedly throughout scripture, we are reassured that our Lord knows us better than anyone else. And when we are fully committed to Him and give Him our very best, He'll bless us every step of the way.

Father, thank You for caring about what's in my heart more than anything else. You are so, so good.

WEDNESDAY, MAY 13

1 Samuel 9:27–11:15 / John 3:1–22 / Psalm 78:42–55

Saved!

For God so loved the world that he gave his one and only Son, that whoever believes in him shall not perish but have eternal life. For God did not send his Son into the world to condemn the world, but to save the world through him.
JOHN 3:16–17 NIV

God loves you so much! There's nothing you can do to cause Him to love you more, and nothing you can do to cause Him to love you less.

But what if. . .
I told a lie that hurt someone I love?
I divorced my spouse?
I'm fighting an addiction?
I had an abortion?

There's not one thing you can add to this list that will change God's promise to you. When His Word says that nothing can separate you from His love, it means zero. . .zilch (see Romans 8:35–39). There's no catch. . .no gimmick. . .no "gotcha" moment coming your way. If you accepted His gift of salvation, there's nothing He won't forgive.

"God so loved the world"—and so, He sent His Son, Jesus, to die for me and for you. If we believe in Him and invite Him into our hearts as Lord and leader of our lives, then we are saved! Saved from our sins, saved from shame, saved from guilt, saved. . .so we can live forever in heaven with Him.

Father God, thank You for loving me so much that You sent Your Son to die on the cross for my sins. I look forward to my forever home in heaven.

THURSDAY, MAY 14

> 1 Samuel 12–13 / John 3:23–4:10 / Psalm 78:56–66

Joy-Full

My joy could not be more complete.
JOHN 3:29 VOICE

What is joy, exactly? Most of us would describe it as a feeling of wonder. Happiness. Pleasure. Joy certainly is a feel-good emotion. But is it something more. . .something felt and experienced on a deeper level than our other emotions?

According to God's Word, joy is when we experience contentment and satisfaction—regardless of our circumstances—because we know God is in control and He has nothing but good plans for His children. Consider these scriptures:

> *And we know that all things work together for good to them that love God, to them who are the called according to his purpose. (Romans 8:28 KJV)*

> *"For I know the plans I have for you," declares the LORD, "plans to prosper you and not to harm you, plans to give you hope and a future." (Jeremiah 29:11 NIV)*

> *The plans of the LORD stand firm forever, the purposes of His heart through all generations. (Psalm 33:11 NIV)*

The truth is, without Jesus, we can't fully experience joy, not on a deep spiritual level. Joy *without* Jesus is nothing more than surface-y, in-the-moment delight. Joy *with* Jesus is deep-soul satisfaction even in the darkest pits of life.

Say yes to a life with Jesus and experience the joy-full life today!

Father God, with You in my life, I have true joy. I am thankful that in each circumstance—the good, the bad, and the awful—I can be content. I couldn't do it without You!

FRIDAY, MAY 15

1 Samuel 14 / John 4:11–38 / Psalm 78:67–72

Divine Watering

Jesus said, . . ."Anyone who drinks the water I give will never thirst—not ever. The water I give will be an artesian spring within, gushing fountains of endless life." The woman said, "Sir, give me this water so I won't ever get thirsty, won't ever have to come back to this well again!"
JOHN 4:13–15 MSG

When we're thirsty, there's nothing quite like a long, cool gulp of water. While taking a drink satisfies our thirst in the moment, it doesn't last. We *will* get thirsty again. Our bodies will eventually send a signal to our brains that we need to take another drink of water. . .and the cycle continues.

While we have physical thirst, we also have spiritual thirst that plagues us from time to time. If we fail to stay in the Word and lose sight of Christ, we will experience this second kind of thirst. When we become spiritually thirsty, we're in desperate need of the heavenly Father's guidance and love and assurance—our faith is dried up, withered, and in need of a divine watering. Without Christ's "living water," our faith can't grow—it can't thrive. But with it, we have life! Life that overflows with meaning and purpose and satisfaction. Life that lasts forever!

If you're in a spiritual drought, dear one, ask Jesus for His living water. . ."an artesian spring within, gushing fountains of endless life." His water will satisfy—for eternity!

Father God, please drench me in Your life-giving water today.

SATURDAY, MAY 16

1 Samuel 15–16 / John 4:39–54 / Psalm 79:1–7

Your Beautiful Heart

But God told Samuel, "Looks aren't everything. . . .
God judges persons differently than humans do. Men and
women look at the face; God looks into the heart."
1 SAMUEL 16:7 MSG

Have you ever been wrongly judged or accused? Maybe you've lost a relationship over a false allegation. Perhaps you've been rejected because of how you look or a past mistake you made. Maybe your social status has caused other women to wrongly judge your character. Whatever your personal experience has been, you know how much hurt and frustration surface-level perceptions can cause. It's grossly unfair when another person decides you're guilty or unworthy before getting to know you or understanding what's in your heart—your true self. It can be downright maddening.

Isn't it wonderful then, that our heavenly Father looks at and cares most about the substance of our hearts? He'll never wrongly accuse you or assume the very worst about you, friend. And what's better is that no matter what's in your heart, He loves you. He whispers for you to come closer to Him. Even when no one else gets you, when no one else seems to care what's beneath the surface, our Lord does!

We serve a mighty God who judges differently. . .praise Him with that beautiful heart of yours!

Father God, thank You for truly seeing me. For loving
me for who I am and for "getting me" even when no
one else in the world does. I love You, Lord!

SUNDAY, MAY 17

1 Samuel 17 / John 5:1–24 / Psalm 79:8–13

Goliath-Sized Battles

[David said,] "I come to you in the name of the LORD of Heaven's Armies—the God of the armies of Israel, whom you have defied. . . . Everyone assembled here will know that the LORD rescues his people."
1 SAMUEL 17:45, 47 NLT

The massive giant Goliath bullied and brutalized, taunted and terrified the men in the Israelite army. Not one soldier was willing to fight him. . .and rightly so! He dwarfed even the largest, most powerful men on the battlefield. Only a complete lunatic would volunteer to go head-to-head with him. And yet. . .David bravely accepted the challenge: "Today the LORD will conquer you, and I will kill you and cut off your head. And then I will give the dead bodies of your men to the birds and wild animals, and the whole world will know that there is a God in Israel!" (verse 46).

This young man, who wasn't even part of the Israelite army, stepped up in complete confidence. He had no intentions of fighting—he had only come to check on his brothers. Onlookers surely wagered that David would undoubtedly lose, but little did they know. . . With one sling and a small stone, David struck the giant dead. His victory was secure with God on his side!

David's sure confidence can be yours too! When you step up and fight the Lord's battles, victory is yours!

Heavenly Father, I have complete confidence that You are with me in every Goliath-sized battle.

MONDAY, MAY 18

1 Samuel 18–19 / John 5:25–47 / Psalm 80:1–7

Returned to God

Turn Your ear toward us, Shepherd of Israel. . . .
Radiate Your light! . . . Arouse Your strength and power,
and save us! Bring us back to You, God. Turn the light of Your
face upon us so that we will be rescued from this sea of darkness.
PSALM 80:1–3 VOICE

If you've ever been lost in the woods, you know how scary it can be—especially in the dark. It's easy to get turned around when you're in an unfamiliar place at night. One path looks just like the next. . . and you feel like you're walking in circles. At some point you may begin to wonder if you'll ever find your way out.

When we get separated from God, it's not all that different. The more we try to navigate in the darkness—without His help—the more lost and confused we become. We can't escape the darkness by ourselves. We need someone to illuminate the right path so we can get back on track—and the light that we need is Jesus! He has the strength and power to rescue us from the "sea of darkness."

If you're lost somewhere in the shadows today, pray these words from Psalm 80. Then look up and let the Lord's light lead you back to Him. . .to a place of peace and safety.

God, thank You for always bringing me back to You. I am never so lost that You can't shine Your light to guide me home.

TUESDAY, MAY 19

1 Samuel 20–21 / John 6:1–21 / Psalm 80:8–19

Abundantly Blessed

Those counting the people reported approximately 5,000 men—not including the women and children. . . . Jesus picked up the bread, gave thanks to God, and passed it to everyone. He repeated this ritual with the fish. Men, women, and children all ate until their hearts were content. When the people had all they could eat, He told the disciples to gather the leftovers.
John 6:10–12 voice

Just when it seemed the people would go home hungry, God provided. With only five loaves of bread and two fish, Jesus fed more than five thousand men, women, and children. They ate until their bellies were full. There were even leftovers!

This is how the Lord provides for us—with blessings in abundance:

God can pour on the blessings in astonishing ways so that you're ready for anything and everything, more than just ready to do what needs to be done. . . . He throws caution to the winds, giving to the needy in reckless abandon. . . . This most generous God. . . is more than extravagant with you. He gives you something you can then give away, which grows into full-formed lives, robust in God, wealthy in every way, so that you can be generous in every way, producing with us great praise to God. (2 Corinthians 9:8–11 msg)

Lord God, You are exceedingly kind. You have blessed me with more than I could possibly need. Help me to pass Your extravagant generosity on to others.

WEDNESDAY, MAY 20

1 Samuel 22–23 / John 6:22–42 / Psalm 81:1–10

Forever Satisfied

Jesus declared, "I am the bread of life. Whoever comes to me will never go hungry, and whoever believes in me will never be thirsty. . . . All those the Father gives me will come to me, and whoever comes to me I will never drive away. . . . For my Father's will is that everyone who looks to the Son and believes in him shall have eternal life."
JOHN 6:35, 37, 40 NIV

Your stomach growls. Your throat is dry. You'd give anything for a slice of your favorite pizza and a tall, frosty glass of sweet tea.

When you feel hunger or thirst, your brain is communicating to your body that you need food and water. And once those immediate needs are met, you feel satisfied. . .but not for long. Eventually you'll be hungry and thirsty again.

But here in John 6, Jesus says, "Whoever comes to me will never go hungry, and whoever believes in me will never be thirsty." How is it possible? Jesus is not speaking about our physical hunger and thirst—he's instead referring to our spiritual longing for righteousness, for a right relationship with God, which can only be satisfied *through* Him. And when we humbly come to Him, we will be satisfied—permanently. . .forever!

What about you? Do you feel a longing for something that's missing in your spiritual walk—are you hungry. . .or thirsty? If so, remember this truth: Your lack can forever be satisfied by the bread of life.

Jesus, thank You for forever satisfying my hunger and thirst.

THURSDAY, MAY 21

1 Samuel 24:1–25:31 / John 6:43–71 / Psalm 81:11–16

Three Things

Jesus said to them, "Very truly I tell you, unless you eat the flesh of the Son of Man and drink his blood, you have no life in you. Whoever eats my flesh and drinks my blood has eternal life, and I will raise them up at the last day. For my flesh is real food and my blood is real drink. Whoever eats my flesh and drinks my blood remains in me, and I in them. . . . This is the bread that came down from heaven. Your ancestors ate manna and died, but whoever feeds on this bread will live forever."
JOHN 6:53–56, 58 NIV

If you've said yes and accepted Jesus' invitation of salvation. . .if you meant it with all your heart, soul, and mind, then you are the recipient of many life-changing blessings, including:

Eternal life—you have a forever home in heaven.

Constant connection with Jesus—He resides in your heart.

Abundant life—life with Jesus has meaning and purpose.

Communion is a reminder of these beautiful blessings. When we eat the bread and drink the juice, we are remembering Jesus' sacrifice on the cross. We're celebrating our transformed lives made possible because of His precious gift—His sacrifice on the cross—so that we can live every day with intention and significance!

Lord Jesus, thank You for Your beautiful sacrifice.
Without You, my life would have no purpose.
Your precious gift changed my life forever.

FRIDAY, MAY 22

1 Samuel 25:32–27:12 / John 7:1–24 / Psalm 82

God's Business

*David answered, "See what I have here? The king's spear. . . .
GOD put your life in my hands today, but I wasn't willing to lift a
finger against GOD's anointed. Just as I honored your life today,
may GOD honor my life and rescue me from all trouble."*

1 SAMUEL 26:22–24 MSG

King Saul had lost his mind. He was paranoid and had made numerous attempts to murder David.

In a setup in a wilderness cave, David was presented with an opportunity to kill Saul. But instead of following through, David chose to spare Saul's life. His act of mercy was quite remarkable. David was in line to take the throne, after all, and he had been on the run for his life for way too long. Saul's death would put an end to all the running, and it would create a direct path to the throne. But David grasped a deeper truth: God's plan involved his obedience. . .and obedience to God didn't include the murder of Saul. God would put David on the throne in His perfect timing and way.

David understood that each one of us is God's business. He is the ultimate decision-maker. He will *always* do what's right for us. And when we obey Him, He will bless us accordingly (John 3:36).

When we allow ourselves to be God's business, life is so much better that way!

***Father God, my heart is grateful because my life is in Your
hands and Your plans for me are right and good.***

SATURDAY, MAY 23

1 Samuel 28–29 / John 7:25–8:11 / Psalm 83

Drink Deeply

On the last day, the biggest day of the festival, Jesus stood again and spoke aloud. If any of you is thirsty, come to Me and drink. If you believe in Me, the Hebrew Scriptures say that rivers of living water will flow from within you. Jesus was referring to the realities of life in the Spirit made available to everyone who believes in Him. But the Spirit had not yet arrived because Jesus had not been glorified.
JOHN 7:37–39 VOICE

If you understand basic biology, you know that without water, human beings can't survive. Our bodies are about 60 percent water. Water refreshes us; it helps regulate body temperature; it helps deliver oxygen throughout our bodies; it aids in our digestive process. . . and more! Water does so much to keep us healthy and functioning.

Just as water is essential to our physical bodies, Jesus is essential to our spiritual lives. And the Holy Spirit is the living water that flows within us once we accept Christ as Lord and Savior. The "rivers of living water" refresh us on a spiritual level. They sustain our faith. They keep our emotional temperatures in check. . .and more! These living waters ensure that we're connected to God. . .which in turn keeps our faith healthy, strong, and thriving.

If you're thirsty today, friend, drink deeply of the living water and refresh your soul!

Jesus, I believe! Fill me with Your living water that will sustain and refresh me—mind, body, and soul.

SUNDAY, MAY 24

1 Samuel 30–31 / John 8:12–47 / Psalm 84:1–4

Stronger!

David strengthened himself with trust in his GOD. He ordered Abiathar the priest, son of Ahimelech, "Bring me the Ephod so I can consult God." . . . Then David prayed to GOD, "Shall I go after these raiders? Can I catch them?" The answer came, "Go after them! Yes, you'll catch them! Yes, you'll make the rescue!"

1 SAMUEL 30:6–8 MSG

David knew that his strength wasn't self-made. He didn't rely on himself, because he understood that whatever wisdom and power *he* could muster would *never* be sufficient. And so, in his uncertainty, David did the wise thing and consulted God before moving ahead. Then, he waited for God to answer.

What about you? Do you ask God *first*? Do you tap into His wisdom and guidance before making decisions—both big and small? Or are you guilty of self-relying all over the place? *I've got this, God. I can handle it myself!* . . . Only to discover what you knew deep in your heart all along: *God, I can't do this without You!*

When we look to God for our next steps, we will *never* make the wrong turn. He knows what's best, and that settles it! Whenever you're uncertain, remember that you belong to the all-knowing, all-seeing God of the universe. He is your strength, your shield, your guide.

When you trust in Him, you are *always* stronger!

You are the God who strengthens me. I trust You today and every day. Show me the way I should go!

Memorial Day MONDAY, MAY 25

2 Samuel 1–2 / John 8:48–9:12 / Psalm 84:5–12

Your Favorite Place

One day spent in your house. . .beats thousands spent on Greek island beaches. I'd rather scrub floors in the house of my God than be honored as a guest in the palace of sin. . . . It's smooth sailing all the way with GOD-of-the-Angel-Armies.
PSALM 84:10, 12 MSG

Where is your favorite place to spend time? On a white sandy beach? In the peaceful mountains? Floating on a quiet lake? In a lush garden? You wouldn't rather be scrubbing floors somewhere, would you? No way!

But the psalmist thinks differently. According to him, not even beautiful Greek island beaches could compare to scrubbing floors in God's house! Is this guy for real? What does he know that we don't? For starters, He understands that time in God's house—in the presence of the Lord—is more valuable than time spent anywhere else in the world.

When you're in the presence of God, you experience life at its fullest and best. Time with Him is like being outside and letting the sun warm your face. . .it's like receiving blessing upon blessing. . .it's "smooth sailing" even when the waves are crashing, because He's always got your back.

Time with the heavenly Father is better than time spent anywhere else! Try it and see for yourself!

Father, with You is exactly where I want—and need—to be!

TUESDAY, MAY 26

2 Samuel 3–4 / John 9:13–34 / Psalm 85:1–7

Heard

"Why, that's very strange!" the man replied. "He healed my eyes. . . . We know that God doesn't listen to sinners, but he is ready to hear those who worship him and do his will."
JOHN 9:30–31 NLT

Good listeners. They're few and far between. Listening more than we talk is tough!

How often have you been talking and noticed that the person across from you is focusing their attention elsewhere—on their phone, smartwatch, television screen, or something other than you? Probably a lot! Distractions are everywhere, and they make it difficult to focus on what's right in front of us—especially when it's another human being. It's irritating when we realize we're only talking to ourselves, yes?

So, isn't it a relief to know that there is someone who always listens to every single word we speak? Our heavenly Father is wholly invested in us, and "he is ready to hear those who worship him and do his will." He doesn't get distracted by anything! God never tunes you out because He's worried that He'll miss something else. Yes, it's true that we need to do our part by following Him—obeying Him and giving Him praise and glory. But when we do, we are heard, friend! Isn't that wonderful?

Heavenly Father, You are so marvelous and perfect— and yet, You hear me. Thank You for listening to me even when no one else does.

WEDNESDAY, MAY 27

2 Samuel 5:1–7:17 / John 9:35–10:10 / Psalm 85:8–13

A Life with Him

I will listen to what God the LORD says; he promises peace to his people, his faithful servants. . . . Surely his salvation is near those who fear him, that his glory may dwell in our land. Love and faithfulness meet together; righteousness and peace kiss each other. . . . The LORD will indeed give what is good. . . . Righteousness goes before him and prepares the way for his steps.
PSALM 85:8–10, 12–13 NIV

Are you aware of God's nearness—not just in good times but also in the very worst? When things are going south in our lives, it's difficult to see beyond our anxiety, suffering, and pain; yet when we walk through the darkest valleys, He is right there with us. All we need to do is look up and grab His hand. And, if we let Him, He will guide us back into the light and bless us with His promises along the way.

When we know and trust God's character, we will recognize His goodness. We can hear Him speak His promises to our hearts. And when we are connected to Him, we will benefit from His rich generosity. A life with Him results in—

- Salvation
- Peace
- Love
- Faithfulness
- Righteousness
- Goodness
- And more!

The heavenly Father is always near, and He is always good!

Heavenly Father, remind me that You're here for me— with every step I take. I trust You, and I know You are good.

THURSDAY, MAY 28

2 Samuel 7:18–10:19 / John 10:11–30 / Psalm 86:1–10

Something Better

"Master God. . .speaking sure words as you do. . .just one more thing: Bless my family; keep your eye on them always. . . . Oh, may your blessing be on my family permanently!"
2 Samuel 7:28–29 msg

We women wrestle quite a bit with confidence, don't we? From a young age, the world trains us to compare and obsess in areas where we believe we fall short—in beauty, in brains, in (fill in the blank). . .and then we churn and worry until our self-confidence all but disappears into the abyss. To make matters worse, our self-confidence rarely resurfaces when our focus remains on the world.

Yet God has something different—something better—for us. When we say yes to Him and become part of His family, our self-confidence is amplified. Why? Because God speaks "sure words." His blessings are abundant and permanent. And they're yours for keeps because God and His promises never change. The blessing giver reminds you of how special you are because He made you to be. . .YOU!

Anytime you feel your confidence begin to waver, stop and have a quiet heart-to-heart with the heavenly Father. Reread this passage from 2 Samuel. Ask God not only to bless you and your family today and forever—but to gift you a big dose of heavenly confidence too!

Confidence giver, thank You for Your heavenly blessings on my family. Your promises are true— I know it! I trust You today, tomorrow, forever!

FRIDAY, MAY 29

2 Samuel 11:1–12:25 / John 10:31–11:16 / Psalm 86:11–17

What's Right in Front of You

O Eternal One, guide me along Your path so that I will live in Your truth. Unite my divided heart.... O Lord, my God! I praise You with all that I am.... For Your loyal love for me is so great it is beyond comparison. You have rescued my soul from the depths of the grave.
Psalm 86:11–13 voice

Whatever hardships we experience, we don't have to sink into hopelessness, depression, and despair. It's tempting to go dark when our lives are overflowing with difficult circumstances. The weak, human side of us even tells us that it's okay to withdraw from our family and friends, to shut down for a while and focus inward, eyes only on our problems. But when we're focused on self, we miss out on the joy that's right in front of us—the joy that was right there all along.

The author of this psalm gets it right. He acknowledges that his life has been hard, but he returns his focus to God, the reason for our joy—the one whose love for us "is beyond comparison." He is good, even in the bad. God was, is, and always will be our hope, strength, and joy. So, when life brings you down, let God lift you back up. Praise Him for His love, His grace, His rescue.

Father, my life is just...hard sometimes. I struggle to see the sunshine beyond the shadows. Help me to recognize Your rescue right in front of me.

SATURDAY, MAY 30

2 Samuel 12:26–13:39 / John 11:17–54 / Psalm 87

With Jesus, We Know...

[Jesus] found Lazarus already four days dead. . . . Martha said, "Master, if you'd been here, my brother wouldn't have died. Even now, I know that whatever you ask God he will give you." Jesus said, "Your brother will be raised up." Martha replied, "I know that he will be raised up in the resurrection at the end of time." "You don't have to wait for the End. I am, right now, Resurrection and Life. The one who believes in me, even though he or she dies, will live. And everyone who lives believing in me does not ultimately die at all. Do you believe this?" "Yes, Master. All along I have believed."
JOHN 11:17, 21–27 MSG

What do you truly know beyond all doubt?

Do you *know* your relationship will last?
Do you *know* you'll get the job?
Do you *know* your car will start in the morning?

Truth is, none of us knows anything—not with 100 percent certainty. But there is *one* exception. We can know that Jesus, the Son of God, died for our sins, rose again, and will come back to take all believers to heaven to live for eternity.

Dear one, have you accepted Jesus as Savior? Do you believe in the Resurrection and the Life? If you haven't already, pray this prayer:

Heavenly Father, thank You for sending Your Son, Jesus, to save me. I believe! Forgive my sins. Change my thoughts, my heart, my life! Make me brand-new!

SUNDAY, MAY 31

2 Samuel 14:1–15:12 / John 11:55–12:19 / Psalm 88:1–9

Our Defender

Mary came in with a jar of very expensive aromatic oils, anointed and massaged Jesus' feet, and then wiped them with her hair. . . . Judas Iscariot. . .said, "Why wasn't this oil sold and the money given to the poor? . . ." He said this not because he cared two cents about the poor but because he was a thief. . . . Jesus said, "Let her alone. She's anticipating and honoring the day of my burial."

JOHN 12:3–7 MSG

When someone jumps into action to defend you, how does it make you feel? Loved? Secure? Worthy? Seen? Mary likely felt all these things when Jesus came to her defense. She had poured expensive oils onto Jesus' feet, and Judas voiced his disapproval. Judas accused Mary of being wasteful because the oil could have been sold and the money given to the poor. (Interestingly, Judas was a thief!) Judas didn't bother to consider Mary's motives. He immediately passed judgment—sadly, Judas was not unlike many people in today's culture. But the beautiful part of this story is Jesus' response. . .because He knew Mary's heart!

Imagine someone lashing out at you or wrongfully accusing you, and Jesus jumps in with: "Let her alone." This is what our Savior does! He will put the bullies in their place if we give Him the space to move. Leave it to Him. He has your back—*always*!

Heavenly Father, thank You for coming to my defense. You know my motives, my heart. I love You.

JUNE 2026

SUNDAY	MONDAY	TUESDAY	WEDNESDAY	THURSDAY	FRIDAY	SATURDAY
	1	2	3	4	5	6
7	8	9	10	11	12	13
14 Flag Day	15	16	17	18	19 Juneteenth	20
21 Father's Day / First Day of Summer	22	23	24	25	26	27
28	29	30				

MONDAY, JUNE 1

2 Samuel 15:13–16:23 / John 12:20–43 / Psalm 88:10–18

Not Ashamed

Many among the chief rulers also believed in [Jesus], but because of the Pharisees they did not confess Him, lest they should be put out of the synagogue, for they loved the praise of men more than the praise of God.

JOHN 12:42–43 SKJV

Throughout His ministry, Jesus called out Pharisees for their hypocrisy, greed, self-righteousness, and pride. Their leadership positions in the community, however, gave them massive influence in every area of Jewish life. If someone got on their bad side, watch out—just look at what they did to Jesus!

So it's unsurprising to read in John 12 that many of the synagogue leaders believed in Jesus but hid their faith out of fear of repercussions from the Pharisees. Verse 43 says it plainly: "They loved the praise of men more than the praise of God."

This scripture calls for a gut check. Do any of your non-Christian friends know that you are a Christian? Would they be surprised to hear that you believe the truth of God's Word? Do you remain quiet when someone mocks God? Whose praise do you seek?

Jesus has placed in your heart His Holy Spirit that is powerful and loving and bold (2 Timothy 1:7). Today, choose to stand up for Jesus, and He will fulfill His promise, "Everyone who acknowledges me publicly here on earth, I will also acknowledge before my Father in heaven" (Matthew 10:32 NLT).

*Jesus, I am not ashamed of You.
I will shine Your light everywhere I go!*

TUESDAY, JUNE 2

2 Samuel 17:1–18:18 / John 12:44–13:20 / Psalm 89:1–6

God's Will Be Done

Absalom and his counselors decided that Hushai's plan was better than Ahithophel's, not knowing that the Eternal One had determined to thwart Ahithophel's good advice and bring about Absalom's destruction.

2 SAMUEL 17:14 VOICE

Absalom had just overthrown his father, King David, and was trying to hold on to Israel's throne. So Absalom asked two advisers what he should do. Ahithophel urged Absalom to immediately chase after David and kill him. That seemed like a good plan to Absalom. But then Hushai told Absalom he would become more famous if he *first* gathered the entire army of Israel and *then* led the troops against David. Absalom's ego liked the sound of Hushai's plan better.

This story is an example of how God can use any situation to make His will be done. Absalom had certainly received solid advice from Ahithophel, but God allowed Hushai's bad advice to sway Absalom's pride to choose unwisely. His vanity resulted in his death and the reinstatement of David as God's chosen, true king of Israel.

If you're unsure what God is doing in your life today, remember the story of Absalom and David. In it, you can see the promise fulfilled that "God causes everything to work together for the good of those who love God and are called according to his purpose for them" (Romans 8:28 NLT).

God, thank You for this look behind the curtain of how You work. I trust You to take care of everything in my life!

WEDNESDAY, JUNE 3

2 Samuel 18:19–19:39 / John 13:21–38 / Psalm 89:7–13

Snap out of It

"Get hold of yourself; get out there and put some heart into your servants! I swear to GOD that if you don't go to them they'll desert. . . . And that will be the worst thing that has happened yet."

2 SAMUEL 19:7 MSG

King David was inconsolable after hearing of his son's death. Never mind that Absalom had been hunting to kill David for the right to rule Israel. . .or that Absalom was an egomaniac who didn't follow the Lord. All David could feel was loss. David's troops, who had bravely saved his life, had expected to celebrate the victory but instead crept home in shame—thinking they had disappointed their king.

That's when Joab told David to snap out of it. Joab, David's nephew and commander of his troops, spoke the truth to the king in love—that God had worked a miracle through David's warriors. Joab risked the consequences of confronting the king, but because he was brave enough to speak up, Israel was able to move ahead in God's plan and heal.

Who do you identify with in this story—David or Joab? Sometimes, like David, we need someone to kick us in the shins to help us get out of our own head and refocus on what God is doing. And sometimes, like Joab, we must bravely confront someone important to us and point out the truth in love.

Lord, whether I'm David or Joab in any situation, help me to do Your will.

THURSDAY, JUNE 4

2 Samuel 19:40–21:22 / John 14:1–17 / Psalm 89:14–18

Call to Worship

Happy are those who hear the joyful call to worship, for they will walk in the light of your presence, LORD. . . . You are their glorious strength. It pleases you to make us strong.
PSALM 89:15, 17 NLT

When do you hear and answer the call to worship? It could be on your way to Sunday morning service. Maybe the call reaches your heart as you sit with a steaming mug of coffee, the morning light falling across the open pages of your Bible. Perhaps it's while celebrating the first steps of a toddler or while watching the fast-beating wings of a hummingbird. Worship, no matter the time or the place, resets our focus on the truth that God is great and He is worthy of every ounce of adoration we can muster. "Let all that I am praise the LORD; with my whole heart, I will praise his holy name," David wrote in Psalm 103:1 (NLT).

Yes, worship raises up and blesses our Father, but worship also blesses us. As we enter into His presence, worship can help us see His perspective, help us to know Him better, and refill our souls with His Spirit. Psalm 89:17 even says that it pleases God to strengthen us in this way! And can't we all use a little more strength today?

"Bless the LORD, O my soul! O LORD my God, you are very great! You are clothed with splendor and majesty" (Psalm 104:1 ESV).

FRIDAY, JUNE 5

2 Samuel 22:1–23:7 / John 14:18–15:27 / Psalm 89:19–29

Pep Talk

"I don't have much more time to talk to you, because the ruler of this world approaches. He has no power over me, but I will do what the Father requires of me, so that the world will know that I love the Father. Come, let's be going."

John 14:30–31 NLT

The urgency in Jesus' voice is obvious. He knows He will be separated from His friends in just a few short hours to face unjustified arrest, interrogation, torture, and death on the cross. But instead of focusing on what was to come for Him, Jesus instead spent time encouraging the disciples. Already in chapter 14, He had promised the coming of His Spirit. The Holy Spirit, He said, will help them understand the parts of His teachings that they simply could not grasp or retain yet (John 14:26). Although Jesus knows the confusion and turmoil that His followers are about to go through, He does His very best to tell them what's to come and promises them peace (John 14:27–29).

You don't know what your tomorrow brings, but Jesus does. His words to the disciples are just as true for you in anything you will face. Today, take comfort from the fact that Jesus is the same yesterday, today, and forever (Hebrews 13:8).

Lord, thank You for Your Word and Your teachings. Please make the Holy Spirit come alive in me so I can understand Your teachings more and more.

SATURDAY, JUNE 6

> 2 Samuel 23:8–24:25 / John 16:1–22 / Psalm 89:30–37

Promises, Promises

I will not break My agreement, or change what was spoken by My lips. Once I have promised by My holy name, I will not lie to David.
PSALM 89:34–35 NLV

God keeps His promises.

It's a simple statement, but it's a truth that's nearly impossible for the world to believe. Why? Because the world is full of broken promises, breached contracts, unfulfilled agreements, double crosses, failed marriage vows, lies, and manipulation—in another word. . .*sin*.

So if you struggle to believe the fullness and truth of the promises in God's Word, you aren't alone. One of Jesus' closest friends and followers, Thomas, didn't believe that the Messiah had *actually* risen from the dead. And what's more—Jesus didn't condemn Thomas for doubting. He simply offered concrete evidence and encouraged Thomas to believe (John 20:27).

Our almighty, powerful God isn't swayed by fads, popular thought, peer pressure, or the tricks and temptations of Satan himself. In His perfection, He chooses not to lie (Numbers 23:19). He is faithful, even when we aren't (2 Timothy 2:13). His perfect ways and Word offer protection (2 Samuel 22:31) and comfort (Psalm 23) to His children. His promises are the unmovable, rock-solid foundation that we can build our lives upon and anchor our hope to (Matthew 7:24–29).

> *Father, when people fail me and I'm left frustrated and disappointed, help me to rely all the more on Your promises. You are always faithful. You keep me headed in the right direction—closer to Your heart.*

SUNDAY, JUNE 7

1 Kings 1 / John 16:23–17:5 / Psalm 89:38–52

Be Back Soon

"I've told you all this so that trusting me, you will be unshakable and assured, deeply at peace. In this godless world you will continue to experience difficulties. But take heart! I've conquered the world."

JOHN 16:33 MSG

John 16:33 wraps up a chapter where Jesus explains to His disciples what to expect in the coming hours and days. Essentially, He says, "I'm going to leave you for a little while, and you're going to be devastated. But then suddenly I'll be back, and you'll be filled with joy." The disciples said they understood what Jesus said (John 16:29–30), but they still couldn't fully grasp how the world would soon be shaken to its core.

Jesus offers us the same promises that He gave the disciples on the night He was betrayed and headed to the cross. Right now He is physically away from us, seated at the right hand of God, waiting the Father's cue to return to earth. And when He does, His followers will be filled with joy, because we already know the end of the story. He's returning to conquer Satan, make all things new, and take us with Him to dwell in heaven!

Today, regardless of what difficulties you're facing, no matter how helpless or hopeless it feels, take heart and grasp hold of the peace of the Holy Spirit. Our Savior is coming back soon.

Jesus, I'm holding tightly to Your promise that You will be back. Come soon, Lord!

MONDAY, JUNE 8

1 Kings 2 / John 17:6–26 / Psalm 90:1–12

Jesus Prays for You

"I am praying not only for these disciples but also for all who will ever believe in me through their message."

JOHN 17:20 NLT

It's no small blessing to know there are people who pray for you. Maybe you have a mother who has held you close in prayer for your whole life. Maybe you've found a friend group who will pray sincerely for each other like James 5:16 encourages us to do. "The earnest prayer of a righteous person," James 5:16 (NLT) says, "has great power and produces wonderful results."

Throughout the entire chapter of John 17, Jesus prays for His disciples—but not just the people who followed and believed in Him while He walked on earth. Instead, He prays for everyone who will ever believe. If you have accepted Jesus as your Savior, that means Jesus prayed this prayer for *you* too! Think of it: Jesus asked His Father to protect you, set you apart from the world and make you holy, help you be wise in God's Word, unite you with other believers, and guard you from Satan's attacks.

Yes, Jesus prayed for you so many years ago in John 17, and what's more is that He is still praying for you as He sits next to His Father in heaven (Romans 8:34)!

Jesus, it gives me such hope and peace to know that You are praying for me. Help me to faithfully pray for others too!

TUESDAY, JUNE 9

1 Kings 3–4 / John 18:1–27 / Psalm 90:13–17

Get Wise

*"Give me an understanding heart so that I can govern your
people well and know the difference between right and wrong.
For who by himself is able to govern this great people of yours?"
The Lord was pleased that Solomon had asked for wisdom.*

1 Kings 3:9–10 NLT

Early in King Solomon's reign, God offered to give him anything he asked for. Solomon could've requested *anything*—immortality, wealth, strength, good looks, love, intelligence, power. It might've been a difficult decision for us, but it seems Solomon didn't hesitate in his answer. He admitted to the Lord that he was inexperienced and didn't know how to effectively lead Israel. And then he humbly asked for God's wisdom to govern His people. God was *delighted* by Solomon's request (1 Kings 3:10 MSG). With God's blessing and help, Solomon grew to be the wisest and the wealthiest man who had ever lived.

"Getting wisdom is the wisest thing you can do!" Solomon wrote in Proverbs 4:7 (NLT). How do we do that? First, by humbly admitting that we don't know everything. Then, just like Solomon, we can ask God to give us His wisdom, the ability to understand His truth in scripture, and sound judgment to put our wisdom and understanding into action. God will delight in granting that request, just as He did for Solomon.

*Father, You are the giver of all wisdom,
sound judgment, and understanding. Please grant me
more of these—more of You—today and every day.*

WEDNESDAY, JUNE 10

1 Kings 5–6 / John 18:28–19:5 / Psalm 91:1–10

God's Temple

"Concerning this Temple you are building, if you keep all my decrees and regulations and obey all my commands, I will fulfill through you the promise I made to your father, David."

1 KINGS 6:12 NLT

The Israelites had one job: Obey God's Law. If they accomplished this task, God promised that He would dwell with them; His presence would live in the temple that King Solomon was building. But all throughout the Old Testament, Israel's kings failed to lead the people in keeping His laws. They wouldn't and couldn't hold up their end of the covenant.

While the temple was a good idea, because of sin, it never really served a lasting purpose. It wasn't until generations later when Jesus—who *is* the presence of God in human form—fulfilled the purpose and goal of the temple (John 1:14; 2:19–22). When Jesus laid down His life as the ultimate sacrifice for sin, He ushered in the new covenant between God and Christ's followers—a covenant based on Jesus' sacrifice and His grace and salvation.

If you have accepted Jesus as your Savior, you are serving as the temple of the Lord. His Holy Spirit lives inside of you, so you take God with you everywhere (1 Corinthians 6:19–20).

Lord, it's an awe-inspiring truth to know that I am Your temple. Thank You for the gift of Your Spirit. Help me to be worthy of the privilege of carrying Your love, light, and might no matter where I go!

THURSDAY, JUNE 11

1 Kings 7 / John 19:6–25 / Psalm 91:11–16

Angels Among Us

For He will tell His angels to care for you and keep you in all your ways. They will hold you up in their hands. So your foot will not hit against a stone.
Psalm 91:11–12 nlv

What does the Bible say about guardian angels? There are a few specific examples in scripture of angels that are sent to take care of God's children. In 1 Kings 19:5, an angel attended to Elijah when he was on the run from the evil Queen Jezebel. In Daniel 6:22, Daniel explains how he survived the night with lions because an angel came and shut the beasts' mouths. Angels show up in the New Testament as well, like in Matthew 4:11 when angels took care of Jesus after His forty-day fast and tempting from Satan. And in Acts 12:7, an angel helped the apostle Peter escape from prison. There's no indication that God assigns one specific angel to each believer, but angels are certainly capable of doing God's work and will in supernatural ways.

Under God's direction, angels are actively present and at work in the world. But they, like we, are God's servants (Hebrews 1:14). God is the one worthy of our praise and in whom we should place our hope and faith.

Father, thank You for sending angels to help do Your work in this world. Today I will raise my voice with Your angels who sing Your praise. Only You are worthy (Revelation 7:12)!

FRIDAY, JUNE 12

1 Kings 8:1–53 / John 19:26–42 / Psalm 92:1–9

Others First

"In the future, foreigners who do not belong to your people Israel will hear of you. They will come from distant lands because of your name, for they will hear of your great name and your strong hand and your powerful arm. And when they pray toward this Temple, then hear from heaven where you live, and grant what they ask of you. In this way, all the people of the earth will come to know and fear you, just as your own people Israel do."

1 KINGS 8:41–43 NLT

King Solomon's prayers during the temple dedication span a large portion of 1 Kings 8, and Solomon's wisdom and understanding of God's nature really shine through in these verses. As you read these passages, notice how Solomon's prayers focus almost entirely on others rather than himself. He unselfishly prays not just for the nation of Israel but also for future followers of God who are not Jewish. His understanding that God is a God for *all* people was centuries ahead of its time.

Jesus came to earth and paid the price for *all* of humanity's sins so we could live in freedom (1 Timothy 2:6). Although Solomon didn't know all the details of this plan, he wisely understood that God loved the whole world, and whoever believes in Jesus will live forever (John 3:16).

Father, there are so many people who need Your love and salvation. Work in their hearts, Lord, and use me to help them find You.

SATURDAY, JUNE 13

1 Kings 8:54–10:13 / John 20:1–18 / Psalm 92:10–15

Confusion

Then the disciple who had reached the tomb first also went in, and he saw and believed—for until then they still hadn't understood the Scriptures that said Jesus must rise from the dead.
JOHN 20:8–9 NLT

John's Gospel describes a scene of confusion at Jesus' tomb on Sunday morning. Before dawn, Mary Magdalene finds the stone rolled away from the grave and runs to tell the disciples that Jesus' body is gone. Peter and John take off in a sprint to see for themselves what's happened. Inside the tomb, they find Jesus' linen burial wrappings and cloth head covering. If this had been a robbery, these expensive garments would've been stolen and sold. The fact that John included these details shows that even though he didn't understand completely, he was beginning to believe that God was at work and that a miracle had occurred.

Every believer goes through times when God's plan feels confusing. We wonder *what* He's doing, *where* our part in all of it is, and sometimes *if* He's working at all. If that's how you feel today, pray and ask God for understanding. You may not have a light bulb moment where every detail becomes clear, but God is faithful to help you begin to see where He is working, where He is headed, and that His way is always perfect (Psalm 18:30).

God, please grant me insight and understanding about what You are doing in my life (Proverbs 2:3). I trust that Your ways are good.

SUNDAY, JUNE 14 — *Flag Day*

1 Kings 10:14–11:43 / John 20:19–31 / Psalm 93

More Powerful

The waters have risen, O Eternal One; the sound of pounding waves is deafening. The waters have roared with power. More powerful than the thunder of mighty rivers, more powerful than the mighty waves in the ocean is the Eternal on high!
PSALM 93:3–4 VOICE

Water has been called the most powerful natural force on earth. Water's power lies in the fact that it's necessary for life and also has the potential to cause major destruction. Ask anyone who has felt the pull of a riptide, had frozen pipes burst, or been behind the wheel of a vehicle in a downpour. In Genesis 6–9 God used water to destroy the evil in the world—saving only Noah, his family, and two of every living creature (or seven pairs, with certain animals). The potential of uncontrolled water is something to be feared.

But here's the good news: Your heavenly Father is the God of water, and the Creator is mightier and more powerful than His creation.

God's unstoppable power is both awe-inspiring and—for our enemy, Satan—terrifying. For those of us counted among His children, we can trust in His power for our every need. He is faithful to protect us, uphold us, provide for us, and equip us to face every challenge and circumstance. Today, ask God to display His power through you. The same Holy Spirit that had the power to raise Jesus from the dead lives in your heart right now.

Father, thank You for being mightier than anything I face!

MONDAY, JUNE 15

1 Kings 12:1–13:10 / John 21 / Psalm 94:1–11

Eternal Gospel

And there are also many other things that Jesus did, and if each of them were written, I suppose that even the world itself could not contain the books that would be written. Amen.

JOHN 21:25 SKJV

The Gospel writers wrote about Jesus' life from unique perspectives and for different audiences. Matthew, Mark, and Luke are known as the synoptic Gospels—meaning each book is a synopsis of Jesus' life (think: "greatest hits"). John's Gospel stands apart and includes scenes from Jesus' ministry that aren't recorded in the first three. Together, the four Gospels tell the same story of Jesus' life, His teaching, and the essential role He plays in God's bigger story of creation's redemption.

But, as John mentions in today's verse, what's recorded in the Gospels doesn't begin to scratch the surface of all the things Jesus did on earth. Someday in heaven we will learn—perhaps from the eyewitnesses themselves—all these other amazing things Jesus did! But in the meantime, the story of Jesus continues to be written through the lives of His followers today. Think of it! If you profess Jesus as your Lord and Savior, His Spirit is alive in you this moment, adding to the record of what Jesus has done. And when you tell others about what He has done for you and the difference He has made in your life, you are adding to the eternal gospel story!

Jesus, thank You for allowing me to be a part of Your story.

TUESDAY, JUNE 16

1 Kings 13:11–14:31 / Acts 1:1–11 / Psalm 94:12–23

The Lord's Discipline

*Blessed is the one you discipline, Lord,
the one you teach from your law.*
PSALM 94:12 NIV

No child enjoys discipline. To a little one, being told no or to have something they want taken away is the worst kind of injustice. Discipline may result in tears, tantrums, and full-body resistance. You might remember what that feels like, but perhaps more recently you've been in the parent role in that scenario. A mother who loves her child wants nothing more than to guide, direct, protect, and help them thrive. When a mother cares about the well-being and future of her child, she'll willingly work on teaching through discipline because she can see how it helps her child to learn and grow and mature.

God, as our loving heavenly Father, also disciplines us—His children. And whether we're young or young at heart, discipline is still difficult to accept. "No discipline is enjoyable while it is happening— it's painful!" Hebrews 12:11 (NLT) says. But the second sentence of the verse offers a promise: "Afterward there will be a peaceful harvest of right living for those who are trained in this way."

God's discipline provides wisdom and perspective and discernment that can only come from Him. Are you willing to endure some discomfort for His greatest blessings?

Father, this is a difficult prayer to pray, but I will follow the example from scripture and ask you to "correct me, Lord, but please be gentle" (Jeremiah 10:24 NLT).

WEDNESDAY, JUNE 17

1 Kings 15:1–16:20 / Acts 1:12–26 / Psalm 95

Cycle Breaker

Asa did what was right in the eyes of the Lord. . . . He sent away the men from the land who sold the use of their bodies in their religion. He took away all the false gods his father had made.
1 Kings 15:11–12 NLV

Asa, the third king of Judah, inherited a load of sinful baggage from the rulers who preceded him. First was Rehoboam, who, during his seventeen-year reign, built pagan shrines to idols throughout the land. He installed male and female shrine prostitutes, and "the people imitated the detestable practices of the pagan nations" (1 Kings 14:24 NLT). Rehoboam and his successor, Abijam, constantly battled the northern kingdom of Israel, causing even deeper disunity among God's chosen people (1 Kings 14:30; 15:6).

Despite all these terrible things, during Asa's forty-one-year reign, he was able to stop some of the generational sin by abolishing shrine prostitution and removing pagan idols. Although he couldn't remove all sinful practices from Judah, it seems he did all that he could and his "heart remained completely faithful to the LORD throughout his life" (1 Kings 15:14 NLT).

If your family tree contains sinful strongholds that have been passed down from your parents or grandparents, take hope and courage from Asa's story. Ask God to strengthen you and equip you to break those cycles, and choose to be faithful to God and His ways.

You have equipped me, Lord, to break sinful generational cycles. Show me how!

THURSDAY, JUNE 18

> 1 Kings 16:21–18:19 / Acts 2:1–21 / Psalm 96:1–8

Obedience

[Elijah] went to Zarephath. As he arrived at the gates of the village, he saw a widow gathering sticks, and he asked her, "Would you please bring me a little water in a cup?" As she was going to get it, he called to her, "Bring me a bite of bread, too."
1 Kings 17:10–11 NLT

The widow at Zarephath was in no position to be hospitable. She had only a handful of flour and a little oil, and once she used these to make one final meal, she and her son fully expected to die of starvation. She had no hope for any other outcome.

But Elijah knew the Lord was working, so he gently encouraged her to bake a little bread for him too, promising that God would provide what they needed.

She must've thought Elijah was nuts, but she did what the prophet asked her to do. Not only was there enough flour and oil to make that meal, but the flour and oil continued to last to make food for herself, Elijah, and her family for many days (1 Kings 17:15–16).

Often in the Bible we see miracles that are tied to a great faith. Here, however, we see a miracle that happens because of obedience. Sometimes that's what God needs from us—a willing heart to take the first step that will lead to seeing Him work in amazing ways!

Father, when my faith is struggling, help me to continue to obey!

Juneteenth   FRIDAY, JUNE 19

1 Kings 18:20–19:21 / Acts 2:22–41 / Psalm 96:9–13

Here He Comes

The LORD said, "Go out and stand on the mountain in the presence of the LORD, for the LORD is about to pass by." Then a great and powerful wind tore the mountains apart. . . , but the LORD was not in the wind. After the wind there was an earthquake, but the LORD was not in the earthquake. After the earthquake came a fire, but the LORD was not in the fire. And after the fire came a gentle whisper.

1 KINGS 19:11–12 NIV

Although the Lord communicated with Elijah through many prophetic messages, this mountaintop experience was unique. God invited Elijah to meet with Him, and the prophet didn't know what to expect.

So Elijah did what God told him to do—stand on the mountain—and then he waited. . .and listened. As a powerful wind kicked up, Elijah might've thought, *Here He comes!* But he knew the Lord well enough to know it wasn't Him. Next came an earthquake, and then a fire. Quite an eventful mountaintop experience—but no Yahweh. . .yet. Elijah continued to listen, and that's when he heard the voice of God. . .in a gentle whisper.

What can we learn from Elijah's experience in discerning God's voice? Be open to whatever way God chooses to show up. Listen and watch—intently and patiently—for Him to arrive and act mightily!

Lord, I stand with my eyes, ears, and heart open to You. Will You meet me here again?

SATURDAY, JUNE 20

1 Kings 20 / Acts 2:42–3:26 / Psalm 97:1–6

Not Condemned

"You rejected this holy, righteous one and. . .killed the author of life, but God raised him from the dead. . . . God was fulfilling what all the prophets had foretold about the Messiah— that he must suffer these things. Now repent of your sins and turn to God, so that your sins may be wiped away."
ACTS 3:14–15, 18–19 NLT

The people whom Peter addressed in Acts 3 were Jews on their way to temple prayers. They'd just witnessed Peter and John heal a crippled beggar and were probably curious to hear what Peter had to say after such a miraculous display of God's power.

Peter boldly explained that the source of the healing was Jesus Christ—the Messiah that the Jews rejected, handed over to Pilate, and ultimately killed. Peter didn't sugarcoat the message: *They themselves* were responsible for Jesus' death. Yet the apostle's sermon didn't contain condemnation but instead an open invitation to God's grace and forgiveness.

That's what is so radical about salvation. For the very people who cheered as Jesus was condemned and slaughtered, God will trade their repentance for His pardon, grace, and eternal life.

The same is true for us today. No matter the sin, God is faithful to forgive a contrite heart. The very blood that Jesus shed on the cross will cover every blemish so we can stand blameless before the Father.

*Jesus, Your salvation is so awesomely powerful.
Thank You for Your work on the cross.*

Father's Day / First Day of Summer   SUNDAY, JUNE 21

1 Kings 21:1–22:28 / Acts 4:1–22 / Psalm 97:7–12

The Truth Standard

The messenger who had gone to summon Micaiah said to him, "Look, the other prophets without exception are predicting success for the king. Let your word agree with theirs, and speak favorably." But Micaiah said, "As surely as the Lord lives, I can tell him only what the Lord tells me."

1 Kings 22:13–14 niv

The royal messenger sent to bring the prophet Micaiah to King Ahab's royal court was probably groaning the whole way. He knew that unlike the rest of Ahab's prophets and advisers, Micaiah wouldn't simply tell the evil king what he wanted to hear. The prophet Micaiah held himself to an unheard standard: He wouldn't prophesy a message unless it was from the Lord.

Micaiah faced the temptation to simply go with the flow. . .to *not* rock the boat. . .to fudge the truth a little to appease King Ahab and save his own neck. But God called Micaiah to a higher standard, and He calls us—His daughters—to the same standard of truth.

So when you're faced with the choice of glossing over what's right or stating the truth, ask the Lord for the strength to choose truth, even when it's not what others want to hear.

Pause, pray, seek wisdom in scripture and from mature Christian friends, and His Spirit will help you. You can bring His love and wisdom to any situation, no matter how difficult.

> ***Lord, help me always remember that above***
> ***all I want to please You, not others.***

MONDAY, JUNE 22

1 Kings 22:29–2 Kings 1:18 / Acts 4:23–5:11 / Psalm 98

Bold Prayers

"Herod Antipas, Pontius Pilate the governor, the Gentiles, and the people of Israel were all united against Jesus, your holy servant, whom you anointed. But everything they did was determined beforehand according to your will. And now, O Lord, hear their threats, and give us, your servants, great boldness in preaching your word."

ACTS 4:27–29 NLT

Jesus told His followers they would be persecuted in His name, and here in Acts 4—just days after Jesus had ascended into heaven—the believers were already dealing with angry Jewish leaders, arrests, and threats against them. And there was more to come.

But instead of going underground, instead of abandoning their faith, instead of trying to come up with a strategy of how to avoid persecution and hardships, the Christians got together and prayed. They didn't ask God to take away their problems but instead prayed for boldness to preach mightily—to spread God's Word even more widely and powerfully.

When we as God's people are on mission with Him, we can boldly ask for confidence like these followers did. We don't have to fear the unknown, but we can trust that He is in control and He works all things together for our good and His glory (Romans 8:28).

God, give me the boldness to live on mission like the early Christians. With You in my corner, I will not quit, I will not give in to fear. I will live every moment courageously for You.

TUESDAY, JUNE 23

2 Kings 2–3 / Acts 5:12–28 / Psalm 99

Keep It Up!

The high priest and his officials, who were Sadducees, were filled with jealousy. They arrested the apostles and put them in the public jail. But an angel of the Lord came at night, opened the gates of the jail, and brought them out. Then he told them, "Go to the Temple and give the people this message of life!"
ACTS 5:17–20 NLT

With the arrival of the Holy Spirit, the apostles displayed mighty acts of healing around Jerusalem. Many people sought them out to experience a miracle, and more and more of those people believed in Jesus Christ. All the while, the believers met regularly—publicly and without fear of repercussion—and their community of faith grew stronger.

All this enraged the Jewish leaders known as the Sadducees. They arrested and jailed the apostles and probably smugly thought this would snuff out the church. If the apostles had any doubts about whether they were following God's will, those misgivings evaporated when an angel showed up and sprung them out of jail. It was a clear "Keep it up!" from heaven itself.

When you find yourself bumping up against frustrations in your own faith, remember this story from Acts 5. Ask God for the strength you need to do His will and do it well, and He will encourage you to "Keep it up!"

Father, I want to do Your will, but sometimes I need a little extra boost to take the next step. Will You give me that boost today?

WEDNESDAY, JUNE 24

2 Kings 4 / Acts 5:29–6:15 / Psalm 100

Church Troubles

> *And in those days, when the number of the disciples was multiplying, a murmuring arose by the Greeks against the Hebrews because their widows were neglected in the daily administration.*
>
> ACTS 6:1 SKJV

As you read Acts, you might think the early church was a perfect community—dynamic preaching, miracles, generosity, fellowship, growth. Maybe you even find yourself disappointed that your own church isn't firing on all those cylinders.

While the early church was certainly expanding and fulfilling Jesus' Great Commission, it was by no means perfect. God's Word even points out some of the very human struggles of all Christians—even those believers who learned from Jesus Himself.

Acts 5:1–11 recounts the hypocrisy of a couple in the church who lied to make themselves appear more generous than they really were—a choice that ended in their demise. And here in Acts 6, we see rumors, grumbling, prejudice, and discrimination rear its ugly head.

The church is made up of sinful individuals, but Jesus' example for us to follow and His grace from His work on the cross equip us to strive, daily, to be worthy to be called the bride of Christ. When you find yourself in a tough situation in the church, remember 1 Peter 4:8 (NLT): "Most important of all, continue to show deep love for each other, for love covers a multitude of sins."

Lord, shower my church with grace to make us worthy to be Your light in this dark world.

THURSDAY, JUNE 25

2 Kings 5:1–6:23 / Acts 7:1–16 / Psalm 101

Attitude Check

Naaman lost his temper. He spun around saying, "I thought he'd personally come out and meet me, call on the name of GOD, wave his hand over the diseased spot, and get rid of the disease. . . ." He stomped off, mad as a hornet.
2 KINGS 5:11–12 MSG

Naaman was a well-regarded army general from Aram. So when he asked the prophet Elisha to heal him of leprosy, Naaman expected a certain level of respect and even special treatment from Elisha. But instead of rolling out the red carpet, Elisha sent a messenger to give Naaman simple instructions on how to be healed. No elaborate to-do, no mystical healing service. Naaman found the whole thing demeaning and had himself a toddler temper tantrum.

Attitude check, Naaman.

But haven't we all been guilty of the same thing? We often expect God to do something specific, to answer our prayers in just the way we think they should be answered. And when God's ways are surprising and *not* what we expect, it's tempting to pout or throw a pity party or even withhold our prayers from God.

Thankfully, Naaman's story doesn't end in a tantrum. The proud man chose to listen to the wisdom of his servants, and he humbly obeyed Elisha's instructions. When he did what God asked of him, he found complete physical healing.

Almighty God, Your ways are not my ways. Give me the wisdom, patience, and humility to follow Your plan no matter what.

FRIDAY, JUNE 26

> 2 Kings 6:24–8:15 / Acts 7:17–36 / Psalm 102:1–7

Pouring Out Problems

A prayer of one overwhelmed with trouble, pouring out problems before the LORD.
TITLE OF PSALM 102 NLT

There are 116 psalms in the Bible that include descriptive titles. Some of these titles identify the writer; other titles are a kind of musical direction for a worship setting. The title of Psalm 102 describes the person and purpose of this prayer, and it's a practical example of how we can talk to God even in our most stressed-out and exhausted state.

From this psalm, we learn that it's okay to cry out to God when we are struggling. . .without fear of His judgment or disappointment. We can tell Him exactly how we feel, how our troubles are affecting us physically, how stress is keeping us from sleeping, and how these things impact our attitude and outlook. Psalm 102 shows us that even in an overwhelmed state, it's important to remind ourselves of the truth of God's mighty power, His faithfulness to us, and His promise to help and strengthen us.

When you feel overwhelmed, follow the example of the writer of Psalm 102 and keep talking to God. Cling to the truth that your Father is faithful to hear you and answer you (Psalm 50:15). Give Him your stresses and burdens and He'll hold you up and help you (Psalm 55:22; Hebrews 4:16). And He will restore your joy (Psalm 51:12; 71:20–21).

Father, You are my safe place when I am overwhelmed. Help me learn to run to You.

SATURDAY, JUNE 27

2 Kings 8:16–9:37 / Acts 7:37–53 / Psalm 102:8–17

Justice

> "Jezebel will be devoured by dogs in the land of
> Jezreel. Her body will be so gruesome that it will
> be like a pile of dung on the surface of a field."
> 2 KINGS 9:36–37 VOICE

There's a good reason why baby girls aren't usually named Jezebel. The only fitting descriptor for this tyrannical Old Testament queen is *evil*.

Jezebel was a foreign princess who married Israel's King Ahab—an evil ruler in his own right. Among other things, Jezebel brought Baal worship to Ahab and Israel. She openly threatened and commanded the execution of many of God's prophets (1 Kings 18), and she orchestrated a murderous scheme to steal a vineyard from an innocent man named Naboth (1 Kings 21).

Finally, here in 2 Kings 9, the Lord revealed Jezebel's fate to the prophet Elisha. It's violent and disgusting, but it's also just, fitting, and well deserved for the atrocities she committed.

While our Father is a God of grace when we repent of our sins, scripture also tells us that the Lord is a just God. Justice is an essential part of God's character and one we can take comfort in as His children. When Christ returns to earth, He will use His power to eradicate Satan and his darkness—resulting in the ultimate justice for Himself and His people.

> *God, thank You for being a righteous and holy*
> *judge. Your justice is as mighty as Your grace,*
> *and I am blessed because You offer both.*

SUNDAY, JUNE 28

2 Kings 10–11 / Acts 7:54–8:8 / Psalm 102:18–28

Growth in Challenges

And at that time there was a great persecution against the church that was at Jerusalem. And they were all scattered out throughout the regions of Judea and Samaria, except the apostles.
ACTS 8:1 SKJV

Before Jesus ascended to heaven, He told His followers that they would face persecution (Luke 21:12–19). The Messiah never downplayed the difficulties Christians would encounter, yet He promised to be with them and give them peace (John 14:18, 27).

These early believers were harassed, beaten, arrested, taken to court, jailed, and ultimately forced to flee from their homes. The hard times the church was going through were foundation-rocking and life-changing. Yet because of these things, the good news spread more quickly and widely. This persecution forced the Christians to Judea and Samaria, fulfilling the second part of Jesus' Great Commission to spread the gospel in Acts 1:8.

That's one of the great mysteries of how God works in every situation. Things seem scary, worrisome, uncertain, and dark—yet when we are faithful to trust and follow Him one step at a time through difficult times, He will work mightily for His glory and our good (Romans 8:28).

What difficulties are you facing today? Ask the Lord to show you one small step you can take to align your hard time with His plan, and then watch what He will do!

Lord, give me a glimpse of what You're doing through my difficulties. I trust You to work mightily in every hard thing I face.

MONDAY, JUNE 29

2 Kings 12–13 / Acts 8:9–40 / Psalm 103:1–9

Authentic Praise!

O my soul, come, praise the Eternal with all that is in me—body, emotions, mind, and will—every part of who I am—praise His holy name. O my soul, come, praise the Eternal; sing a song from a grateful heart; sing and never forget all the good He has done.
PSALM 103:1–2 VOICE

If anyone in the Bible understood authentic praise, it was David. Physically, he used his body to dance in worship of the God who created him (2 Samuel 6:14). Emotionally, David focused his innermost feelings on the Lord—even when he struggled and suffered—often pouring out his feelings at God's feet as an act of faith (Psalm 22). Mentally, he thought about and meditated on God day and night (Psalm 63). It's no exaggeration to say that David lived a life of praise and worship.

What did David praise God for? His all-encompassing forgiveness, healing, salvation, love, compassion, blessings, righteousness, and justice—just to name a few things. David constantly reminded himself of the goodness of God, and when David faced really hard times, those reminders helped sustain him.

God created you to worship Him (Isaiah 43:21), and daily praise is one of the best ways to get to know your heavenly Father better. Study David's praise in the psalms, and practice praising God with all that is in you—body, heart, and mind.

O my Savior and God, You are worthy of my worship. Create in me a sincere heart of praise!

TUESDAY, JUNE 30

2 Kings 14–15 / Acts 9:1–16 / Psalm 103:10–14

Absolute God

Measure how high heaven is above the earth; God's wide, loving, kind heart is greater for those who revere Him. You see, God takes all our crimes—our seemingly inexhaustible sins—and removes them. As far as east is from the west, He removes them from us.

Psalm 103:11–12 voice

"How big is God?"

You might remember asking this question when you were a child. It's a mystery that humankind has tried to solve since the beginning of creation—a puzzle whose answer can leave us both overwhelmed and comforted.

First John 4:16 tells us that God is love, so we could say that His "bigness" corresponds with how large, how encompassing, how fully enveloping His love is. And—as Psalm 103 clearly describes—His love for us, His children, reaches far beyond the limits of heaven itself. Think of it: Jesus demonstrated the vastness of that love by closing the gap between heaven and earth when He willingly came as a baby, lived as a man, and died on a cross. His death and resurrection completed the purpose of that love by removing our sins without a trace so that we can be with Him for all of time, forevermore.

God is absolute, limitless love. And He is absolute, limitless forgiveness. He created you and invites you to experience the joy of both. Let's praise His name for His absolute bigness!

Father, I am in awe of Your love. Your kindness and goodness are overwhelming in the very best way.

JULY 2026

SUNDAY	MONDAY	TUESDAY	WEDNESDAY	THURSDAY	FRIDAY	SATURDAY
			1	2	3	4 Independence Day
5	6	7	8	9	10	11
12	13	14	15	16	17	18
19	20	21	22	23	24	25
26	27	28	29	30	31	

WEDNESDAY, JULY 1

2 Kings 16–17 / Acts 9:17–31 / Psalm 103:15–22

When the Scales Fall Away

So Ananias departed and entered the house. And laying his hands on him he said, "Brother Saul, the Lord Jesus who appeared to you on the road by which you came has sent me so that you may regain your sight and be filled with the Holy Spirit." And immediately something like scales fell from his eyes, and he regained his sight. Then he rose and was baptized; and taking food, he was strengthened.

ACTS 9:17–19 ESV

Saul had a Damascus Road encounter with Jesus that changed his entire life. He went from being a Pharisee bent on persecuting believers to being a mighty man of God who relentlessly shared the gospel with the Gentile community. And all it took was divine appointment with the Lord.

For your identity to now be secured in Christ alone means that you had an encounter with Him too. It may have looked different from Paul's, but the results were the same. The scales that covered your eyes—the ones making you unaware of or unconcerned with your sinful nature—have also been graciously removed. And you received spiritual eyes, enabling you to recognize what pleases God and pursuing that righteousness. You're now His child, fully and completely loved. Don't let anything keep you from walking in faith as you follow the Lord's will for your life with passion and purpose.

Lord, thank You for removing the scales from my eyes so I could see the truth and live in it.

THURSDAY, JULY 2

2 Kings 18:1–19:7 / Acts 9:32–10:16 / Psalm 104:1–9

Miracles

Now as Peter went here and there among them all, he came down also to the saints who lived at Lydda. There he found a man named Aeneas, bedridden for eight years, who was paralyzed. And Peter said to him, "Aeneas, Jesus Christ heals you; rise and make your bed." And immediately he rose. And all the residents of Lydda and Sharon saw him, and they turned to the Lord.

Acts 9:32–35 esv

Miracles still happen today. They may look different from what Aeneas experienced from God through Peter, but make no mistake, the Lord is still in the business of miracles here and now.

Where have you seen God move in your life? Did He restore a marriage on divorce's doorstep? Did financial relief show up at just the right time? Did He bring a prodigal home? Did your prayers for a job pay off? Did you find a doctor who was able to effectively treat your ailment? Were you able to forgive the unforgivable? Has your heart toward the situation softened unexpectedly?

As a believer, you can know that God is constantly at work in your life, on your behalf. If you take notice, you'll see His fingerprints everywhere. You will see His unmistakable intervention throughout your day. And it will deepen your faith as you realize God is with you always. . .and He's intimately involved in your life every day.

Lord, help me to see Your hands at work in my life and to praise You for every good thing.

FRIDAY, JULY 3

> 2 Kings 19:8–20:21 / Acts 10:17–33 / Psalm 104:10–23

Sustain and Satisfy

You send fresh streams that spring up in the valleys, in the cracks between hills. Every animal of the open field makes its journey there for drink: wild donkeys lap at the brooks' edges. Birds build their nests by the streams, singing among the branches. And the clouds, too, drink up their share, raining it back down on the mountains from the upper reaches of Your home, sustaining the whole earth with what comes from You. And the earth is satisfied.
Psalm 104:10–13 voice

We serve a God that sustains and satisfies. Notice in today's verses the attention and oversight He gives to details. The Lord fully knows what this world needs so it can be a source of life for all living creatures. He understands where water needs to flow, both when and how much. He's instilled in animals an innate road map so they can find the resources they need to survive. In thoughtful and purposeful ways, God cares diligently for the earth He created.

Knowing that, imagine then how much more His eyes are trained on those whose identity rests in Him. No matter what you're facing, God sees the complexity of it. He appreciates every emotion and feeling you're grappling with. And you can be certain that His arms are wrapped tightly around you as He leads the way forward. The Lord will sustain and satisfy you, fully and completely.

Lord, grow my faith so I learn to trust You in my lacking.

Independence Day   SATURDAY, JULY 4

2 Kings 21:1–22:20 / Acts 10:34–11:18 / Psalm 104:24–30

To Pursue Righteousness

Josiah was 8 years old when he inherited the throne. His reign in Jerusalem lasted 31 years. His mother was Jedidah (daughter of Adaiah from Bozkath). Josiah was righteous in the Eternal's eyes. He continually did what was right, just as his ancestor David had. He did not ever step away from the righteous path.

2 KINGS 22:1–2 VOICE

What a breath of fresh air Josiah was, especially after a string of very corrupt kings who turned their backs on God. No doubt his mother (or other influence in his life) instilled in him a deep longing for righteousness and an unshakable love for the Lord. Scripture tells us that this king remained consistently faithful, never veering from the godly path laid before him. And God saw it all.

Since we are believers who have been accepted into His family, our greatest desire should be to live in ways that bless the Lord. We should want to embrace a righteous life that brings honor to our Father in what we say and what we do. Just as He loves us deeply, our heart should feel the same toward Him. And while perfection is never the goal or expectation, we can choose to be women who are intentional to follow God's commands to love and live faithfully.

Lord, let me seek Your help daily to stay on the path of righteousness so You're delighted in how I live my life here and now. I know obedience leads to freedom!

SUNDAY, JULY 5

2 Kings 23 / Acts 11:19–12:17 / Psalm 104:31–35

Reestablishing Righteousness

The Passover had not been observed from the time when the judges judged Israel, even throughout all the generations of Israel's kings and Judah's kings. But during King Josiah's 18th year, the Passover was celebrated in honor of the Eternal One in Jerusalem. In addition, Josiah destroyed the clairvoyants, necromancers, household gods, idols, and every other corruption in Judah and in Jerusalem, so that he could make things right according to the laws and commands of the covenant book Hilkiah the priest had discovered in the Eternal's house.

2 KINGS 23:22–24 VOICE

Simply put, Josiah cleaned house. He reestablished worship and praise in the nation. He prioritized holiness within its borders. The king removed any idols, evildoers, or items created to replace the one true God, eliminated all types of corruption, and once again recognized the Passover. Following the Lord's commands was his highest priority.

Ask yourself if you need to clean house, just like Josiah did. Are there changes that need to happen so your focus is back on God? Do you need to reorder your day? Are there plans in place that need to be rearranged? Have you forgotten how very loved and valued you are in the eyes of the Lord and anchored your identity in all the wrong places?

Let God help you reestablish your faith in Him alone. Let Him reignite your heart for righteousness.

Lord, help me desire godliness above worldliness every day and in every way.

MONDAY, JULY 6

2 Kings 24–25 / Acts 12:18–13:13 / Psalm 105:1–7

Sharing God's Goodness

Come, offer thanks to the Eternal; invoke His holy name. Tell other people about the things He has done. Sing songs of praise to Him; tell stories of all His miracles. Revel in His holy name. May the hearts of the people who seek the Eternal celebrate and experience great joy. Seek the Eternal and His power; look to His face constantly.

Psalm 105:1–4 voice

The psalmist understands the importance of cultivating a grateful heart and offering credit where credit is due. They know the value of sharing the good and mighty things God has done in their life with others. And they recognize the power of testimony, especially in bringing encouragement for those struggling to stand strong in the storms of life. Do you?

The truth is that we have a loving Father in heaven who's intimately involved in the lives of those who love Him. His plans for our future are detailed and well crafted. We were created on purpose and for a purpose. Because of God's great love, we are protected and secure in His arms. We are accepted and celebrated! And the Lord always equips us for what's ahead, ensuring we can be confident in each next step.

Be quick to share God's goodness with others. Tell them how He's impacted your life. And give Him thanks for loving you fully and completely.

Lord, I cannot imagine my life without You.
My heart for You is so full of gratitude.

TUESDAY, JULY 7

> 1 Chronicles 1–2 / Acts 13:14–43 / Psalm 105:8–15

Names Matter

Tamar, gave birth to Judah's youngest children, Perez and Zerah, giving Judah a total of five sons. Perez fathered Hezron and Hamul. Zerah fathered five sons: Zimri, Ethan, Heman, Calcol, and Dara. The son of Carmi (the grandson of Zimri) was Achar, the troublemaker in Israel who violated the ban against taking the spoils of Jericho. The son of Ethan was Azariah.
1 CHRONICLES 2:4–8 VOICE

The books of Chronicles reveal the significance of the Davidic covenant as the everlasting foundation for why the nation of Israel could have hope. First Chronicles (among other things) focuses on King David and is filled with his victories and genealogies. When reading through this book, however, it's tempting to skip over all the names of who came from whom. It may even seem unimportant.

But consider that God chose to include each name for divine reasons. They do matter. And one powerful takeaway for believers is to recognize that He loved these people enough to put their names in His book. We hold that same value to God today.

He knows your name and the family line where you came from. Your name—your life—matters greatly, and as a believer, never forget that your name is written in the Lamb's Book of Life. And it will never be overlooked.

Lord, I realize everything in scripture is important. If names matter to You, they should matter to me. Thank You for writing my name in Your book. That matters to me most.

WEDNESDAY, JULY 8

1 Chronicles 3:1–5:10 / Acts 13:44–14:10 / Psalm 105:16–28

A Heart for Obedience

Then, He sent His servant Moses and Aaron, the men He had chosen. They did all the signs He planned for them to do among the Egyptians, and they performed miracles in the land of Ham. He sent darkness to cover the land; they did not stray from His word.
Psalm 105:26–28 voice

If you're a believer, it means you're chosen too. God knew through His foreknowledge that when presented with the gospel, you would choose to follow Him. And now that your identity is anchored in Christ, you're empowered to obey His commands and follow the divine purpose placed on your life. Whatever beautiful plans God has designed for your life, you will be equipped to walk them out. Just as Moses and Aaron did.

Were they perfect in executing His will? Not a chance. Did they always respond in a posture of surrender? Nope. Did they face fear and worry along the way? Oh, yes. But even in their flawed faith, these two men were intentional to do as God commanded.

We can have the same heart for obedience as they did. We can seek the Lord's ways and will and lean into His strength to follow through. We can ask for wisdom to know the path forward. And we can pray for peace through the process.

Lord, give me the courage to say yes to Your plans and purposes for my life, and make me confident to follow through without hesitation.

THURSDAY, JULY 9

> 1 Chronicles 5:11–6:81 / Acts 14:11–28 / Psalm 105:29–36

At His Command

At His command, their waters turned to blood; their fish began to die. Throngs of frogs covered the land, invading even in the chambers of their kings. At His command, a swarm of flies arrived, and gnats came over all their land. He caused hail to fall instead of rain; lightning flashed over all their land. He struck their vines and their fig trees; He destroyed the trees over all their land. At His command, locusts came; young locusts marched beyond number, and they ate up all the plants that grew and all the fruits over their land.

PSALM 105:29–35 VOICE

Did you notice the number of times this passage of scripture said the words *at His command* and the obedience that followed immediately? God spoke, and nature responded without question. Be it water or hail, frogs or gnats, lightning or locusts, they did as they were told. They surrendered their natural patterns and behavior when directed. All of creation knows who the Creator is, and it submits to His will.

As believers, we should take joy in letting God lead us, even if we don't know what's ahead. We can trust Him when the path goes a different direction than expected. We are safe in His capable hands because we're loved deeply and completely. *At His command* are words that should bring comfort, trusting His will is always for our good and His glory.

Lord, help me always trust You without question.

FRIDAY, JULY 10

1 Chronicles 7:1–9:9 / Acts 15:1–18 / Psalm 105:37–45

The God Who Provides

Then He brought His people out of slavery, weighed down with silver and gold; and of all His tribes, not one of them stumbled, not one was left behind. Egypt was glad to see them go, for Pharaoh's people had been overcome with fear of them. He spread out a cloud to cover His people and sent a fire to light their way at night. They asked, and He sent them coveys of quail, satisfying their hunger with the food of heaven. He split the rock and water poured out; it flowed like a river through the desert. For He remembered His holy covenant with Abraham, His servant.

PSALM 105:37–42 VOICE

Throughout the entire exodus from slavery in Egypt and the forty years of wandering in the wilderness, God always provided what the Israelites needed. It wasn't necessarily in the ways they groaned for, but as their Father, He met each need in the right way according to His perfect will.

As His children, we can expect the same. God is kind and generous, and His plans for us are good ones! But He loves us too much to spoil us with short-lived and unfulfilling answers to our prayers. Instead, the Lord promises to meet our every need in ways that will bless us and bring glory to His name.

Lord, I trust Your answers to my prayers, even if they're not what I'd asked for. I know Your heart for me is always good.

SATURDAY, JULY 11

1 Chronicles 9:10–11:9 / Acts 15:19–41 / Psalm 106:1–12

The Goodness of God's Presence

David said, "Whoever strikes the Jebusites first shall be chief and commander." And Joab the son of Zeruiah went up first, so he became chief. And David lived in the stronghold; therefore it was called the city of David. And he built the city all around from the Millo in complete circuit, and Joab repaired the rest of the city. And David became greater and greater, for the Lord of hosts was with him.

1 Chronicles 11:6–9 esv

Did you notice what it was that made David become greater and greater? It wasn't his wise decision-making skills. It wasn't grit on the battlefield. It wasn't a good PR campaign. Instead, it was solely because God was with him.

The Lord's presence didn't mean his days would be easy. They weren't without struggles and strife. And scripture shares with us many of the ups and downs David navigated throughout his life. But when the Lord is with you and you purpose to live righteously, following His commands, divinely placed blessings will bloom in significant and meaningful ways.

What role is faith playing in your life right now? Are you standing strong in your identity as a child of God, or are you letting the world define you? Are you deepening your relationship through time in the Word and in prayer, or are your priorities upside-down? Recommit your heart to Him today, and watch how that blesses your life.

Lord, bless me with Your goodness.

SUNDAY, JULY 12

1 Chronicles 11:10–12:40 / Acts 16:1–15 / Psalm 106:13–27

Trading the Glory of God

The people made a golden calf in Horeb and bowed to worship an image they had made. They traded the glory of God for the likeness of an ox that eats grass. They forgot about God, their True Savior, who had done great things for them in Egypt—miracles in the land of Ham and amazing deeds at the Red Sea.
PSALM 106:19–22 VOICE

To say the Israelites made some pretty bad decisions may be the understatement of the year. Amen? Just think of all they'd seen God do on their behalf! From freeing them out of Pharaoh's slavery to parting the Red Sea to keeping their clothes and shoes from wearing out for forty years, the Lord had moved mightily in their presence. But they often "traded the glory of God" for something worldly.

Let's make sure we stand confidently in our identity in Christ, choosing to stay focused on His goodness in our lives and rejecting any earthly imitations. Let's dig into scripture so it piles up in our heart, always ready to remind us that we are loved and cherished. Let's cultivate an attitude of gratitude for all God has done. . .and all He promises to do. And let's be inspired by the glory of God, unwilling to trade it for anything this world may offer in its place.

The Lord's presence is our greatest gift. May we never take it for granted.

Lord, I am so grateful for who You are to me!

MONDAY, JULY 13

1 Chronicles 13–15 / Acts 16:16–40 / Psalm 106:28–33

Praying and Praising

Picture this: It's midnight. In the darkness of their cell, Paul and Silas—after surviving the severe beating—aren't moaning and groaning; they're praying and singing hymns to God. The prisoners in adjoining cells are wide awake, listening to them pray and sing. Suddenly the ground begins to shake, and the prison foundations begin to crack. You can hear the sound of jangling chains and the squeak of cell doors opening. Every prisoner realizes that his chains have come unfastened.
ACTS 16:25–26 VOICE

When you pray and praise God in the midst of hardship, it rumbles in the spiritual realm. It sends ripples through the unseen places and shakes the foundation of the evil one. This intentional choice strengthens you from within because it changes your perspective from victim to victor. And from His throne in heaven, your Father hears you and moves on your behalf. You are His child, and the Lord protects and provides for you with deep love.

What circumstances are you navigating today that feel overwhelming? Where do you feel trapped? Where has life beat you down, making it feel impossible to find your footing again? Friend, pray and praise God right now. Rather than moan and groan about it, thank God for all He's doing to remedy the situation. You can trust He's working all things for your good and His glory!

Lord, I know You see every detail, and I'm standing in faith that You will take care of me!

TUESDAY, JULY 14

1 Chronicles 16–17 / Acts 17:1–14 / Psalm 106:34–43

God Will Not Be Contained

Go and tell My servant David the Eternal One says: You may not build a house for Me to live in; I have never lived in a house, from the day I brought Israel out of Egypt until today. I have always moved from tent to tent, from one home to another. In all these places where I have walked with Israel, did I ever ask any of the judges I commanded to shepherd Israel, "Why have you not built for Me an expensive house of cedar?"

1 CHRONICLES 17:4–6 VOICE

God was clear. He commanded the prophet Nathan to tell David that He could not be contained in a building. He didn't need a fancy place to inhabit on earth. And while David's heart was pure and good, wanting to honor the Lord with a nice home rather than a temporary one, God spoke with clarity. He could not be confined.

Sometimes we try to put Him in a box too. We come up with formulas for how to interact with God, what and how to pray, assuming our blueprint will help bring our prayers to fruition. Even if done with wholesome motives, we try to fit the Lord into our plans or procedures, and our God cannot be controlled.

As God's children, we can trust He'll be with us always, and His Word will reveal ways we can best connect our heart to His.

Lord, thank You for being in control!

WEDNESDAY, JULY 15

> 1 Chronicles 18–20 / Acts 17:15–34 / Psalm 106:44–48

A Limitless God

Nevertheless, He saw their great struggle, took pity on them, and heard their prayers; He did not forget His covenant promises to them but reversed their fortune and released them from their punishment because of His loyal love. He changed the hearts of all who held them captive so that they would show compassion on them.

PSALM 106:44–46 VOICE

These verses are filled with some power-packed truths about God. Did you find them? We're told He sees the struggles we're facing, and His heart is tendered by them. Our prayers are heard. We're reminded that the Lord never forgets His promises and follows through faithfully. And we learn that God can change hearts when necessary, filling them with compassion when they were once filled with coldness.

The reality is that God can do anything at any time in any way that pleases Him. He is limitless. He's unbound by anything worldly or heavenly. His powers are infinite and unmatched. God is inexhaustible, which is a sweet reminder for us, His children. His love and compassion are immeasurable. His mercy is vast. And the Lord's grace is never ending. Let this bring comfort to your heart today.

Because your identity is in Christ, this amazing God is yours always. He's with you now, and you'll be with Him in eternity forever.

Lord, what a privilege it is to be Your daughter forevermore! I love You with all my heart.

THURSDAY, JULY 16

1 Chronicles 21–22 / Acts 18:1–23 / Psalm 107:1–9

When Discouragement Settles In

In the course of listening to Paul, a great many Corinthians believed and were baptized. One night the Master spoke to Paul in a dream: "Keep it up, and don't let anyone intimidate or silence you. No matter what happens, I'm with you and no one is going to be able to hurt you. You have no idea how many people I have on my side in this city." That was all he needed to stick it out. He stayed another year and a half, faithfully teaching the Word of God to the Corinthians.

ACTS 18:8–11 MSG

While we may know that with God's provision we're equipped and capable to do what He's called us to do, discouragement can sometimes still settle in. Today's passage of scripture reveals this is true for Paul, and we can assume every other believer doing God's work has also felt this from time to time. The issue is that we're limited by our human condition and battling against the evil plans of the enemy. It's bound to happen, even to the strongest believer.

But God sees you, weary warrior. And He will restore your strength and resolve when it's needed. The Lord will bring much-needed encouragement that will refresh your spirit and get you back in the game. You are highly valued to your heavenly Father, and He'll stop at nothing to reignite your heart and mind for the purpose He created specifically for you.

Lord, inspire me again!

FRIDAY, JULY 17

1 Chronicles 23–25 / Acts 18:24–19:10 / Psalm 107:10–16

Desperate Conditions

Then you called out to GOD in your desperate condition; he got you out in the nick of time. He led you out of your dark, dark cell, broke open the jail and led you out. So thank GOD for his marvelous love, for his miracle mercy to the children he loves; he shattered the heavy jailhouse doors, he snapped the prison bars like matchsticks!

PSALM 107:13–16 MSG

What is your "desperate condition" today? Is there a health challenge that feels hopeless? Did the hard conversation go south, and you're not sure what to do next? Was the wedding called off unexpectedly? Were you overlooked for the promotion again? Have you lost control of your child, unsure how to get things back on track in a positive way? Are the bills piling up with no way to pay them off? Regardless of what circumstances feel like darkness and oppression, God will lead you out. Pray for freedom. Ask for remedies and results. Cry to the Lord for comfort and peace.

Being a child of God carries with it beautiful blessings. Never forget that you are deeply loved by the Father who created you, and you're perfectly loved every minute of every day. Even though life is challenging at times, you are always safe and secure in His very capable hands, and He will protect your life.

Lord, hear my cry for help, and come quickly.
I need what only You can provide.

SATURDAY, JULY 18

1 Chronicles 26–27 / Acts 19:11–22 / Psalm 107:17–32

The Storms Will Come

In their distress, they called out to the Eternal, and He saved them from their misery. He commanded the storm to calm down, and it became still. A hush came over the waves of the sea, the sailors were delighted at the quiet, and He guided them to their port. May they erupt with praise and give thanks to the Eternal in honor of His loyal love and all the wonders He has performed for humankind!

PSALM 107:28–31 VOICE

Nowhere in the Bible does it say that Christians will live on easy street. We're not promised a problem-free existence. Instead, we can expect storms to blow through from time to time. We should know that big waves of discouragement and disappointment are headed our way. But rather than be caught off guard and sit in despair when they do, we should trust that God allowed them only because He'll use them for our benefit. Remember, Romans 8:28 (ESV) tells us that "for those who love God all things work together for good, for those who are called according to his purpose." And because as a believer your identity is in Christ, you can be confident that you were created on purpose and for a purpose.

Just as the Lord guided these sailors to safety, He will do the same thing for you. Yes, tumultuous waters will come, but God will calm them at the right time and in the right ways.

Lord, I trust You.

SUNDAY, JULY 19

> 1 Chronicles 28–29 / Acts 19:23–41 / Psalm 107:33–38

Fatherly Wisdom Passed Down

To you, my son Solomon, maintain a relationship with the God of your father and serve Him with a complete heart in all your thoughts and actions. The Eternal searches all hearts for their desires and understands the intentions of every thought. If you search for Him as He searches you, then He will let you find Him. But if you abandon Him, then He will reject you forever. Realize that the Eternal has chosen you to build a temple as a sanctuary. You must be resolute and do it!

1 CHRONICLES 28:9–10 VOICE

David's fatherly advice to his youngest son was solid. He knew his death was near and that God had passed the task of building a temple on to Solomon, so he once again imparted godly truth.

The amazing thing about God's Word is how what was important back then is also important today. It's a relevant document of His love and goodness, and it reveals the Lord's commands and blueprints for living righteously. As believers, we should embrace David's fatherly wisdom for our own lives.

So, let's maintain a relationship with and serve our Father wholeheartedly. Let's seek Him every day and in all things. And let's take our calling seriously and walk it out with God's guidance and wisdom. It's our privilege to delight the heart of the Lord and bless Him with our lives.

Lord, my identity is in Christ, and my life is in Your hands!

MONDAY, JULY 20

2 Chronicles 1–3 / Acts 20:1–16 / Psalm 107:39–43

Wisdom

God answered Solomon, "Because this was in your heart, and you have not asked for possessions, wealth, honor, or the life of those who hate you, and have not even asked for long life, but have asked for wisdom and knowledge for yourself that you may govern my people over whom I have made you king, wisdom and knowledge are granted to you. I will also give you riches, possessions, and honor, such as none of the kings had who were before you, and none after you shall have the like."

2 CHRONICLES 1:11–12 ESV

God appeared to Solomon and asked him what he wanted. The Lord was poised to bless the new king as he reigned over a great number of His people. And rather than ask for worldly items, vengeful actions, or personal gain, Solomon asked for. . .wisdom. He wanted to know the best ways to govern the Israelites—the people God put him in charge of. And because this request deeply pleased the Lord, it was granted. Not only that but also wealth and respect to boot.

Above all else, our greatest request should be for His wisdom. We need it! And God promises to abundantly equip His children who wholeheartedly seek His help. The Lord knows we need it as we pursue our divine purpose and walk it out well. We're capable of great things when we lean into godly discernment. Let's ask Him for wisdom every day.

Lord, bless me with Your wisdom.

TUESDAY, JULY 21

2 Chronicles 4:1–6:11 / Acts 20:17–38 / Psalm 108

Setting an Example

And when they came to him, he said to them: "You yourselves know how I lived among you the whole time from the first day that I set foot in Asia, serving the Lord with all humility and with tears and with trials that happened to me through the plots of the Jews; how I did not shrink from declaring to you anything that was profitable, and teaching you in public and from house to house, testifying both to Jews and to Greeks of repentance toward God and of faith in our Lord Jesus Christ."

Acts 20:18–21 esv

As he was about to leave the Ephesian elders, Paul asked them to remember the example he set for living a godly life. It was marked with humility, courage, and accurate teaching. And Paul—in all he did and said both privately and publicly—testified of the goodness of God and faith in Jesus.

The takeaway for today's believers is to remember that our life also preaches. When others know that our identity is in Christ, they watch how we live. They listen to our words and observe how we navigate the ups and downs that come our way. Never forget that your faith is always on display, even when you don't always recognize it is.

We have a beautiful opportunity to set an example of righteous living. Let's make sure we honor God in how we live each day.

Lord, may my life always glorify You!

WEDNESDAY, JULY 22

2 Chronicles 6:12–7:10 / Acts 21:1–14 / Psalm 109:1–20

Taking Our Hurt to God

My enemies have opened their wicked, deceit-filled mouths and blown their foul breath on me. They have slandered me with their twisted tongues and unleashed loathsome words that swirl around me. Though I have done nothing, they attack me. Though I offer them love and keep them in my prayers, they accuse me; though I treat them well, they answer me with evil; though I give them love, they reply with a gesture of hatred.

PSALM 109:2–5 VOICE

This world has a unique way of making us doubt our value and worth. Be it slander and gossip or calculated attacks on our reputation, it can knock us down, especially when we've done nothing to invite this hurtful treatment. And it often deeply affects how we as women feel about ourselves. Even though we know we're daughters of the King, there are times we forget what it means. That beautiful truth loses its power in our heart, and we become discouraged and insecure.

Like the psalmist, let's make sure we take that hurt right to God. We can't always reason with people, nor should we have to defend ourselves. That's our Father's job and joy. Talking to the Lord helps us take the burden off our shoulders and lay it at His feet. It brings comfort to our weary spirit and creates peace inside. And it offers shelter where we feel safe and secure in His very capable arms.

Lord, help me and heal me.

THURSDAY, JULY 23

2 Chronicles 7:11–9:28 / Acts 21:15–32 / Psalm 109:21–31

We Are Known by His Name

If I close up the heavens and their rain and send any of the disasters you described—drought, locusts, pestilence—to ravish the land and people; and My people (who are known by My name) humbly pray, follow My commandments, and abandon any actions or thoughts that might lead to further sinning, then I shall hear their prayers from My house in heaven, I shall forgive their sins, and I shall save their land from the disasters.

2 Chronicles 7:13–14 voice

The temple had been constructed to spec, God had filled it with His presence, and then He came to Solomon and spoke today's verses. It was a reminder of the covenant the Lord made with his father, David, to follow His laws and commands. In return, God promised to keep the kingship of Israel in the family line.

This reminder to follow and obey the Lord is for us too. We are to keep His ways and be led by His will every day because our identity is in Christ alone. As believers, we're known by His name. And this gives us confidence to stay the course that faith provides us through God's Word.

Lord, thank You for the blessings that come from obedience. Help me demonstrate my love for You through daily devotion and following Your commands with passion and purpose. Strengthen me to live each day for You. I am honored to be known by Your name.

FRIDAY, JULY 24

2 Chronicles 9:29–12:16 / Acts 21:33–22:16 / Psalm 110:1–3

A Heart Change

Then he said, "You have been chosen by the God of our ancestors to know His will, to see the Righteous One, and to hear the voice of God. You will tell the story of what you have seen and heard to the whole world. So now, don't delay. Get up, be ceremonially cleansed through baptism, and have your sins washed away, as you call on His name in prayer."
ACTS 22:14–16 VOICE

In Acts 22:14–16, Paul is recounting his Damascus Road moment where he encountered the Lord who called him out for persecuting Christians. In that moment, not only did his name change (was previously known as Saul), but his heart did too. And once the scales fell from Paul's eyes, Ananias spoke to him about the divine calling and purpose for his new life.

Be encouraged, friend! When you accept Jesus as your personal Savior, your heart is changed as well. Your identity in the world's offerings is replaced by an identity anchored in Christ. The things here will continue to grow strangely dim as your eyes focus on heavenly promises. And as you seek a deeper relationship with God daily, your divine calling and purpose will continue to unfold at the right time.

Your testimony will bring hope to others who need to know there's a better way of living. Like you, they'll desire to a life committed to loving and serving Jesus.

Lord, let my heart always be focused on You!

SATURDAY, JULY 25

2 Chronicles 13–15 / Acts 22:17–23:11 / Psalm 110:4–7

His Promises Are Unchangeable

Remember, as you prepare to fight against us, that the True God is on our side and is leading us. His priests will blow the signal trumpets to alert Him that you are here to fight us, and He will rescue us from our enemies as He promised. O Israelites, God's chosen people, do not fight against the Eternal One, the True God of your fathers, because you will not succeed.
2 Chronicles 13:12 voice

Abijah, king of Judah, was speaking these words to Jeroboam and all the soldiers from the Northern Kingdom. It was a warning and a promise. They had rebelled against God, worshipping false gods, and they denied David's descendants as the rightful kings over the nation of Israel.

Notice Abijah's confidence in God. He knew the Lord was on his side, would lead their battle plans, and was ready to rescue them at the trumpet's alert. Rather than worry if the Lord would be true to His word, this king banked on it. And God honored his faith and kept true to every promise.

As daughters of our heavenly King, we can stand strong in this confidence too because God's promises are unchangeable. For every pledge we find in the Word, we can cling to them with unshakable faith. There's nothing for us to worry about. Our Father sees us and will never forsake us.

Lord, make my faith confident and assured that You will always keep Your word.

SUNDAY, JULY 26

2 Chronicles 16–17 / Acts 23:12–24:21 / Psalm 111

It Starts with Fear

The fear of the LORD is the beginning of wisdom; all those who practice it have a good understanding. His praise endures forever!
PSALM 111:10 ESV

Why is *fear* the beginning of wisdom for the believer? It's because our quest for a righteous life must start with a heart of worship and humility toward God. Fear of the Lord means we're in awe of Him and His ways. It's admiration and amazement. And there must be respect for God if we want to correctly apply His knowledge to our lives. It's meekly asking for the Lord's wisdom in the circumstances we're trying to navigate. This helps us live in ways that bless us and others and bring glory to His name.

Do you need guidance in your marriage or as you try to parent teenagers? Are you at a loss on how to move forward in your career? Are the choices confusing on managing your health, and you don't know the best decision for your circumstances? Are you unsure how to have that honest and difficult conversation with a friend? Is your schedule out of control and you're uncertain about how to better prioritize your day? Are you struggling to know when it's time to move in a different direction?

As His daughter, you're invited to ask for wisdom! So, humble yourself before the Lord today and make your request known.

Lord, I'm humbly asking for Your wisdom in my choices today!

MONDAY, JULY 27

2 Chronicles 18–19 / Acts 24:22–25:12 / Psalm 112

A Life Marked

Good comes to all who are gracious and share freely; they conduct their affairs with sound judgment. Nothing will ever rattle them; the just will always be remembered. They will not be afraid when the news is bad because they have resolved to trust in the Eternal. Their hearts are confident, and they are fearless, for they expect to see their enemies defeated. They give freely to the poor; their righteousness endures for all time; their strength and power is established in honor.

PSALM 112:5–9 VOICE

There are beautiful and powerful truths unpacked in today's verses. It's a timely reminder for believers that how we live our lives matters. How we treat those around us makes a difference. How we respond to celebrations and challenges carries weight. Our confidence in God's faithfulness counts. Sound judgment is important. Trusting Him in all things is significant. And our willingness to be kind and generous toward others has bearing. When our lives are marked in such ways, scripture tells us that good will come our way.

What is the Holy Spirit speaking to you right now? How is God bringing sweet conviction? Where are you seeing a necessary shift in your life? Because your identity is secure in Jesus, there's no condemnation. But the Lord will continue to shape you into the woman He created you to be. Let His redirection settle into your spirit today, and follow His leading.

Lord, let my life be marked by steadfast faith.

TUESDAY, JULY 28

2 Chronicles 20–21 / Acts 25:13–27 / Psalm 113

When God Fights Our Battles

"Stand and watch, but do not fight the battle. There, you will watch the Eternal save you, Judah and Jerusalem." Do not fear or worry. Tomorrow, face the army and trust that the Eternal is with you. Jehoshaphat bowed his head low, and all the assembly fell prostrate before the Eternal and worshiped Him with reverence. They trusted the Lord completely.

2 Chronicles 20:17–18 voice

As Jehoshaphat was corporately praying and asking the Lord for help against an incoming army, the Spirit of God fell on Jahaziel, a Levitical singer, and he spoke what was put on his heart. They were not to worry or fear, for the battle was the Lord's. Today's verses are part of what Jahaziel shared.

There are times when the battle is ours. In His strength and with His direction, we're to stand strong and navigate the choppy waters. We're given words to share or actions to take. While leaning on God for help, we're active and working toward the right outcome. But other times we're to watch as the Lord fights on our behalf. Our role is to be in prayer and be steadfast in our faith, trusting that He is working all things out for our good and His glory.

The challenge comes in discerning what we're to do as His daughters. That's where prayer comes in! Ask God to clarify, and then obey.

Lord, help me discern my role in the battle, and strengthen me to obey.

WEDNESDAY, JULY 29

2 Chronicles 22–23 / Acts 26 / Psalm 114

Godly Leadership

*Then Jehoiada made a covenant between himself,
all the people, and the king, promising to follow the Eternal.
Because of this covenant, all the people demolished
Baal's temple, destroyed the altars and icons there,
and killed Mattan, the priest of Baal, in front of the altars.*

2 CHRONICLES 23:16–17 VOICE

When a godly person is in charge, good things happen. Holy things happen. Righteousness is prioritized. And while the road is often difficult and challenging, pushing for God-fearing leadership is always the right idea. When Jehoiada removed Athaliah, he restored the temple and the Davidic monarchy. He paved the way for a renewed covenant of obedience for himself, the people, and the king.

Not only can you be someone who helps promote those who love the Lord and follow His commands, but you can also choose to be that person yourself. Whether it's the CEO of a company, the lead volunteer, a small group facilitator, a community activist, a town council member, or mom and wife to your family, you are called to stand for godly principles. It's Jesus in you that will help usher in righteous living. And God will honor and bless your obedience.

You are the Lord's child, secure in Christ and focused on heavenly things. Make sure your life reflects that truth every day and in every way.

*Lord, help me be an advocate for godly leadership.
Give me courage to speak up and confidence to
stand steadfast in what's right in Your eyes.*

THURSDAY, JULY 30

2 Chronicles 24:1–25:16 / Acts 27:1–20 / Psalm 115:1–10

Wholeheartedly

Amaziah was twenty-five years old when he became king and reigned twenty-nine years in Jerusalem. His mother was Jehoaddin from Jerusalem. He lived well before GOD, doing the right thing for the most part. But he wasn't wholeheartedly devoted to God.

2 CHRONICLES 25:1–2 MSG

God wants our wholehearted devotion. He wants us to be all in—fully engaged and always seeking a deeper connection with Him. Revelation 3:15 in The Voice translation says, "I know your works. You are neither cold with apathy nor hot with passion. It would be better if you were one or the other, but you are neither."

Sometimes as believers, we start out strong but our faith wanes. We give up our quiet time with God. We stop praying with fervor. We find excuses to not attend church or be part of a small group. And we find ourselves faithful. . .*for the most part*.

Let's not forget that our faith in Christ makes us capable of great things. God created us on purpose and for a purpose, and His plan is that we stand confident in that calling and walk it out daily. And because we have a loving Father who knows the ins and outs of every detail this life brings our way, we're to "love the Lord [our] God with all [our] heart and with all [our] soul and with all [our] mind and with all [our] strength" (Mark 12:30 ESV).

Lord, help me love You with wholehearted devotion.

FRIDAY, JULY 31

2 Chronicles 25:17–27:9 / Acts 27:21–28:6 / Psalm 115:11–18

Fanning the Flames of Our Devotion

He acted just as his father Amaziah and his grandfather Joash had—following the Eternal initially, then turning away from Him. While Zechariah the seer was alive, Uzziah followed the True God, listening to Zechariah's messages from God as Joash had listened to Jehoiada's counsel, and the True God blessed the king in battles, in building, and in wealth as long as he was obedient.

2 Chronicles 26:4–5 voice

The Bible is filled with examples of how God blesses obedience, and today's passage of scripture also speaks to that unwavering truth. Without fail, His goodness always follows intentional choices to obey His will and ways.

Let's not be women who start this journey of faith strong and eventually let our passion for God fade. Instead, let's choose now to fan the flames of our devotion to doing what He asks every day. Remember that faith is a verb. It's active. And our obedience should never be rooted in manipulation, so the Lord blesses us. It should be our greatest desire to live rightly with Him. Our identity is in Christ, and our life should boldly reflect that.

Where do you need to surrender your will to His and obey God? In what areas has your faith in Him diminished? Ask the Lord to equip you to walk out His will with courage and confidence.

Lord, let my life bring You glory through my imperfectly perfect desire to live righteously.

AUGUST 2026

SUNDAY	MONDAY	TUESDAY	WEDNESDAY	THURSDAY	FRIDAY	SATURDAY
						1
2	3	4	5	6	7	8
9	10	11	12	13	14	15
16	17	18	19	20	21	22
23 / 30	24 / 31	25	26	27	28	29

SATURDAY, AUGUST 1

2 Chronicles 28:1–29:19 / Acts 28:7–31 / Psalm 116:1–5

Do Right in the Eyes of the Lord

Hezekiah began to reign when he was twenty-five years old, and he reigned twenty-nine years in Jerusalem. . . . And he did what was right in the eyes of the Lord, according to all that David his father had done.

2 Chronicles 29:1–2 esv

During his reign from age twenty-five to age fifty-four, King Hezekiah nobly "did what was right in the eyes of the Lord." Whether we're in a similar age bracket or not, in every stage of life, we all have areas of influence right where we are this very moment and need to ask ourselves, "Am I doing what's right in the eyes of the Lord?" Let's pray for ourselves and for all believers everywhere—young or old, in big circles of influence or small—to make an impact. An impact to help both individuals and society as a whole to do what is good and right according to God's Word and His perfect ways.

Heavenly Father, thank You for Hezekiah's example and inspiration. He was human, so I know he wasn't perfect, but he is recorded in history as faithful and honoring to You. I want to be known for the same. Forgive and help me with my imperfections in all ages and stages of my life, and help me to walk so closely with You and do right in Your eyes each day.

SUNDAY, AUGUST 2

2 Chronicles 29:20–30:27 / Romans 1:1–17 / Psalm 116:6–19

We Need Each Other

First of all, I keep thanking my God, through Jesus Christ, for all of you. This is because the whole world knows of your faith in Christ. God knows how I work for Him. He knows how I preach with all my heart the Good News about His Son. He knows how I always pray for you. I pray that I might be able to visit you, if God wants me to. I want to see you so I can share some special gift of the Holy Spirit with you. It will make you strong. Both of us need help. I can help make your faith strong and you can do the same for me. We need each other.
ROMANS 1:8–12 NLV

When we're counting blessings, we should feel extra grateful for family and friends who also boldly follow Jesus. We all dearly need each other, and together we are stronger and braver—and more peaceful and joyful too! We encourage one another by sharing the gifts we've received from the Holy Spirit, by sharing how God is working in our lives, and by sharing truth from the Bible with each other. And we just get to have fun being together and worshipping God together too!

Heavenly Father, thank You for the family and friends in my life who help make my faith in You stronger and bolder. Help me to encourage them and make them stronger and bolder too.

MONDAY, AUGUST 3

> 2 Chronicles 31–32 / Romans 1:18–32 / Psalm 117

Clear in His Creation

Through everything God made, they can clearly see his invisible qualities—his eternal power and divine nature. So they have no excuse for not knowing God. Yes, they knew God, but they wouldn't worship him as God or even give him thanks. And they began to think up foolish ideas of what God was like. As a result, their minds became dark and confused. Claiming to be wise, they instead became utter fools. And instead of worshiping the glorious, ever-living God, they worshiped idols made to look like mere people and birds and animals and reptiles. So God abandoned them to do whatever shameful things their hearts desired.
ROMANS 1:20–24 NLT

No person can say they know nothing about God. We can see Him in the tiny details of a beautiful flower and in the vast magnificence of a mountain range. . . In the extraordinary way our human bodies are designed and in the way animals know how to hunt for their food or build themselves a home. . . And on and on! Our Creator God is awesome and worthy of all our praise! He clearly revealed Himself in His creation, so there is no excuse for denying or ignoring Him—and there are, sadly, terrible consequences for those who do.

Almighty God, thank You for making Yourself known. I pray for more people to acknowledge You in Your creation and that they have forgiveness of sins and relationship with You through the grace of Jesus.

TUESDAY, AUGUST 4

2 Chronicles 33:1–34:7 / Romans 2 / Psalm 118:1–18

When You're in Trouble

Give thanks to the Lord, for He is good. His loving-kindness lasts forever. Let Israel say, "His loving-kindness lasts forever." Let the house of Aaron say, "His loving-kindness lasts forever." Let those who fear the Lord say, "His loving-kindness lasts forever." I cried to the Lord in my trouble, and He answered me and put me in a good place.
Psalm 118:1–5 NLV

Troubles come and go constantly, it seems. So when we feel overwhelmed by them, we need to stop to praise God as we remember how He has helped us out of troubles in the past. This will calm our anxious hearts as we trust that He will surely help again now and in the future. Psalm 118 encourages us that we can always cry out to God in our troubles, and He will help us get back into a good, safe place. We can say confidently, "The Lord is with me. I will not be afraid of what man can do to me. The Lord is with me. He is my Helper. I will watch those lose who fight against me. It is better to trust in the Lord than to trust in man. It is better to trust in the Lord than to trust in rulers" (Psalm 118:6–9 NLV).

Dear Lord, I trust You more than any person or leader. I know You are always with me, and I don't need to feel anxious about anything, even in the midst of trouble. Remind me that You will always help me get to good, safe places.

WEDNESDAY, AUGUST 5

2 Chronicles 34:8–35:19 / Romans 3:1–26 / Psalm 118:19–23

A Young Brave King

[Josiah] took his place of authority beside the pillar and renewed the covenant in the Lord's presence. He pledged to obey the Lord by keeping all his commands, laws, and decrees with all his heart and soul. He promised to obey all the terms of the covenant that were written in the scroll. And he required everyone in Jerusalem and the people of Benjamin to make a similar pledge. The people of Jerusalem did so, renewing their covenant with God, the God of their ancestors. So Josiah removed all detestable idols from the entire land of Israel and required everyone to worship the Lord their God. And throughout the rest of his lifetime, they did not turn away from the Lord, the God of their ancestors.
2 Chronicles 34:31–33 nlt

Josiah had become king at only eight years old, and that's hard to comprehend! But as he grew and matured, the most important thing about him was that throughout his lifetime he helped his people worship and not turn away from the one true God. With all his heart and soul, Josiah sought to keep the Lord's commands, laws, and decrees, and he removed all false gods and detestable idols from the land of Israel.

Heavenly Father, show me any idols I'm keeping in my own life, and help me to remove them. Thank You for the inspiration and example that such a young, brave king gives us. Help me to remember Josiah's sincerity and commitment to worshipping and obeying You alone.

THURSDAY, AUGUST 6

2 Chronicles 35:20–36:23 / Romans 3:27–4:25 / Psalm 118:24–29

By Putting Trust in Christ

This is what we have come to know. A man is made right with God by putting his trust in Christ. It is not by his doing what the Law says. Is God the God of the Jews only? Is He not the God of the people who are not Jews also? He is for sure. He is one God. He will make Jews and the people who are not Jews right with Himself if they put their trust in Christ. Does this mean that we do away with the Law when we put our trust in Christ? No, not at all. It means we know the Law is important.

ROMANS 3:28–31 NLV

Take a deep, grateful breath—it's so freeing to know we can't work our way to heaven with good deeds and obeying God's law. We certainly aren't perfect, so how would we ever know if we were doing a good enough job? Thankfully, our salvation and eternal life depend *totally* on putting our trust in Jesus Christ. He did the work on the cross that saves us. He paid the price for our sin with His blood. Our salvation is a gift that makes us right with God. Hallelujah! It's *amazing* grace, for sure!

Dear Lord, I'm beyond grateful for Your gift of salvation. Remind me to continue to respect the importance of Your law and obedience to You, but as I do my best imperfectly, I'm so thankful that nothing can ever snatch me out of Your hand (John 10:28).

FRIDAY, AUGUST 7

Ezra 1–3 / Romans 5 / Psalm 119:1–8

Should We Keep on Sinning?

God's law was given so that all people could see how sinful they were. But as people sinned more and more, God's wonderful grace became more abundant.... Well then, should we keep on sinning so that God can show us more and more of his wonderful grace? Of course not! Since we have died to sin, how can we continue to live in it?
ROMANS 5:20, 6:1–2 NLT

What an immeasurable blessing, that trusting in Jesus as Savior makes us right with God because of His grace! But that sure doesn't mean we should purposefully or carelessly choose to disobey our heavenly Father—who simply wants us to obey because He loves us and desires what's best for us. In fact, God's Word warns us that if we cherish sin in our hearts, He's not inclined to listen to our prayers (Psalm 66:18). The bottom line is, even though we are covered fully by God's grace, we shouldn't play around with sin or stand around on the edges of it. To have good relationship and communication with God and not reap the consequences of sin, we have to do our best to avoid it and confess it quickly when we do mess up.

Heavenly Father, even though I am saved through trust in Jesus, I don't want to purposefully go against Your Word. Help me to repent and run away from sin. I love You and want to please You.

SATURDAY, AUGUST 8

Ezra 4–5 / Romans 6:1–7:6 / Psalm 119:9–16

Seek, Rejoice, Delight

How can a young person stay on the path of purity? By living according to your word. I seek you with all my heart; do not let me stray from your commands. I have hidden your word in my heart that I might not sin against you. Praise be to you, Lord; teach me your decrees. With my lips I recount all the laws that come from your mouth. I rejoice in following your statutes as one rejoices in great riches. I meditate on your precepts and consider your ways. I delight in your decrees; I will not neglect your word.

PSALM 119:9–16 NIV

The Bible is not typical reading material. It's a living and active book from God (Hebrews 4:12), and it's His main way of speaking into our lives and guiding and correcting us. We have so many stressors in life, plus a sin nature and an enemy named Satan, all trying to keep us from reading our Bibles. But it's essential that we regularly seek God through His Word, especially with *all the things* going on in our lives. So we have to be so intentional and fight the temptation and sin. We have to ask God to help us crave spending time in His Word every day and to truly hide it in our hearts and rejoice in it.

Heavenly Father, I want to delight in Your Word and in relationship with You more than anything else.

SUNDAY, AUGUST 9

Ezra 6:1–7:26 / Romans 7:7–25 / Psalm 119:17–32

The Struggle with Sin

I do not understand myself. I want to do what is right but I do not do it. Instead, I do the very thing I hate. . . . This has become my way of life: When I want to do what is right, I always do what is wrong. My mind and heart agree with the Law of God. But there is a different law at work deep inside of me that fights with my mind. This law of sin holds me in its power because sin is still in me. There is no happiness in me! Who can set me free from my sinful old self? God's Law has power over my mind, but sin still has power over my sinful old self. I thank God I can be free through Jesus Christ our Lord!
ROMANS 7:15, 21–25 NLV

The struggle is real! The sin struggle, that is! We all can relate, unfortunately. But mercifully, we don't have to stay mired in the muck of that struggle. Every time we find ourselves mentally falling and slipping around in it, we can keep coming back to this powerful, liberating truth: Because of Jesus Christ, we are never held captive by sin. He gives us the power to avoid it, climb out of it, turn away from it, and confess in this life—and He frees us from its eternal consequences forever.

> *Lord Jesus, I'm totally dependent on You for the forgiveness of and freedom from sins. I'm so grateful for the true liberty that only You can give and that no one can ever take away.*

MONDAY, AUGUST 10

Ezra 7:27–9:4 / Romans 8:1–27 / Psalm 119:33–40

Turn My Eyes from Worthless Things

Teach me your decrees, O Lord; I will keep them to the end. Give me understanding and I will obey your instructions; I will put them into practice with all my heart. Make me walk along the path of your commands, for that is where my happiness is found. Give me an eagerness for your laws rather than a love for money! Turn my eyes from worthless things, and give me life through your word. Reassure me of your promise, made to those who fear you. Help me abandon my shameful ways; for your regulations are good. I long to obey your commandments! Renew my life with your goodness.

Psalm 119:33–40 nlt

"Turn my eyes from worthless things"—what a needed prayer in this broken world! It seems we are bombarded nearly every waking moment with worthless things before our eyes because of smartphones and social media that are so easily accessible every second of the day. It takes great intention, with much discipline, to say, "I will not set before my eyes anything that is worthless" (Psalm 101:3 esv). And it takes loving and living in God's holy Word.

Dear Lord, I sure need Your help to turn my eyes from worthless things. Please forgive me for my weaknesses and mistakes at this. I truly want to do so much better at focusing on what pleases You and brings You glory and helps build Your kingdom.

TUESDAY, AUGUST 11

Ezra 9:5–10:44 / Romans 8:28–39 / Psalm 119:41–64

The Most Powerful Love

Who shall separate us from the love of Christ? Shall trouble or hardship or persecution or famine or nakedness or danger or sword? . . . No, in all these things we are more than conquerors through him who loved us. For I am convinced that neither death nor life, neither angels nor demons, neither the present nor the future, nor any powers, neither height nor depth, nor anything else in all creation, will be able to separate us from the love of God that is in Christ Jesus our Lord.

ROMANS 8:35, 37–39 NIV

We can't deny our uncertainties and insecurities. There might be days when we feel unloved and uncared for and maybe scared that we'll never be loved and cared for again. And so we have to keep coming back to Romans 8, where we're assured that God's love is unlike any other kind of love, and absolutely nothing can ever stop it. God lavishes His love on us in all kinds of ways and through many different people and sources. As we intentionally look for His love and thank Him for it, we begin to notice it all the more—and thus fill up with gratitude, confidence, and peace.

Heavenly Father, please remind me that I am never, ever uncared for or unloved. You love me better and more powerfully than I can possibly imagine. Help me to better notice all the detailed ways You do. I love You too, Lord!

WEDNESDAY, AUGUST 12

Nehemiah 1:1–3:16 / Romans 9:1–18 / Psalm 119:65–72

Nehemiah Sat Down and Wept

The words of Nehemiah son of Hakaliah: In the month of Kislev in the twentieth year, while I was in the citadel of Susa, Hanani, one of my brothers, came from Judah with some other men, and I questioned them about the Jewish remnant that had survived the exile, and also about Jerusalem. They said to me, "Those who survived the exile and are back in the province are in great trouble and disgrace. The wall of Jerusalem is broken down, and its gates have been burned with fire." When I heard these things, I sat down and wept. For some days I mourned and fasted and prayed before the God of heaven.

NEHEMIAH 1:1–4 NIV

The prophet Nehemiah served as the cupbearer for the Persian king Artaxerxes. Nehemiah had found favor with the king, so when Nehemiah wanted to go back to his homeland and help build the walls around Jerusalem, the king allowed him to go. Nehemiah organized and led a team of builders, and within fifty-two days they were able to rebuild the city's walls. That was incredibly quick for such an enormous job, and it showed that God's power was clearly at work. Nehemiah loved and respected God passionately, and he continued to help the Jewish people want to honor and obey Him too.

Lord God, like Nehemiah, let me weep for the destruction and sins that hurt Your heart. Let me be one who confesses and who helps restore and rebuild. Let me help bring people back to honoring and obeying You.

THURSDAY, AUGUST 13

Nehemiah 3:17–5:13 / Romans 9:19–33 / Psalm 119:73–80

The Sense to Follow His Commands

You made me; you created me. Now give me the sense to follow your commands. May all who fear you find in me a cause for joy, for I have put my hope in your word. I know, O Lord, that your regulations are fair; you disciplined me because I needed it. Now let your unfailing love comfort me, just as you promised me, your servant. Surround me with your tender mercies so I may live, for your instructions are my delight. Bring disgrace upon the arrogant people who lied about me; meanwhile, I will concentrate on your commandments. Let me be united with all who fear you, with those who know your laws. May I be blameless in keeping your decrees; then I will never be ashamed.

Psalm 119:73–80 nlt

Sometimes we might wonder, *Is it just too hard to obey God in this broken, modern world?* But this psalm is so straightforward: God made us! He created us by His perfect design. So of course He can give us the good sense to follow His commands. We simply have to ask for His help and His wisdom. We have to truly want to receive them—especially through spending time in His Word, where He comforts and encourages, teaches and matures us.

Lord, I want the words of this passage in Psalms to be a sincere prayer in my mind and heart too. I have put my hope in Your Word.

FRIDAY, AUGUST 14

Nehemiah 5:14–7:73 / Romans 10:1–13 / Psalm 119:81–88

Call on the Name of the Lord

If you openly declare that Jesus is Lord and believe in your heart that God raised him from the dead, you will be saved. For it is by believing in your heart that you are made right with God, and it is by openly declaring your faith that you are saved. As the Scriptures tell us, "Anyone who trusts in him will never be disgraced." Jew and Gentile are the same in this respect. They have the same Lord, who gives generously to all who call on him. For "Everyone who calls on the name of the LORD will be saved."

ROMANS 10:9–13 NLT

This passage is the message we need to spread far and wide! For God "wants everyone to be saved and to understand the truth" (1 Timothy 2:4 NLT) and so should we! There is not a single person on the planet whom He does not love and long for them to believe in Him as the risen Savior. He is the only one who has conquered sin through His work on the cross and gives life forever to all who turn away from sin to trust and follow Him. What simple yet profound and priceless good news we have to share with all who will listen!

Lord Jesus, help me to share Your precious, powerful name and the good news of the gospel with as many dear people as I can throughout my whole life.

SATURDAY, AUGUST 15

Nehemiah 8:1–9:5 / Romans 10:14–11:24 / Psalm 119:89–104

Bringing the Good News

How, then, can they call on the one they have not believed in? And how can they believe in the one of whom they have not heard? And how can they hear without someone preaching to them? And how can anyone preach unless they are sent? As it is written: "How beautiful are the feet of those who bring good news!"

Romans 10:14–15 NIV

How am I bringing the good news to people? This is a question we need to ask ourselves daily. Our world is broken and hurting in myriad ways. There is such a vast number of needs, such endless evil, it seems. It can feel totally overwhelming at times. But we are to not be overcome by evil but overcome evil with good (Romans 12:21). In everything we do to encourage and help others, we can pray, "Jesus, let Your love flow through me. Give me opportunities to tell people that I'm inspired by You and that though this world will pass away, our hope and salvation are found in You alone."

Lord, make me willing to move my feet, do good deeds, and share the best news ever—that You died on the cross to save from sin all who believe in You. Motivate me more to be bold and active about sharing the gospel. Fill me with Your love and joy, and make it so contagious to those around me!

SUNDAY, AUGUST 16

Nehemiah 9:6–10:27 / Romans 11:25–12:8 / Psalm 119:105–120

Total Makeover

And so, dear brothers and sisters, I plead with you to give your bodies to God because of all he has done for you. Let them be a living and holy sacrifice—the kind he will find acceptable. This is truly the way to worship him. Don't copy the behavior and customs of this world, but let God transform you into a new person by changing the way you think. Then you will learn to know God's will for you, which is good and pleasing and perfect.
ROMANS 12:1–2 NLT

Our heavenly Father wants to give total, incredible makeovers to all who trust in Jesus as Savior and choose to follow Him. He wants to change lives and minds and identities in the best kind of way! He doesn't want us to act like the sinful people who delight in the ways of this world. He wants to renew our minds to be like His, to help us see things the way He does and do the things He wants us to do. He will fill us with the fruit of His Spirit— love, joy, peace, patience, kindness, goodness, faithfulness, gentleness, and self-control. And He will grow us in grace and truth and help us serve and care for others so that others will want to know Him as Savior too.

Heavenly Father, I want a total makeover! Please give me the new life and mind You want for me, through Jesus Christ—a life and mind that match up with Yours.

MONDAY, AUGUST 17

Nehemiah 10:28–12:26 / Romans 12:9–13:7 / Psalm 119:121–128

Let God Handle It

Do not repay anyone evil for evil. Be careful to do what is right in the eyes of everyone. If it is possible, as far as it depends on you, live at peace with everyone. Do not take revenge, my dear friends, but leave room for God's wrath, for it is written: "It is mine to avenge; I will repay," says the Lord. On the contrary: "If your enemy is hungry, feed him; if he is thirsty, give him something to drink. In doing this, you will heap burning coals on his head."
ROMANS 12:17–20 NIV

When someone mistreats us, our first reaction is often to want to retaliate in the same kind of way. But God's Word tells us not to. It tells us not to repay evil for evil. As followers of Jesus, we're called to a higher standard, and God wants us to let Him handle the situation. He knows exactly what happened and exactly what is fair—much better than we do. So when we feel angry about an injustice done against us, we have to choose to stop and calm down. We have to remember that God knows and cares and wants us to live in peace while He does the hard work of making things right and fair.

Heavenly Father, please help me to live in peace even when I feel angry about injustice and ways I've been mistreated. Help me to let You handle the situation with Your perfect plans and ways.

TUESDAY, AUGUST 18

Nehemiah 12:27–13:31 / Romans 13:8–14:12 / Psalm 119:129–136

God's Wonderful Word

Your Laws are wonderful, and so I obey them. The opening up of Your Word gives light. It gives understanding to the child-like. I opened my mouth wide, breathing with desire for Your Law. Turn to me and show me loving-favor, as You always do to those who love Your name. Set my steps in Your Word. Do not let sin rule over me. Set me free from the power of man, and I will obey Your Law. Make Your face shine upon Your servant and teach me Your Law. Tears flow from my eyes because of those who do not keep Your Law.
PSALM 119:129–136 NLV

As we mature in our faith and grow closer to God through our relationship with Jesus, this passage from Psalms should be more and more relatable. The more we spend time learning from God's Word, the more we should crave coming to it and learning even more. Also, we should increasingly weep for those who don't love God's Word and feel motivated to pray for and show God's love to them—and to share the good news of Jesus as much as possible.

Heavenly Father, You give light and love through Your living and active Word. I want to crave it as much as I need air to breathe. I want to obey You and feel Your face shine on me with blessing.

WEDNESDAY, AUGUST 19

Esther 1:1–2:18 / Romans 14:13–15:13 / Psalm 119:137–152

Abound in Hope

May the God of hope fill you with all joy and peace in believing, so that by the power of the Holy Spirit you may abound in hope.
ROMANS 15:13 ESV

It's good to really think about what our hopes and goals are and why. From time to time, we need to evaluate them and think about how they change with life and experience and maturity. The reason we have any hope for good things at all is because God is the giver of hope. Every good and perfect gift comes from Him, James 1:17 tells us. And our ultimate, final hope is in the promise of heaven, where there will be no more sickness, sadness, or pain—only perfect paradise forever as God dwells with us. With each new day, we can choose to let God direct our hopes and goals, according to His will. We can trust in His good gifts and grow stronger and stronger in faith, by the power of the Holy Spirit within us, to be ready for whatever life brings us—until one day all our hopes are fulfilled in perfect paradise.

> *Heavenly Father, thank You for giving me hope. Please match my hopes and goals to Your will and plans for my life. Remind me that all gifts and good things come from You. Keep me trusting that You have good plans for me here on earth and a perfect forever waiting for me in heaven with You.*

THURSDAY, AUGUST 20

Esther 2:19–5:14 / Romans 15:14–21 / Psalm 119:153–168

Esther's Confidence and Courage

"For if you keep silent at this time, relief and deliverance will rise for the Jews from another place, but you and your father's house will perish. And who knows whether you have not come to the kingdom for such a time as this?" Then Esther told them to reply to Mordecai, "Go, gather all the Jews to be found in Susa, and hold a fast on my behalf, and do not eat or drink for three days, night or day. I and my young women will also fast as you do. Then I will go to the king, though it is against the law, and if I perish, I perish."

ESTHER 4:14–16 ESV

Esther knew she could be killed for her boldness in speaking up to the king in defense of her people. But she trusted in the one true God. And because of her courage, her people, the Jews, were saved from the destruction intended by Haman's evil plans. As we read the whole story of Esther and look to her example, we can be filled with extra faith and hope and courage for whatever hard situations we find ourselves in. God worked out His good plans to protect His people through Esther, and He is working out good plans for each of us today too.

Heavenly Father, I want to have the confidence and courage of Esther in any difficult or dangerous situation I face. Fill me up with trust and peace in Your power and perfect plans.

FRIDAY, AUGUST 21

Esther 6–8 / Romans 15:22–33 / Psalm 119:169–176

Come and Find Me

O LORD, listen to my cry; give me the discerning mind you promised. Listen to my prayer; rescue me as you promised. Let praise flow from my lips, for you have taught me your decrees. Let my tongue sing about your word, for all your commands are right. Give me a helping hand, for I have chosen to follow your commandments. O LORD, I have longed for your rescue, and your instructions are my delight. Let me live so I can praise you, and may your regulations help me. I have wandered away like a lost sheep; come and find me, for I have not forgotten your commands.

PSALM 119:169–176 NLT

We just get lost sometimes in all kinds of ways in this sinful world, don't we? We go down wrong paths and then can't seem to find our way back to Jesus. But He's our loving good shepherd (John 10) who seeks out His sheep. We just have to admit it when we've wandered away and pray, "Come and find me, Jesus!" And we have to be willing to be found and directed off the wrong path we've gone down. We have to *want to* get back to following and obeying the leading of Jesus and all the goodness of the commands and wisdom in God's Word.

Lord Jesus, I'm so sorry that I've wandered away from You. Forgive me and come and find me, please!

SATURDAY, AUGUST 22

Esther 9–10 / Romans 16 / Psalm 120–122

Watch Out

And now I make one more appeal, my dear brothers and sisters. Watch out for people who cause divisions and upset people's faith by teaching things contrary to what you have been taught. Stay away from them. Such people are not serving Christ our Lord; they are serving their own personal interests. By smooth talk and glowing words they deceive innocent people. . . . I want you to be wise in doing right and to stay innocent of any wrong. The God of peace will soon crush Satan under your feet.

ROMANS 16:17–20 NLT

Paul's warnings to his dear friends and fellow believers are for us today too. We have to watch out for false teachers. We're warned about them in multiple other places in the Bible as well. For example, Jesus Himself said, "Beware of false prophets, who come to you in sheep's clothing but inwardly are ravenous wolves" (Matthew 7:15 ESV). Peter said, "There will be false teachers among you, who will secretly bring in destructive heresies, even denying the Master who bought them, bringing upon themselves swift destruction" (2 Peter 2:1 ESV). And John said, "Do not believe every spirit, but test the spirits to see whether they are from God, for many false prophets have gone out into the world" (1 John 4:1 ESV).

Heavenly Father, help me to test the spirits as Your Word instructs. Give me wisdom and discernment and protect my mind from being deceived and drawn away from the whole truth of Your whole Word.

SUNDAY, AUGUST 23

Job 1–3 / 1 Corinthians 1:1–25 / Psalm 123

Learning from Job

"Naked I came from my mother's womb, and naked shall I return. The Lord gave, and the Lord has taken away; blessed be the name of the Lord."

JOB 1:21 ESV

Job's faith in God was tested in such excruciating ways. It's hard to fully imagine the pain and sorrow he endured. Yet after losing so much, Job "fell on the ground and worshiped" (Job 1:20 ESV). However, we find that as Job's story goes on, he was tested even more, but he did not continue to praise God through it all. In fact he was quite angry for a while. In the end, though, after God reminded Job of His greatness and goodness, Job cried out in repentance, "I hate the things that I have said. And I put dust and ashes on myself to show how sorry I am" (Job 42:6 NLV). Like Job, when we cry out to God with angry words, we should stop and realize God's power and love over all things, in ways we cannot understand. And we need to apologize for our disrespect to God. After Job had repented, God blessed Job again even greater than before.

Heavenly Father, help me to have faith and strength like Job through grief and pain and hardship. Help me also to learn from Job that if I speak in anger to You, I need to repent and restore good relationship with You and continue to trust in You.

MONDAY, AUGUST 24

Job 4–6 / 1 Corinthians 1:26–2:16 / Psalm 124–125

What If?

What if the Lord had not been on our side? Let all Israel repeat: What if the Lord had not been on our side when people attacked us? They would have swallowed us alive in their burning anger. The waters would have engulfed us; a torrent would have overwhelmed us. Yes, the raging waters of their fury would have overwhelmed our very lives. Praise the Lord, who did not let their teeth tear us apart! We escaped like a bird from a hunter's trap. The trap is broken, and we are free! Our help is from the Lord, who made heaven and earth.

Psalm 124 NLT

Like this psalm urges all of Israel, we also should ask ourselves repeatedly: "What if the Lord had not been on our side?" We can think back over our lives and all the ways God has helped and provided. He's given us miracles big and small. And how he continues to do so now and will in the future. He sustains and protects our lives in endless ways! In fact, our every single breath is a miracle from Him. And while our health and lives are not guaranteed in this world, we do have guaranteed eternal life waiting for us in perfect paradise in heaven.

Heavenly Father, I truly don't know where I'd be without You on my side. You are my provider and protector. You give me life now and forever. I'm full of gratitude, and I want to count my blessings and praise You!

TUESDAY, AUGUST 25

Job 7–9 / 1 Corinthians 3 / Psalm 126–127

Real Wisdom

Do not deceive yourselves. If any of you think you are wise by the standards of this age, you should become "fools" so that you may become wise. For the wisdom of this world is foolishness in God's sight.

1 Corinthians 3:18–19 niv

This broken world promotes a counterfeit kind of wisdom that is the opposite of God's good wisdom. So how do we know the difference? We keep asking God for help through prayer and His Word. For example, this passage teaches us:

"Who is wise and understanding among you? Let them show it by their good life, by deeds done in the humility that comes from wisdom. But if you harbor bitter envy and selfish ambition in your hearts, do not boast about it or deny the truth. Such 'wisdom' does not come down from heaven but is earthly, unspiritual, demonic. For where you have envy and selfish ambition, there you find disorder and every evil practice. But the wisdom that comes from heaven is first of all pure; then peace-loving, considerate, submissive, full of mercy and good fruit, impartial and sincere." (James 3:13–17 niv)

Heavenly Father, help me recognize the fake stuff of the world and reject it—I want Your real wisdom to fill my mind and guide my steps through life. I want to humbly seek Your will and Your ways.

WEDNESDAY, AUGUST 26

Job 10–13 / 1 Corinthians 4:1–13 / Psalm 128–129

Servants of Christ

So look at Apollos and me as mere servants of Christ who have been put in charge of explaining God's mysteries. Now, a person who is put in charge as a manager must be faithful. As for me, it matters very little how I might be evaluated by you or by any human authority. I don't even trust my own judgment on this point. My conscience is clear, but that doesn't prove I'm right. It is the Lord himself who will examine me and decide. So don't make judgments about anyone ahead of time—before the Lord returns. For he will bring our darkest secrets to light and will reveal our private motives. Then God will give to each one whatever praise is due.

1 CORINTHIANS 4:1–5 NLT

We can be so grateful for pastors and teachers of the Bible. But we can also remember, as Paul instructed, that they are "mere servants of Christ." While we respect and appreciate and honor them, we can't forget that Jesus is our greatest teacher. Any other teacher who is worthy of our trust will point constantly to Him and not contradict Him. And all are known completely, inside and out, and will be judged by Him.

Lord, thank You so much for good, humble teachers of Your Word. As I respect and learn from them, help me to not forget that they are merely Your servants and to never hold any of them on a higher pedestal than You.

THURSDAY, AUGUST 27

Job 14–16 / 1 Corinthians 4:14–5:13 / Psalm 130

Count on the Lord

From the depths of despair, O Lord, I call for your help. Hear my cry, O Lord. Pay attention to my prayer. Lord, if you kept a record of our sins, who, O Lord, could ever survive? But you offer forgiveness, that we might learn to fear you. I am counting on the Lord; yes, I am counting on him. I have put my hope in his word. I long for the Lord more than sentries long for the dawn, yes, more than sentries long for the dawn. O Israel, hope in the Lord; for with the Lord there is unfailing love. His redemption overflows. He himself will redeem Israel from every kind of sin.

Psalm 130 nlt

Sometimes we do find ourselves in the depths of despair, and often it's because of our own sinful choices. Yet Psalm 130 reminds us of our hope in Jesus Christ. We all have a sin problem, and Jesus is the one and only solution. We can count on Him and cry out to Him. We can remember that His Word promises us time and again of His endless mercy and grace when we admit our sin and ask for His forgiveness.

Lord, thank You that I don't have to remain in the depths of despair. I confess my sin to You: ____. And I'm counting on You and hoping in Your Word. I'm so grateful for Your unfailing love!

FRIDAY, AUGUST 28

Job 17–20 / 1 Corinthians 6 / Psalm 131

Mind, Body, and Soul

Don't you realize that your body is the temple of the Holy Spirit, who lives in you and was given to you by God? You do not belong to yourself, for God bought you with a high price. So you must honor God with your body.
1 CORINTHIANS 6:19–20 NLT

There is so much advice about keeping our bodies healthy these days. And that's wonderful, especially since the Bible teaches us to honor God with our bodies. But our heavenly Father wants us to know that "physical training is of some value, but godliness has value for all things, holding promise for both the present life and the life to come" (1 Timothy 4:8 NIV). In other words, we need to have the right perspective about keeping our bodies in good health and appearance. That's important, absolutely, but we can easily go overboard and let the focus become on pride in ourselves and our looks rather than on honoring God with the care of our bodies. So we need to regularly refix our thoughts and goals on godliness and good health in honor and worship of the one who knows and loves us most of all, from the inside out.

Heavenly Father, I want to honor You—mind, body, and soul. Please give me wisdom about physical training and care of my body—and even more importantly, help me to grow in godliness and deeper faith in and dependence on You!

SATURDAY, AUGUST 29

Job 21–23 / 1 Corinthians 7:1–16 / Psalm 132

When He Tests Me

"[God] knows where I am going. And when he tests me, I will come out as pure as gold. For I have stayed on God's paths; I have followed his ways and not turned aside. I have not departed from his commands, but have treasured his words more than daily food."

JOB 23:10–12 NLT

Job's words here are ones we should reflect on regularly, asking ourselves, *Can I say the same as Job did? Am I staying on God's paths? Where have I veered off onto my own and need to turn back to Him? Am I following His ways? Have I departed from any of His commands? Am I treasuring God's Word and time with Him more than anything else? What will God's tests reveal about me?* These aren't easy questions to answer. We have to be truly humble and willing to admit our faults and mistakes—and our desperate need of a Savior from our sins. Thankfully God's grace to us through Jesus Christ is endless, and He removes our sins as far as the east is from the west (Psalm 103:12) when we're repentant and dependent on Him.

Lord, I want to come out as pure gold when You test me, and I know that is only possible because of Your mercy and grace to forgive me of sin. Help me to stay on Your paths and to love and obey You wholeheartedly.

SUNDAY, AUGUST 30

Job 24–27 / 1 Corinthians 7:17–40 / Psalm 133–134

The World Will Pass Away

For this world as we know it will soon pass away.
1 CORINTHIANS 7:31 NLT

Whether we find ourselves in times of blessing or of sorrow, on a mountaintop or in a valley of life, it's so important to remember that this world is coming to an end someday. And so

> *we do not lose heart. Though outwardly we are wasting away, yet inwardly we are being renewed day by day. For our light and momentary troubles are achieving for us an eternal glory that far outweighs them all. So we fix our eyes not on what is seen, but on what is unseen, since what is seen is temporary, but what is unseen is eternal. (2 Corinthians 4:16–18 NIV)*

We can't get too attached or overwhelmed or caught up in all that we see and experience right now on earth because it will all be over eventually—and that's no reason for despair for those who trust in Jesus. Because "the world and its desires pass away, but whoever does the will of God lives forever" (1 John 2:17 NIV).

> *Lord Jesus, remind me how temporary everything of this world is, whether good or bad. That's okay, because my identity and hope and peace forever are completely found in You! Thank You for the perfect eternal paradise that You are preparing for all who trust in You.*

MONDAY, AUGUST 31

Job 28–30 / 1 Corinthians 8 / Psalm 135

Careful with Freedom

You must be careful so that your freedom does not cause others with a weaker conscience to stumble. For if others see you—with your "superior knowledge"—eating in the temple of an idol, won't they be encouraged to violate their conscience by eating food that has been offered to an idol? So because of your superior knowledge, a weak believer for whom Christ died will be destroyed. And when you sin against other believers by encouraging them to do something they believe is wrong, you are sinning against Christ.

1 CORINTHIANS 8:9–12 NLT

Jesus gives us grace that covers our sin, and we can feel so wonderfully free because of that! But we are also called to be very careful to avoid sin—especially thinking of other believers and how our actions can influence and even harm them. Romans 5:21–6:2 (NLT) says,

> *God's wonderful grace rules instead, giving us right standing with God and resulting in eternal life through Jesus Christ our Lord. Well then, should we keep on sinning so that God can show us more and more of his wonderful grace? Of course not! Since we have died to sin, how can we continue to live in it?*

Lord Jesus, I'm so grateful to have freedom from sin because You paid the price to save me from it. But please give me wisdom and discernment about avoiding and fleeing from sin. Help me to be a true encouragement to fellow believers.

SEPTEMBER 2026

SUNDAY	MONDAY	TUESDAY	WEDNESDAY	THURSDAY	FRIDAY	SATURDAY
		1	2	3	4	5
6	7 Labor Day	8	9	10	11	12
13	14	15	16	17	18	19
20	21	22 First Day of Autumn	23	24	25	26
27	28	29	30			

TUESDAY, SEPTEMBER 1

Job 31–33 / 1 Corinthians 9:1–18 / Psalm 136:1–9

A Love That Never Quits

*Thank God! He deserves your thanks. His love never quits. . . .
Thank the miracle-working God, His love never quits. The God
whose skill formed the cosmos, His love never quits. The God
who laid out earth on ocean foundations, His love never quits.
The God who filled the skies with light, His love never quits.*
PSALM 136:1, 4–7 MSG

When was the last time you told God "thank You"?

When we pray, we often get caught up in our thoughts. . .what's weighing on our minds in the moment—our worries, stresses, hardships, needs, and wants. We spend an exorbitant amount of time praying for *me*, don't we? We even talk to God about our families, friends, and acquaintances—because they have the same kinds of troubles and needs that we do.

But when we say those "me" prayers, we're missing what's more important: purposeful time praising the heavenly Father, telling Him "thank You" for loving me. . .for never giving up on me. . .for being consistent and faithful. No one is more deserving of our thanks. Yet, we've probably said more thank-yous to the people in our circle than to God.

Today, focus on the one who calls you His, the one whose love never quits. Tell Him how thankful you are to be loved by Him!

*Miracle-working God, Lord of lords, I am Yours!
Thank You for loving me with Your forever-and-always love.*

WEDNESDAY, SEPTEMBER 2

Job 34–36 / 1 Corinthians 9:19–10:13 / Psalm 136:10–26

Songs of Comfort

People call out to God when they feel the crush of oppression. They implore Him for deliverance from the strong hand of tyranny. But none of them pleads in this way: "Where is God, my Creator, who gives songs of comfort in the silence and suffering of night?"

JOB 35:9–10 VOICE

Shhh. . . Hush your heart, friend. Do you hear it?

Christ is singing a song of comfort to your heart.

When you're weak and weary, crushed and craving the goodness of our God, cry out to Him. When your stressed-out, panic-laden brain tells you that the Almighty doesn't want to hear your complaints and worries and fears, silence the lies. Tell those thoughts swirling in your mind to "shut it." You can battle negative notions with the truth of God's Word, which tells us to pray about *all* things: "Is anyone among you suffering? Then he must pray. Is anyone cheerful? He is to sing praises" (James 5:13 NASB).

The bottom line is that no matter what you're experiencing—sunshine, rain, or a torrential thunderstorm—you have 24/7 access to your Creator. He wants you to share your heart with Him. And He will give you "songs of comfort in the silence and suffering of night."

When you say yes to Jesus, you never have to do life solo. He's always with you, always loving you.

Heavenly Father, thank You for the songs of comfort You sing to my heart. Help me to quiet my spirit so I can hear the words.

THURSDAY, SEPTEMBER 3

Job 37–39 / 1 Corinthians 10:14–11:1 / Psalm 137

Startled

Pause where you are, and ponder the wonders of God. Do you know how God orchestrates these marvels?... Do you know how those same clouds are hung up in the sky or how they move?
Job 37:14–16 voice

Have you ever plopped yourself in the middle of nature and basked in your surroundings? No distractions, nothing to disturb the peace in your heart and mind—just you and your God, *together*, soaking up the wonders of His creation. Diverse birds chirping their harmonious chorus, a soft wind causing the leaves to dance on the trees, the warm sun reflecting off a babbling brook, fluffy cotton candy clouds suspended in an azure sky... God's creation is truly stunning, isn't it?

As Christ followers, we know God *created*, but the busyness of our world provides a constant distraction from the miracle of it all. And friend, if we don't pause our frantic, hurried hearts, we'll miss it! We'll fail to experience the wonder and awe of all the heavenly Creator fashioned for our enjoyment. But when we take time to slow down and appreciate the natural world around us, we invite our hearts and minds to be startled by God's sheer power, wisdom, and creativity.

"Pause where you are, and ponder the wonders of God." You'll be so glad you did!

Creator God, when I look up at the night sky, I am amazed by Your artistry. Thank You for creating this beautiful, colorful world!

FRIDAY, SEPTEMBER 4

Job 40–42 / 1 Corinthians 11:2–34 / Psalm 138

Encouraged

I praise your name for your unfailing love and faithfulness; for your promises are backed by all the honor of your name. As soon as I pray, you answer me; you encourage me by giving me strength.
PSALM 138:2–3 NLT

So many things encourage our hearts. . . An unexpected delivery of flowers. An uplifting note from a neighbor. A much-needed hug from a close friend. A praise song with a message our soul needs to hear. Encouragement comes to us in simple and sometimes miraculous ways, doesn't it?

But what about days when we feel lost, hopeless, alone? *That's* when we need encouragement most—and sadly, when we least often feel it. On those down days, your soul needs support, stat! What can you do to get the positivity flowing?

- Open your Bible and start reading—see what God speaks to your heart through scripture.
- Cozy up in a quiet place and talk to God—share your thoughts, feelings, and concerns.
- Listen to some praise and worship music and steep your soul in the inspiring lyrics.
- Some quality R & R will refresh your weary soul.

Say a prayer of thanksgiving today for the encouragement the heavenly Father provides to you, His beautiful daughter. If you don't know where to begin, pray the words from today's scripture.

Encouragement giver, thank You for answering my prayers when I need Your hope, strength, and grace. You always know just what I need.

SATURDAY, SEPTEMBER 5

Ecclesiastes 1:1–3:15 / 1 Corinthians 12:1–26 / Psalm 139:1–6

Eternity in Your Heart

*[God]. . .has made everything beautiful in its time.
He has also set eternity in the human heart.*
ECCLESIASTES 3:11 NIV

Every time we reach a goal. . .or splurge for that big-ticket item. . . are we done wanting and wishing?

Isn't it true that we *immediately* begin to yearn for something else—something *more*? We set a new, "bigger" goal. . .or we begin saving for the next thing. Truth is, our wants and wishes *never* run out—we're *never* completely satisfied. There's always some void in our lives that we're trying to fill.

Why do you think this is true?

Perhaps the answer lies here in Ecclesiastes 3. Might our unrest here on earth have something to do with this desire that has been placed inside each of us? If the true desire of our hearts is for the eternal, then worldly things will *never* satisfy. No matter what we accomplish—success, wealth, fame—it will never be enough to fill the God-sized hole in our hearts.

No matter how long we search, this world can never give our lives purpose and meaning. But when we have a personal relationship with Jesus, the longing in our hearts will be filled by Him. Only God and His promises will *forever* satisfy our souls.

*Father God, when I met You, I realized I could stop
searching for purpose and meaning in the world.
You alone satisfy the desires of my heart.*

SUNDAY, SEPTEMBER 6

Ecclesiastes 3:16–6:12 / 1 Corinthians 12:27–13:13 / Psalm 139:7–18

You Matter

You are Christ's body—that's who you are!... Only as you accept your part of that body does your "part" mean anything.... But it's obvious by now, isn't it, that Christ's church is a complete Body and not a gigantic, unidimensional Part? It's not all Apostle, not all Prophet, not all Miracle Worker, not all Healer, not all Prayer in Tongues, not all Interpreter of Tongues.
1 CORINTHIANS 12:27, 29–31 MSG

You matter—a lot!

If you find that hard to believe, consider this: In all of creation, there's no one else just like you. Even if you have an identical twin, you aren't *exactly* the same. You have unique talents and abilities. You have your own style and mannerisms. You love certain foods and colors and flowers. Best of all, you have your own special role to play in God's family.

God's family needs a variety of "parts" working together to build His kingdom. And just like parts of our bodies have a unique role but work together in harmony, *that* is how the body of Christ works. Those who teach, those who pray, those who help, those who organize...each role is necessary for the body of Christ to function as it should.

What's *your* role? Whatever your special gifting is, God made you for it...you matter! Never forget that!

Lord, You knew I needed this important reminder today. I was created for a purpose...Your purpose. I matter—a lot!

MONDAY, SEPTEMBER 7 — *Labor Day*

Ecclesiastes 7:1–9:12 / 1 Corinthians 14:1–22 / Psalm 139:19–24

Colorful Living

I'm still convinced that the good life is reserved for the person who fears God, who lives reverently in his presence, and that the evil person will not experience a "good" life. No matter how many days he lives, they'll all be as flat and colorless as a shadow.
ECCLESIASTES 8:12–13 MSG

Imagine living in a black-and-white world. No brilliant pinky-orange sunrises or sunsets. . .no multicolored happy floral bouquets. . .no crisp green spring shoots. . .no sparkling aqua ocean waters. . . Just shades of black, gray, and white. Sounds rather dull, doesn't it? A colorful world is *way* more interesting. Color makes the world more vivid. . .brilliant. . .pleasing.

If your life feels lackluster today, examine your relationship with the heavenly Father. Is He as close as your best friend? Do you trust Him with things you wouldn't trust with anyone else? Do you listen closely when He speaks? Or has your relationship been distant? Have you been treating the King of kings like a stranger?

If you're craving some color in your life, remember that is what we get with Jesus in our lives. Without Him, our lives are uninteresting. . .bleak. . .flat. But with Him? With Him, our lives reflect the beautiful, multifaceted colors of our world. With Him, our lives are interesting. . .promising. . .bold!

Creative God, draw me closer to You. I want my life to radiate the colorful hues of a good life—with You at its center!

TUESDAY, SEPTEMBER 8

Ecclesiastes 9:13–12:14 / 1 Corinthians 14:23–15:11 / Psalm 140:1–8

Drenched in Grace

Because God was so gracious, so very generous, here I am. And I'm not about to let his grace go to waste. Haven't I worked hard trying to do more than any of the others? Even then, my work didn't amount to all that much. It was God giving me the work to do, God giving me the energy to do it.
1 Corinthians 15:10 MSG

Grace is the undeserved favor given to us by God. And our generous, loving heavenly Father has drenched us in His grace.

God's grace is given freely, which is important (that's *HIS* part); however, it's the way we receive His grace (*OUR* part) that makes all the difference. We can receive His grace either passively or actively. Passive receiving of God's grace says, "Thanks, Lord. I'll gladly take Your grace. But I'm just going to sit right here with it." Active receiving of His grace says, "I am so grateful, God. Show me what You would have me do with it. Now let's get to work!"

The kicker here is that while God will *equip* us and *encourage* us to do His work. . .He'll never *make us* do the work. That's a choice we get to make when we receive His generous grace. You can either waste it or work it!

What will *you* do with His generous grace today?

Father God, I want to be a worker, not a waster. Would You please show me what I can do with Your generous grace?

WEDNESDAY, SEPTEMBER 9

Song of Solomon 1–4 / 1 Corinthians 15:12–34 / Psalm 140:9–13

Awake!

It's resurrection. . .always resurrection, that undergirds. . .the way I live. If there's no resurrection, "We eat, we drink, the next day we die," and that's all there is to it. But. . .don't let yourselves be poisoned by this anti-resurrection loose talk. . . . Awaken to the holiness of life. . . . Ignorance of God is a luxury you can't afford.
1 CORINTHIANS 15:32–34 MSG

Do you know anyone who seems to be living life asleep? These people just go through the motions. They're comfortable with the status quo. They see no need to stretch and grow and accept new challenges. So they settle in, and life passes them by. Consider these words in 1 Corinthians: "We eat, we drink, the next day we die." If death is the end—if there's really nothing more to life than this—then why bother striving for more? This sleep-living is what Paul warns us against. He calls it poison, which threatens our faith.

Paul teaches that we should live with the resurrection of Christ as our focus. When we say yes to Christ, our perspective shifts from the temporary to the eternal. We begin to live for much more than the moment. We live with purpose—a pursuit of the holy life. So we surround ourselves with Christ followers, we embrace the transformed life we've been gifted, and we wake up to the beautiful future the Lord has in store for us!

*Father God, I want to live awake—
fully aware of You and my purpose as Your child.*

THURSDAY, SEPTEMBER 10

Song of Solomon 5–8 / 1 Corinthians 15:35–58 / Psalm 141

A Wonderful Secret

But let me reveal to you a wonderful secret. We will not all die, but we will all be transformed!. . . For. . .our mortal bodies must be transformed into immortal bodies. Then, when our dying bodies have been transformed. . . : "Death is swallowed up in victory. O death, where is your victory? O death, where is your sting?"
1 Corinthians 15:51, 53–55 NLT

Want to know a wonderful secret?

These bodies of ours aren't meant to last forever. They'll eventually grow old and wrinkly, get sick and die. *Wait a minute!* you're probably thinking, *I thought this secret was supposed to be a good secret!* True, but this is the much *less* wonderful half of the secret. The second half—the beautiful, miraculous, amazing other half—is this: After death, we'll be completely transformed. We'll receive new, perfect bodies that will remain young and healthy and last for all eternity!

In the here and now, we may be cursing our failing bodies. We may be fighting every extra pound, every crease on our aging faces, every ache and pain. But in these moments, we can rejoice. Because when we know Jesus as Lord, we can grab on to this lovely promise. . .this wonderful secret: "When our dying bodies have been transformed into bodies that will never die, this Scripture will be fulfilled: 'Death is swallowed up in victory'" (1 Corinthians 15:54 NLT).

Father God, thank You for this lovely reminder.
My mind (and heart!) needed it today.

FRIDAY, SEPTEMBER 11

Isaiah 1–2 / 1 Corinthians 16 / Psalm 142

Devoted

Finally, brothers and sisters, I call on you to follow your leaders. People like those in the house of Stephanas. . .they have devoted their lives to serving God's people—I urge you to submit to the authority of such leaders, to every coworker, and to those who offer their backs and shoulders for the work. . . . They have been a breath of fresh air for me as I know they are for you, so respect and honor those like them.
1 Corinthians 16:15–16, 18 voice

Paul is describing believers who "have devoted their lives to serving God's people." They are loyal, faithful, and committed to growing the kingdom of Christ. They willingly offer themselves for the work—without selfish expectation. They wholeheartedly set themselves apart to be used by God for His good purpose. When they accepted Christ, their hearts went all in for their heavenly Father. Does this describe you?

Perhaps you've had the pleasure of interacting with selfless people in your church community. Quiet leaders take care of needs behind the scenes. They see a need and do whatever they can to meet it. They know and understand their gifts and stay busy putting those gifts to work for the Lord and in service to others. They put others' needs before their own. These selfless people are "a breath of fresh air" to all who know them. May that be said of me, and may it be said of you too!

Father, I am wholly devoted to working for You!

SATURDAY, SEPTEMBER 12

Isaiah 3–5 / 2 Corinthians 1:1–11 / Psalm 143:1–6

Only God

We think you ought to know. . .about the trouble we went through in the province of Asia. We were crushed and overwhelmed beyond our ability to endure, and we thought we would never live through it. In fact, we expected to die. But as a result, we stopped relying on ourselves and learned to rely only on God. . . . And he did rescue us from mortal danger, and he will rescue us again.

2 CORINTHIANS 1:8–10 NLT

Paul's letter to the Corinthians reads like an epic novel.

"We were crushed and overwhelmed."

"We expected to die." . . .

Throughout his lifetime, Paul's sufferings were colossal, to say the least. They were literally life-threatening. He faced nearly every trouble imaginable—including imprisonment, wrongful accusation, beatings, stoning, shipwrecks, a snakebite, and more. Most of us will never experience even a handful of these trials in our lifetime. It's a miracle that Paul didn't just throw in the towel. (We certainly wouldn't have blamed him if he had.) But Paul chose the better way. . . He stopped relying on himself and instead chose to place his trust wholly in God—the only one capable of saving us.

When you feel like giving up, alter your thinking and instead give everything to God. He will rescue you with His grace and comfort, love and compassion.

Lord, when I face troubles of any kind, help me to remember that I can't save myself. . .only You can do that. Thank You!

SUNDAY, SEPTEMBER 13

Isaiah 6–8 / 2 Corinthians 1:12–2:4 / Psalm 143:7–12

Wholehearted Trust

If you wake me each morning with the sound of your loving voice, I'll go to sleep each night trusting in you. Point out the road I must travel; I'm all ears, all eyes before you. Save me from my enemies, GOD—you're my only hope! Teach me how to live to please you, because you're my God. Lead me by your blessed Spirit into cleared and level pastureland.
PSALM 143:8–10 MSG

When you wholeheartedly trust someone, you believe—with 100 percent confidence—that they will keep their promises. You trust them with your feelings and have faith that they, under no circumstances, will ever take advantage of you. You never question their motives. This person makes you feel safe and loved.

The prayer of David in Psalm 143 expresses this deep kind of trust in his heavenly Father. God had proven faithful in the past, and so David has complete confidence that God will prove faithful in the future. He asks God to guide him, to save him, to teach him. . .and he, in turn, will do what God says. Because David has wholehearted trust!

Dear one, you can trust just like David. Anytime you feel doubt sneaking into your heart, repeat this prayer from Psalm 143:8–10. God is worthy and deserving of your trust. He will never fail you!

God, You are unlimited in Your power and love and grace. You're my God, and I am so very grateful for Your faithfulness to me.

MONDAY, SEPTEMBER 14

Isaiah 9–10 / 2 Corinthians 2:5–17 / Psalm 144

Life-Giving Fragrance

Thanks be to God, who. . .uses us to spread the aroma of the knowledge of him everywhere. For we are to God the pleasing aroma of Christ among those who are being saved and those who are perishing. . . . Unlike so many, we do not peddle the word of God for profit. On the contrary, in Christ we speak. . .as those sent from God.
2 Corinthians 2:14–15, 17 niv

We love a good fragrance, don't we? Whether your sniffer prefers floral, fruity, woodsy, or musky, your favorite perfume probably elicits a joyous feeling whenever you get a whiff.

Have you ever been stopped on the street by another woman who asked, "What are you wearing? You smell *so* good!" Just as women are drawn to the lovely scent of our perfumes, they are attracted to the godly characteristics that make us stand apart from the crowd. This is what today's verses from 2 Corinthians are getting at: As Christ followers, we are "the pleasing aroma of Christ." Our kindness, our courage, our values, our generosity, our faith in action . . .all give off a pleasing fragrance that lingers in the air.

When we live our days in obedience to God and His Word, others can't help but take notice. Other women will want to know what scent we're wearing, so they can wear the same fragrance! Our lovely "aroma" brings life!

Heavenly Father, I am humbled to be Your life-giving fragrance to the world. I want to represent You so well that others will want to know You too.

TUESDAY, SEPTEMBER 15

Isaiah 11–13 / 2 Corinthians 3 / Psalm 145

Captivated

One generation after another will celebrate Your great works; they will pass on the story of Your powerful acts to their children. Your majesty and glorious splendor have captivated me; I will meditate on Your wonders, sing songs of Your worth. . . . There is nothing greater than You, God, nothing mightier than Your awesome works. I will tell of Your greatness as long as I have breath.

Psalm 145:4–6 voice

When something captivates us, it has our rapt attention. . .we're captured by how wonderful. . .beautiful. . .charming. . .or entertaining it is. And we want to share it with everyone!

While the trappings of the world will tempt us at times, nothing worldly is powerful enough to hold our attention for long. They're nothing more than mere distractions. Before long, our souls will long for more. . .something that will captivate us today, tomorrow, and for years to come.

We were created to live for something vastly bigger than ourselves. The heavenly Father planted this longing deep in our hearts. If you have already said yes to the King of kings and Lord of lords, then you certainly have had the pleasure of experiencing what it's like to be truly captivated. . .by His power, majesty, and glory. It's all so wonderful that you can't help but celebrate and share His wonders with future generations.

Tell of His greatness as long as there's breath in your lungs!

Father God, I am captivated by You. Nothing in this world can compare to Your splendor.

WEDNESDAY, SEPTEMBER 16

Isaiah 14–16 / 2 Corinthians 4 / Psalm 146

Real Blessing!

Get help from the God of Jacob, put your hope in GOD and know real blessing! GOD made sky and soil, sea and all the fish in it. He always does what he says—he defends the wronged, he feeds the hungry. GOD frees prisoners—he gives sight to the blind, he lifts up the fallen. GOD loves good people, protects strangers, takes the side of orphans and widows, but makes short work of the wicked. GOD's in charge—always. Zion's God is God for good! Hallelujah!
Psalm 146:5–10 msg

Where is your hope today? As a daughter of the Most High, have you placed *all* your hope in Him?

When we place our hope in God, He makes good on His promises—He always does what He says He will do:

He defends.
He protects.
He provides.
He frees.

He heals.
He lifts.
He loves.

Whatever hardship we face, the heavenly Father has our backs. He takes care of us *and* handles our problems. Is there any human here on earth who can do all these things for you—*always*? Not a chance!

Friend, if you haven't already done so, place your hope in the King of kings and Lord of lords today. Then claim His "real" blessings as yours.

He is so, so good! Praise His holy name!

Lord Jesus, all my hope is in You. I want to experience the fullness of Your blessings in my life today and all my days to come.

THURSDAY, SEPTEMBER 17

Isaiah 17–19 / 2 Corinthians 5 / Psalm 147:1–11

Taste of Heaven

When these bodies of ours are taken down like tents and folded away, they will be replaced by resurrection bodies in heaven. . . . We've been given a glimpse of the real thing, our true home, our resurrection bodies! The Spirit of God whets our appetite by giving us a taste of. . .a little of heaven in our hearts so that we'll never settle for less.

2 Corinthians 5:1, 4–5 msg

Imagine you are presented with a choice between two homes:

The first is a tattered and torn tent. The roof sags and leaks. It's missing a pole needed for stability, and the zipper is broken. Whatever the weather, you'll be exposed to it in this tent-home.

The second is a gorgeous two-story brick home with lush outdoor gardens and an in-ground pool. Full of spacious rooms, it boasts a state-of-the-art kitchen, four full bathrooms complete with Jacuzzi tubs, and more. It's a home most people could only dream of owning.

Which would you choose? The lovely brick home, of course!

This is not unlike the little bit of heaven the Lord puts in our hearts. When He shows us the wonder. . .the beauty that awaits us in eternity. . .the new bodies we'll be given, we'll never settle for that ragged, worn-out tent. We'll always choose the beauty and splendor of our forever home in heaven!

God, thank You for putting this little bit of heaven in my heart so I will never settle for anything less than Your eternal promise.

FRIDAY, SEPTEMBER 18

Isaiah 20–23 / 2 Corinthians 6 / Psalm 147:12–20

Big, Spacious Life!

Dear Corinthians, I can't tell you how much I long for you to enter this wide-open, spacious life. We didn't fence you in. The smallness you feel comes from within you. Your lives aren't small, but you're living them in a small way.

2 CORINTHIANS 6:11–12 MSG

When we walk with God, He never calls us to small living. A boring, uneventful life isn't what He has planned for me or for you—not today, not ever! But if "small" is what you've been feeling, then you need to take a long look inward and let the truths of 2 Corinthians 6 sink deep into your heart.

You need to hear this right now: "The smallness you feel comes from within you." (The truth is painful sometimes, isn't it?)

While our lives might be small, the fact of the matter is that it's because we've *chosen* to live small. It's not the heavenly Father's doing. God hasn't fenced you in. He has a great big spacious life in store for you. You only need to accept His invitation and say yes!

So, today, instead of complaining about your boring little life, break down those fences of your own making and ask God what big ideas He has for you—and then obey. You'll soon find yourself enjoying the wonders of the "wide-open, spacious life" that He has called you to!

Heavenly Father, thank You for waking me up from small living. With You in the lead, I will experience a great big fulfilling life!

SATURDAY, SEPTEMBER 19

Isaiah 24:1–26:19 / 2 Corinthians 7 / Psalm 148

More Jesus

The path of the righteous is level; you, the Upright One, make the way of the righteous smooth. Yes, LORD, walking in the way of your laws, we wait for you; your name and renown are the desire of our hearts. My soul yearns for you in the night; in the morning my spirit longs for you.

ISAIAH 26:7–9 NIV

Today's culture tells us we need more. . .that we deserve more. . . that we should always want something better, nicer, newer. . . But even when we get that "next big thing," there's always something bigger to wish for, and so it goes. This kind of thinking has created a worldwide pandemic of discontent and frustration. People are unhappy and insecure, depressed and anxious. And there's no cure—not without Jesus.

While we Christ followers live in this "more is more" world and we're tempted to cave to its greedy ways, we have a beautiful gift: We walk with the one who fully satisfies. When we belong to Him, our yearnings undergo a lovely transformation. Instead of more money, a bigger house, a luxury car, a designer wardrobe. . . we only long for Jesus. When we are content in Him, our souls are completely satisfied, and the temporary things of the world no longer have first place in our hearts.

Does your heart desire more of Jesus?

Jesus, You are all I want. You are all I need. You satisfy my soul!

SUNDAY, SEPTEMBER 20

Isaiah 26:20–28:29 / 2 Corinthians 8 / Psalm 149–150

Generosity-Rich

The churches in Macedonia. . .are being tested by many troubles, and they are very poor. But they are also filled with abundant joy, which has overflowed in rich generosity. . . . They gave not only what they could afford, but far more. And they did it of their own free will. . . . They even did more than we had hoped, for their first action was to give themselves to the Lord and to us.
2 CORINTHIANS 8:1–3, 5 NLT

When we become Christ followers, we gain the promise of everlasting life, freedom from our sins, brothers and sisters in Christ, and more! We gain blessing upon blessing.

Among those blessings is indescribable joy that overflows from our hearts and spills into every area of our lives. This incredible joy creates the "rich generosity" described in scripture. Although the people in Macedonia were living far from easy street, their joy resulted in "rich generosity." They freely gave more than anyone expected. No one forced them. . .no one had to beg. Why? Because "their first action was to give themselves to the Lord. . . , just as God wanted them to do" (2 Corinthians 8:5 NLT). *That* made all the difference!

What about you? Do you have the abundant joy of Jesus? If you're unsure, do a heart check today. Your first step? Make sure you've given yourself fully to the Lord. Everything else will fall into place!

Father God, please infuse me with Your indescribable joy so I can experience a generosity-rich life.

MONDAY, SEPTEMBER 21

Isaiah 29–30 / 2 Corinthians 9 / Proverbs 1:1–9

Astonished

*God can pour on the blessings in astonishing ways. . . .
He throws caution to the winds, giving to the needy
in reckless abandon. His right-living, right-giving ways
never run out, never wear out. This most generous God. . .
He gives you something you can then give away.*

2 CORINTHIANS 9:8–10 MSG

We've all had the pleasure of connecting with generous people—in our churches, in our businesses, in our neighborhoods. . . We're blessed to share the world with bighearted people who provide meals for the hungry, leave exorbitant tips where they dine, create and deliver care packages for the sick, and generously give of their time and treasures. These men and women are beautiful examples of Christians who serve well.

Yet. . . Not one comes close to the extravagant generosity of our God, who gives in "reckless abandon." His wells of blessing never run dry. . .there is a continuous supply flowing into our lives. These blessings are so abundant that we always have more than enough—so there's plenty to give away and share with others!

When you get distracted and fail to notice the abundant blessings of Christ, it's time to slow down. . .quiet your heart. . .and ask the heavenly Father to help you see "His right-living, right-giving ways" that "never run out, never wear out." Get ready to be astonished at how He's actively pouring into your life!

Generous Father, quiet my heart so I can enter Your presence with a spirit of thanksgiving for Your extravagant generosity.

First Day of Autumn   TUESDAY, SEPTEMBER 22

Isaiah 31–33 / 2 Corinthians 10 / Proverbs 1:10–22

What Fuels You?

For though we walk in the world, we do not fight according to this world's rules of warfare. The weapons of the war we're fighting are not of this world but are powered by God and effective at tearing down the strongholds erected against His truth. We are demolishing arguments and ideas, every high-and-mighty philosophy that pits itself against the knowledge of the one true God. We are taking prisoners of every thought, every emotion, and subduing them into obedience to the Anointed One.
2 Corinthians 10:3–5 voice

When we accept Jesus as our Savior, we are transformed. Although we are still *in* the world, we are no longer *of* the world. What once drove our desires and influenced our thoughts and emotions is replaced by something so much greater and stronger—the power of the living God! When we fully submit to the heavenly Father, our lives become fully fueled by our new purpose as kingdom builders here on earth.

Lies? They are demolished by God's truth.

False arguments and philosophies? They are destroyed by the knowledge of the one true God.

Our wayward thoughts and misguided emotions? They become obedient to Christ!

When we live in obedience to the heavenly Creator, our lives are enhanced. . .full of purpose and peace and powerful truth.

Heavenly Father, my desire is to live a life fully powered by You and Your Word. Help me to live well. . .in complete obedience to You!

WEDNESDAY, SEPTEMBER 23

Isaiah 34–36 / 2 Corinthians 11 / Proverbs 1:23–26

In His Sights

So, with confidence and hope. . .strengthen those with feeble hands, shore up the weak-kneed and weary. Tell those who worry, the anxious and fearful, "Take strength; have courage! There's nothing to fear. . . . Right here is your God!"
ISAIAH 35:3–4 VOICE

Do you ever feel weak-kneed and weary? Worried? Anxious? Fearful? Hopeless? We all have hard times when our focus veers off course and we take our eyes off Jesus. That's when we lose sight of the might and glory of our God. When our attention turns inward instead of upward, we become timid and discouraged.

But we must remember that just because we've lost sight of Jesus, that doesn't mean He's lost sight of us. Here's what His Word says:

> "I'll never let you down, never walk off and leave you." (Hebrews 13:5 MSG)
>
> "And be sure of this: I am with you always, even to the end of the age." (Matthew 28:20 NLT)
>
> "This is my command—be strong and courageous! Do not be afraid or discouraged. For the LORD your God is with you wherever you go." (Joshua 1:9 NLT)

When we're fully rooted in the Word, our strength and hope, confidence and courage never leave us. Even in tough times, we can tap into the power of our heavenly Father. All we need to do is look up, and we'll see that He was right there all along, waiting for us to see the light.

Father, lift my head so my focus is on You alone.

THURSDAY, SEPTEMBER 24

Isaiah 37–38 / 2 Corinthians 12:1–10 / Proverbs 1:27–33

Delighted!

In order to keep me from becoming conceited, I was given a thorn in my flesh. . . . Three times I pleaded with the Lord to take it away from me. But he said to me, "My grace is sufficient for you, for my power is made perfect in weakness." Therefore I will boast all the more gladly about my weaknesses, so that Christ's power may rest on me. That is why, for Christ's sake, I delight in weaknesses, in insults, in hardships, in persecutions, in difficulties. For when I am weak, then I am strong.

2 Corinthians 12:7–10 niv

When we are delighted, we feel joy. We are extremely pleased, excited even. The things that delight our souls can be exhilarating—consider riding a roller coaster at your favorite theme park or attending your best friend's wedding—but they can also be basic, like walking through the grass in your bare feet or dancing in the rain.

Good things do—and should—delight us. But what about the not-so-good things? Does it make any sense to feel joy in hard times? According to scripture. . .yes! This is because we can tap into God's grace and power at any time. And so, even in our weakness, we can be quite strong. God will sustain us. And that should delight your soul—and mine!

> *Father, I am delighted! Life won't always be perfect, but You promise to be with me every step of the way. You will provide the strength and courage I need.*

FRIDAY, SEPTEMBER 25

Isaiah 39–40 / 2 Corinthians 12:11–13:14 / Proverbs 2:1–15

Wisdom Is Yours!

My child, listen to what I say, and treasure my commands. Tune your ears to wisdom, and concentrate on understanding. Cry out for insight, and ask for understanding. Search for them as you would for silver; seek them like hidden treasures. Then you will understand what it means to fear the LORD, and you will gain knowledge of God. For the LORD grants wisdom! From his mouth come knowledge and understanding. He grants a treasure of common sense to the honest. He is a shield to those who walk with integrity.

PROVERBS 2:1–7 NLT

Proverbs is a beautifully practical book overflowing with reliable advice for daily living. It lays out clear instruction on how to apply God's Word to our lives. In addition to truth-filled guidance, it explains the value of wisdom and understanding.

Today's scripture passage advises readers on wisdom, understanding, and insight. It says that we should "concentrate," "cry out," "ask," "search," and "seek" for these things. Are they a priority in *your* life? If we're obeying God's Word, our answer should be *yes*! We should "search for them as [we] would for silver; seek them like hidden treasures."

Have a heart-to-heart with God today and ask Him to supply you with wisdom. He will come through. Wisdom will be yours!

Wisdom giver, thank You for the book of Proverbs and the wisdom and guidance it provides. I want to live Your way. So please help me to prioritize wisdom in all I do.

SATURDAY, SEPTEMBER 26

Isaiah 41–42 / Galatians 1 / Proverbs 2:16–22

Chosen

*"'You're my servant, serving on my side. I've picked you.
I haven't dropped you.' Don't panic. I'm with you. There's
no need to fear for I'm your God. I'll give you strength.
I'll help you. I'll hold you steady, keep a firm grip on you."*
ISAIAH 41:9–10 MSG

If you've ever been rejected, you know how much it stings.

Why does it hurt so much to be excluded? It's because we were made for relationship. So we crave acceptance. We want to belong. We want to be chosen. Sadly, human beings excel at rejecting each other—acceptance and love don't always come easily. So if we're depending on others to make us feel whole and complete and like we truly fit in, we're setting ourselves up for disappointment.

However, there is someone we can depend on—God will always make us feel confident and secure. He will never reject us. He will choose us today, tomorrow, forever. Scripture tells us:

He picked us.
He's with us.
He's our God.
He'll hold us steady.
He'll keep a firm grip on us.

When human relationships fail you—and they will—you can always look to the one who never fails and never changes, our God and Savior. If you haven't already, choose Him—choose the one who has chosen you!

*Heavenly Father, thank You for always choosing me.
Because I am Your child, I will always belong to You!*

SUNDAY, SEPTEMBER 27

Isaiah 43:1–44:20 / Galatians 2 / Proverbs 3:1–12

God's Woman

I tried keeping rules and working my head off to please God, and it didn't work. So I quit being a "law man" so that I could be God's man. . . . I identified myself completely with him. . . . It is no longer important that I appear righteous before you or have your good opinion, and I am no longer driven to impress God. Christ lives in me. The life you see me living is not "mine," but it is lived by faith in the Son of God, who loved me and gave himself for me.

GALATIANS 2:19–20 MSG

Sometimes we get so wrapped up in following rules that we lose sight of the bigger, more important picture. We miss what matters, and we become little more than self-absorbed women trying to win the approval of God (and others).

If this describes you, sister, it's time to stop the madness! No amount of rule following will bring more joy, contentment, or significance to your life. The apostle Paul, who wrote today's scripture, experienced this for himself. He tried rule following and working to gain God's approval. . .and "it didn't work"! So he focused instead on being "God's man." He realized *that* was the most important element in living out his faith.

Let's follow the advice of Paul and become God's women. Let's live exclusively for the one who died so that we might live.

Lord, I need You. My ability to follow rules and work to exhaustion doesn't change a thing—but living for You and with You does!

MONDAY, SEPTEMBER 28

Isaiah 44:21–46:13 / Galatians 3:1–18 / Proverbs 3:13–26

God Goes Before You

I will smash down gates of bronze and cut through bars of iron. And I will give you treasures hidden in the darkness—secret riches. I will do this so you may know that I am the LORD, the God of Israel, the one who calls you by name.

ISAIAH 45:2–3 NLT

Are there people in your life who have sacrificed for you? Perhaps your parents gave up new cars and vacations so they could help pay for your education. Maybe your sister gave up an evening out with friends to care for you while you were sick. As women, we frequently sacrifice for those we care about in a variety of ways, don't we?

We tend to forgo our own pleasures and treasures to benefit those we love. And while our sacrifices might seem significant, none come close to those of our heavenly Father, who sacrifices on another level for those He loves. He loves you and me so much that He not only makes a way for us but provides "treasures" and "secret riches" for us. More significantly, He sent His Son to die on the cross for our sins so we can live in heaven for eternity with Him.

The God who "calls you by name" does what He says He will do. He makes good on His promises—every single one!

*Thank You for loving me so much, Father—
for always making a way for me. I love You!*

TUESDAY, SEPTEMBER 29

Isaiah 47:1–49:13 / Galatians 3:19–29 / Proverbs 3:27–35

Who Are You?

For you are all children of God through faith in Christ Jesus. And all who have been united with Christ in baptism have put on Christ, like putting on new clothes. . . . And now that you belong to Christ, you are the true children of Abraham. You are his heirs, and God's promise to Abraham belongs to you.
Galatians 3:26–27, 29 nlt

I am Terry and Kathy's daughter.
I am John's wife and Keane and Kiley's mother.
I am a writer and editor.
I love autumn, the beach, and books.

When asked who we are, most of us would share our names, family members and relationships, professions, and favorite things. But do any of these descriptors share the most meaningful thing about us?

When we accept Christ as Lord and leader of our lives, our identities change. In addition to who we already are, we become something more—we become children of God! As His heirs, we have hope, joy, forgiveness, unconditional love, belonging, freedom, eternal life, purpose—too many blessings to name. Is there anything more wonderful than that?

So the next time someone asks, "Who are you?" Will you say, first and foremost, "I am a child of God"?

> *Father God, thank You for adopting me into You family, for making me Your heir. I have no confusion about who—or whose—I am! Thank You, Lord!*

WEDNESDAY, SEPTEMBER 30

Isaiah 49:14–51:23 / Galatians 4:1–11 / Proverbs 4:1–19

Shine Bright

I have pointed you in the way of wisdom; I have steered you down the path to integrity. So get going. And as you go, know this: with integrity you will overcome all obstacles. . . . Tighten your grip around wise advice. . . . Protect Wisdom. . . . The way of those who do right is like the early morning sun that shines brighter and brighter until noon.

PROVERBS 4:11–13, 18 VOICE

Have you ever been in the presence of a woman who had "it"? She was a complete joy to be around. She radiated goodness and grace. This woman was anything but ordinary. She was also humble and kind. She made you want to be a better you!

If you've been blessed to know someone like this, thank the Lord for putting her in your life. Then ask Him to help make you into that kind of woman too.

He will "[point] you in the way of wisdom." He has "steered you down the path to integrity." In short, our relationship with the one who created us makes life worth living. When we walk closely with Him, we shine—and others can't help but notice. Just like the woman who has "it," you'll stand out in the crowd and others will want in on your secret. Just be sure to give full credit to your master designer.

Father God, my Creator, help me to shine so others will want to know You too.

OCTOBER 2026

SUNDAY	MONDAY	TUESDAY	WEDNESDAY	THURSDAY	FRIDAY	SATURDAY
				1	2	3
4	5	6	7	8	9	10
11	12 Columbus Day	13	14	15	16	17
18	19	20	21	22	23	24
25	26	27	28	29	30	31 Halloween

THURSDAY, OCTOBER 1

Isaiah 52–54 / Galatians 4:12–31 / Proverbs 4:20–27

A Heart of Wisdom

My son, pay attention to what I say; turn your ear to my words. Do not let them out of your sight, keep them within your heart; for they are life to those who find them and health to one's whole body. Above all else, guard your heart, for everything you do flows from it.
PROVERBS 4:20–23 NIV

Through the eyes of a young child, Mommy is often the smartest, wisest, most beautiful and amazingly fun superhero on earth. The spongelike nature of a child soaks up every word and example Mommy offers. Under her guidance, care, and protection, her little one finds peace and joy and deep contentment in childhood.

That's the kind of life that awaits God's beloved children when we let the wisdom of His Word sink deep into our hearts. Meditating on scripture, asking God for His guidance in every decision, and listening intently for the Holy Spirit's instruction are all ways to join our hearts with His. And when He asks us to step out of our comfort zone or to be convicted and corrected, we must choose to be moldable and to obey His prompting. A humble heart that rests in God's presence, in tune with His Word, is a heart that is protected and safe from the fears, worries, and frustrations of this world.

Father, I'm inching ever close to You as I listen intently to Your voice. Fill my heart with Your wisdom today and every day.

FRIDAY, OCTOBER 2

Isaiah 55–57 / Galatians 5 / Proverbs 5:1–14

It's Beyond Me

My intentions are not always yours, and I do not go about things as you do. My thoughts and My ways are above and beyond you, just as heaven is far from your reach here on earth.
ISAIAH 55:8–9 VOICE

"God, I trust You, but *what* are you doing?" If you've been a Christian for more than twenty-four hours, you've likely prayed something similar. We believe the truth that God is in control of everything (Isaiah 45:7) and that His ways are always good (Psalm 145:9). But when He leads us in a direction that is not the way we would go, when it seems like He's slow to answer our prayers, we start to wonder. . .

While God welcomes our questions, we are only fooling ourselves when we think we know better than the Creator of the universe and veer off the path He's set before us. It's important to remember that while God cares deeply about what we are going through in this moment, He also sees the entire picture of our lives—mind, heart, body, and soul—for all of eternity. He's leading us on from point A to B and from B to C as a victorious, perfectly loving Father. Humbly ask for His guidance and follow where He leads—even or *especially* when it's not what you expect.

I don't always understand Your ways, Lord. But my soul is at rest because I trust You with all my heart.

SATURDAY, OCTOBER 3

Isaiah 58–59 / Galatians 6 / Proverbs 5:15–23

Less Is More

"If you spend yourselves in behalf of the hungry and satisfy the needs of the oppressed, then your light will rise in the darkness, and your night will become like the noonday. The LORD will guide you always; he will satisfy your needs in a sun-scorched land and will strengthen your frame. You will be like a well-watered garden, like a spring whose waters never fail."
ISAIAH 58:10–11 NIV

The world whispers to our hearts that the only way to find happiness and contentment is more—more fame, more money, more influence, more youth and beauty, more and better stuff. Getting ahead means bettering ourselves and diminishing others who aren't worth our time.

But God's Word clearly and firmly states the opposite. The Lord tells us to look outward, instead of focusing inward by satisfying our own appetites for more. He urges us to spend ourselves—our time, money, and effort—on meeting the needs of others who are marginalized, frustrated, down-and-out. What God promises in return is His light to guide our steps, His provision to meet our needs, and His strength to endure through any circumstance. He is the living water that will nourish a richly contented life that can be found only in a close relationship with God.

Father, I've spent too much time chasing after things that don't matter. Help me take my eyes off of my own desires and see others as You see them. Give me Your heart, Lord.

SUNDAY, OCTOBER 4

Isaiah 60–62 / Ephesians 1 / Proverbs 6:1–5

Overwhelming Joy

I am overwhelmed with joy in the LORD my God! For he has dressed me with the clothing of salvation and draped me in a robe of righteousness. I am like a bridegroom dressed for his wedding or a bride with her jewels.

ISAIAH 61:10 NLT

Even if you consider yourself a generally happy person, it's unlikely that you would describe yourself as being "overwhelmed with joy" all day, every day. Overwhelming joy is usually reserved for big, momentous life events. . .an eager anticipating of a marriage, a baby, a baptism, a miraculous healing, an answered prayer, and the list goes on.

But here in Isaiah 61, the prophet writes of experiencing overwhelming joy because of God's salvation—the same salvation that is offered to us today. Consider all the ways that God provides for you and blesses you in big and small ways. If you profess Jesus as your Lord, you've received the gift of His righteous holiness. You are chosen. Your eternity is secure in the arms of the Father. Isaiah writes that the Lord delights in you and rejoices over you (62:4–5). All of these things—and more!—are reasons to let tidal waves of overwhelming joy crash through your heart and mind today. Hallelujah!

I'm bursting at the seams with gratitude, Father! I praise You for Your power, for Your goodness, for Your ancient plan that has always included me as part of Your family. Help me to share this joy with everyone I meet.

MONDAY, OCTOBER 5

Isaiah 63:1–65:16 / Ephesians 2 / Proverbs 6:6–19

The Hustle

For it's by God's grace that you have been saved. You receive it through faith. It was not our plan or our effort. It is God's gift, pure and simple You didn't earn it, not one of us did, so don't go around bragging that you must have done something amazing. For we are the product of His hand, heaven's poetry etched on lives, created in the Anointed, Jesus, to accomplish the good works God arranged long ago.

EPHESIANS 2:8–10 VOICE

There's nothing the world loves more than the hustle—the seemingly superwoman effort of an upwardly mobile, bootstrap-pulling boss babe who takes names and gets the job done.

And while God's Word certainly praises hard work (Proverbs 6:6–11 for example), one of the most beautiful aspects of salvation is that we *don't* have to work for it—in fact, we couldn't earn it even if we tried. Jesus has already done the hard work to secure salvation by dying on the cross. He is our Savior, Redeemer, brother, and friend who offers grace to anyone who will humbly accept His gifts of forgiveness, a loving relationship with God, and eternal life in His presence.

Take time today to celebrate the peace of knowing that you didn't have to save yourself and you don't have to hustle to maintain your salvation. And praise God for that beautiful gift!

Jesus, I spend my days working hard at so many things, but I am forever grateful for Your ultimate sacrifice that paid for my eternity.

TUESDAY, OCTOBER 6

Isaiah 65:17–66:24 / Ephesians 3:1–4:16 / Proverbs 6:20–26

Come Confidently

[Jesus'] faithfulness to God has made it possible
for us to have the courage we need and the ability
to approach the Father confidently.
EPHESIANS 3:12 VOICE

Even the most self-confident people experience moments of social intimidation. Whether it's something as monumental as an important job interview or as mundane as making a call to schedule an appointment, there are lots of reasons that someone could feel unsure, uncomfortable, or anxious around others.

Perhaps the Christians in Ephesus were feeling intimidated to pray, and that's why Paul wrote in Ephesians 3:12 that it was Jesus' obedience on the cross that paved the way for God's children to come to the Father confidently, to talk to Him about everything, and to ask for anything.

"Keep on asking, and you will receive what you ask for," Jesus said about prayer in Matthew 7:7–8 (NLT). Jesus went on to say that as our loving Father, God will give good gifts to His children. What are some of the good gifts we can boldly ask for? God's presence and nearness (Psalm 145), wisdom (James 1:5), and His help in everything (Isaiah 41:10).

Whatever you need today, you can find it in God's presence. There's no need to timidly knock, because you'll find the door wide open and the Father beckoning you warmly into His throne room. You are welcome and at home with Him there.

Jesus, thank You for leading me boldly into the presence of God!

WEDNESDAY, OCTOBER 7

Jeremiah 1–2 / Ephesians 4:17–32 / Proverbs 6:27–35

Set Apart and Appointed

The word of the LORD came to me, saying, "Before I formed you in the womb I knew you, before you were born I set you apart; I appointed you as a prophet to the nations."

JEREMIAH 1:4–5 NIV

Jeremiah's calling from God was clear before he was born. He was a prophet to the kingdom of Judah, and his main objective was to deliver bad news to God's people: Judgment was coming. But as difficult as Jeremiah's job was, and even in the face of persecution and more than one near-death situation, Jeremiah faithfully delivered God's messages. He faithfully took part in God's grand plan of restoration and redemption.

Just as God knew Jeremiah, God knew you and set you apart long before you were born. He created you with a specific calling in mind. Whether that calling is through your vocation, your ministry, or even your own interests and circle of influence, God made you with a particular role to fill and place to serve. Your life, your passions, and your story are part of God's plan to restore and redeem His creation.

What if you haven't yet heard a *specific* assignment from God? Continue to ask Him to reveal it in His time, and be open to the Holy Spirit's prompting. Then as you wait, work to fulfill the mission that's common to all Christians: Love God, love others, and encourage others to follow Jesus.

I'm here, Lord, willing to be used by You.

THURSDAY, OCTOBER 8

Jeremiah 3:1–4:22 / Ephesians 5 / Proverbs 7:1–5

Opportunities

So be careful how you live. Live as men who are wise and not foolish. Make the best use of your time. . . . Do not be foolish. Understand what the Lord wants you to do.
EPHESIANS 5:15–17 NLV

The older you get, the faster time flies. If you've lived long enough to know the truth of that sentence, then you can understand Paul's words in Ephesians 5. "Don't waste your time on things that aren't important," he urged the Christians in Ephesus. "Make the most of every opportunity you have."

What opportunities is he talking about? No matter who you are or how you spend your days, you have chances to impact others for Jesus. Sure, maybe that means sharing the good news of salvation and leading a friend or family member to Jesus, but it also could simply mean showing some small act of kindness to someone who needs it. Perhaps it's offering a sympathetic ear to someone going through a tough time. It means giving when there's a need you can meet, offering a word of encouragement just because, and choosing to display patience when you're running late.

To understand what the Lord wants you to do, ask Him to lead you. Spend time with Him and His Word to know Him better. And then choose to act on opportunities to do good, promote truth, live in contentment and gratitude, and love others above all.

Father, give me Your wisdom to know how to best use my time.

FRIDAY, OCTOBER 9

Jeremiah 4:23–5:31 / Ephesians 6 / Proverbs 7:6–27

Arm Yourself

Put on the whole armor of God, that you may be able to stand against the schemes of the devil.
EPHESIANS 6:11 SKJV

Preparation is essential in every area of life. Want to pass a test? Put in the necessary study time. Want to win the big game? Practice drills and memorize plays and work as a team. Need to nail a job interview? Write out answers to the types of questions you might be asked by a potential employer. Want to be less hurried in the morning? Lay out clothes the night before.

Preparation is also essential for the daily spiritual battles we face against the father of all lies, the prince of darkness, the tempter, the deceiver—Satan. How do we prepare for such an important fight? God supplies us with every piece of His armor we need—truth, righteousness, peace, faith, salvation, and the Bible. Yes, the armor is a gift from God, but it's our job to prepare by *putting on* the armor. That means reading and meditating on scripture on a regular basis. It means putting faith into action by standing up for what's true. It means working toward harmony in our relationships, talking to God, and being in community with other believers, fellow armor-bearers in Christ.

God, I take comfort in knowing that in the final battle, You win and Satan loses. But while the devil still poses a threat, I am thankful that You supply me with ways to stand against him.

SATURDAY, OCTOBER 10

Jeremiah 6:1–7:26 / Philippians 1:1–26 / Proverbs 8:1–11

Listen

To whom can I give warning? Who will listen when I speak? Their ears are closed, and they cannot hear. They scorn the word of the Lord. They don't want to listen at all.
JEREMIAH 6:10 NLT

Like many other Old Testament prophets, Jeremiah had bad news for the people of Judah: Judgment was coming, and it was going to be ugly. God had warned them for generations to stop worshipping idols. Yet nobody in Judah would heed Jeremiah's prophecy. Like a strong-willed child in the throes of a tantrum, Judah's leaders and people seemed to stomp their feet and say, "You aren't the boss of me!" And when Jeremiah continued to warn of the coming destruction, they simply stopped listening—acting as if they ignored the prophecy long enough it would go away.

But God cares too much to let His people continue being sinful, spoiled, strong-willed brats when it comes to His laws. His plan was to redeem Judah—which ultimately *did* happen—but not without generations of suffering that they brought on themselves.

The lesson here? When the Holy Spirit sends up a red flag in your heart, indicating that you aren't following God's plan. . .when the warning signs are there that you're playing with fire. . .open your heart, listen to what God is saying, and humbly change your ways.

Lord, I want to be sensitive to Your prompting and never be so strong-willed that I refuse to listen to Your voice. Help me humbly accept Your correction.

SUNDAY, OCTOBER 11

Jeremiah 7:26–9:16 / Philippians 1:27–2:18 / Proverbs 8:12–21

Get Wise

"I, Wisdom, live together with good judgment. I know where to discover knowledge and discernment. All who fear the Lord will hate evil. Therefore, I hate pride and arrogance, corruption and perverse speech. Common sense and success belong to me. Insight and strength are mine."
PROVERBS 8:12–14 NLT

The book of Proverbs uses a literary device called *personification* when Wisdom is portrayed as a woman. It's a way to make the abstract idea of wisdom come alive and help us understand how we can live more wisely.

Throughout Proverbs 8, Wisdom describes some of her attributes like good judgment, knowledge, discernment, common sense, insight, and strength of character. She stands for God's truth and rejects the evil things of the world like pride, arrogance, corruption, and lies. "Choose my instruction rather than silver, and knowledge rather than pure gold," Wisdom urges the reader in verses 10–11 (NLT). "For wisdom is far more valuable than rubies. Nothing you desire can compare with it."

Wisdom aligns with the mind of God, and seeking wisdom is one of the wisest things we can do. Meditating on Proverbs is a good place to start. Another place to see wisdom in action is in the Gospels—Matthew, Mark, Luke, and John. There, you'll find the perfect wisdom role model: Jesus Christ.

Father, I want to reflect Your wisdom in my life. I'm holding to Your promise in James 1:5 that You will gladly give me wisdom when I ask.

MONDAY, OCTOBER 12 — *Columbus Day*

Jeremiah 9:17–11:17 / Philippians 2:19–30 / Proverbs 8:22–36

Keys to Wisdom

The one who listens to me, who carefully seeks me in everyday things and delays action until my way is apparent, that one will find true happiness. For when he recognizes and follows me, he finds a peaceful and satisfying life and receives favor from the Eternal.
PROVERBS 8:34–35 VOICE

In cartoons and pop culture, wisdom is often illustrated as an owl or an elderly, bespectacled, white-bearded professor-type. These characters can give us the wrong impression that wisdom isn't for us—after all, we aren't owls or geriatric men. But the truth is that wisdom is an important, attainable, everyday tool that we should use in all areas of life. Here are some simple keys to wisdom:

1. *Ask* God to lead your everyday decisions. Even seemingly mundane choices, when made wisely, can bring Him glory in big ways and small ways.
2. *Wait* for God to show you His wisdom when you face an important decision. This will give you confidence that you are on mission with His plan.
3. *Rest* in the wise choices you've made. When you're in step with God, you don't have to second-guess or revisit your decisions. He will bless you with peace of mind.

Proverbs 8:22 says that God formed wisdom before He created anything else. It's the bedrock on which He built everything. When we seek His wisdom, God's blessings will follow.

Father, help me develop more common sense and discernment every day, even in the small things.

TUESDAY, OCTOBER 13

Jeremiah 11:18–13:27 / Philippians 3 / Proverbs 9:1–6

Progress > Perfection

I don't mean to say that I have already achieved these things or that I have already reached perfection. . . . No, dear brothers and sisters, I have not achieved it, but I focus on this one thing: Forgetting the past and looking forward to what lies ahead, I press on to reach the end of the race and receive the heavenly prize for which God, through Christ Jesus, is calling us.

PHILIPPIANS 3:12–14 NLT

Progress is better than perfection.

For the type A folks among us, that truth is a bitter pill to swallow. Because if perfection is the goal of our Christianity, why *wouldn't* we strive to be perfect? The short answer is that perfection is unattainable. Even if we somehow managed to live a day without sin, we simply cannot sustain it indefinitely.

Paul, in his letter to Christians in Philippians, illustrated this idea of "progress over perfection" in chapter 3, where he describes his pursuit of Christlikeness as an athlete who is training to run a race. Every day you can choose to pursue small choices that will lead you to wisdom and maturity. You've already chosen to spend time today reading His Word—that's great! Come back tomorrow and do it again!

You're building your spiritual muscles and becoming more complete in Christ, one moment, one choice, at a time. That's progress that is better than perfection!

Jesus, I will take small steps to be more like You!

WEDNESDAY, OCTOBER 14

Jeremiah 14–15 / Philippians 4 / Proverbs 9:7–18

Don't Worry

Don't worry about anything; instead, pray about everything. Tell God what you need, and thank him for all he has done. Then you will experience God's peace, which exceeds anything we can understand.

PHILIPPIANS 4:6–7 NLT

"Don't worry" might be the simplest—yet the most difficult to follow—command in God's Word. Why? Because our minds *love* to anxiously mull over the "what ifs" in life. Worry gives the human brain something to chew on, to puzzle out, and to think. . .and think. . . and think some more. The problem is that our minds don't naturally gravitate toward positive "what if" outcomes. Instead, worry can leave us spiraling out of control as our thoughts and fears run wild with worst-case scenarios.

Thankfully, God's Word gives us practical steps to banish worry. It all starts with choosing to pray rather than worry. Talk to God about what's troubling you—the big things and the small—and trust Him to take care of it. That's not a once-and-done prayer but instead a moment-by-moment surrender. Recall the times that He's taken care of your worrisome "what ifs" in the past, and take comfort that He continues to be in control.

Father, I am worried, and I can't seem to shake it. I can't handle this on my own, so please take these anxious thoughts. I will hand them to You again and again until I make room in my heart and mind for the gift of Your peace.

THURSDAY, OCTOBER 15

Jeremiah 16–17 / Colossians 1:1–23 / Proverbs 10:1–5

Praying for Others

*I have never stopped praying for you. . . . I ask God that you
may know what He wants you to do. I ask God to fill you
with the wisdom and understanding the Holy Spirit gives. . . .
I pray that God's great power will make you strong,
and that you will have joy as you wait and do not give up.*
COLOSSIANS 1:9, 11 NLV

"Pray about everything," Paul wrote in Philippians 4:6 (NLV), and that includes praying for others. Whether it's close family and friends, coworkers, acquaintances, or even people you've never met, God wants to hear about the people on your heart—because they are on His heart too.

You may often ask God to bless them with health or safety or healing—all good things—but sometimes these requests can get repetitive and scratch just the surface of their needs. The prayers Paul describes in Colossians 1:9–14 are excellent examples of how and what to pray for others. You can ask the Holy Spirit to lead them in the Lord's will, for strength and endurance in whatever troubles they are facing, and that they experience true joy in Christ. Pray that their story can be a shining example of God's faithfulness that leads others to the light of Jesus. Pray for others. . .and never stop.

*God, thank You for giving me people who are dear to me.
As much as I love them, I know You love them more!*

FRIDAY, OCTOBER 16

Jeremiah 18:1–20:6 / Colossians 1:24–2:15 / Proverbs 10:6–14

Rooted

Let your roots grow down deeply in Him,
and let Him build you up on a firm foundation.
COLOSSIANS 2:7 VOICE

A tree's roots serve two main functions: to anchor the tree in the earth and to extract water and nutrients from the soil. Throughout a tree's life, its roots will continue to grow. In times of ample water, nutrients, and sunlight, its roots may grow faster. And in times of drought, its roots may grow more slowly—but they are always growing. For a mature tree, its roots below ground may be two to three times bigger than the canopy of limbs and leaves that reach toward the sun.

Whether you are a new Christian or have followed Jesus for decades, your roots are growing. By spending time in the Word and reading this devotion today, you're adding to the strength of your faith by tapping into the goodness of God. When you choose to spend time with God in prayer, when you seek out biblical teaching, when you strengthen your fellowship with other believers, your roots are entwining with Jesus.

When life whips up a storm, those connections—those anchor points—will help you stand firm in your joy, hope, and faith. When your faith feels dried up in a season of drought, the fullness of your roots in Jesus can help you endure until a time of refreshing rain returns.

Jesus, You are my firm root system. Please help my faith
flourish so I can withstand the difficult times!

SATURDAY, OCTOBER 17

Jeremiah 20:7–22:19 / Colossians 2:16–3:4 / Proverbs 10:15–26

A Teachable Spirit

He who listens to teaching is on the path of life, but he who will not listen to strong words goes the wrong way. . . . The one who talks much will for sure sin, but he who is careful what he says is wise.
PROVERBS 10:17, 19 NLV

When a person earnestly seeks answers, wisdom, and guidance, that person can be described as *teachable*—one of the most underrated characteristics today. But the world shouts that only *you* can determine what's right for you, and how *dare* someone else try to impose their thoughts and opinions on you! The gall!

God's Word urges us to be teachable—to listen to the prompting of the Holy Spirit, to heed scripture's warnings, instruction, and wisdom, and to be open to the guidance of people who are more mature in their faith than we. The first step to having an open heart toward God's teaching is admitting that we don't know everything, and that's okay. The next step in becoming more teachable is simply spending more time listening and less time talking. Listening—to God and others—allows for observation and time for information to sink in for greater understanding. Finally, when we speak, we must choose our words carefully. That's the kind of humble, teachable spirit that God honors and blesses (1 Peter 5:5).

Lord, my aim is to be teachable, moldable in Your hands. Please teach me every day to be more like Jesus!

SUNDAY, OCTOBER 18

Jeremiah 22:20–23:40 / Colossians 3:5–4:1 / Proverbs 10:27–32

Dressing for Forgiveness

Put on your new nature, and be renewed as you learn to know your Creator and become like him. . . . Since God chose you to be the holy people he loves, you must clothe yourselves with tenderhearted mercy, kindness, humility, gentleness, and patience. Make allowance for each other's faults, and forgive anyone who offends you. Remember, the Lord forgave you, so you must forgive others. Above all, clothe yourselves with love, which binds us all together in perfect harmony.
COLOSSIANS 3:10, 12–14 NLT

Whether you're a lay-out-clothes-the-night-before gal or a snag-clothes-off-the-floor-and-give-them-a-sniff girlie, each day you choose what clothing to take off and put on your body. Dressing is an intentional action—it doesn't happen by accident.

In the same way, we must choose to take off our old, smelly, wrinkly, pre-Jesus sinful nature. The wardrobe of our old nature looks like judgment, hatred, pride, selfishness, cruelty, and anxiety. But it's not enough to just lay aside those things; we must then *put on* our new, beautiful, forgiven, and saved nature from Christ. That wardrobe looks like empathy, compassion, consideration for others, wholesome harmony, patience, and humility.

Clothed in our new nature, we're equipped to forgive—lavishly and freely—as Colossians 3:13 tells us to. Will it be easy? Not always. But the harmony in our relationships that results from working toward forgiveness is well worth the effort of dressing ourselves like Jesus.

Jesus, I need a wardrobe makeover. Show me how to dress!

MONDAY, OCTOBER 19

Jeremiah 24–25 / Colossians 4:2–18 / Proverbs 11:1–11

Every Opportunity

Be wise when you engage with those outside the faith community; make the most of every moment and every encounter. When you speak the word, speak it gracefully (as if seasoned with salt), so you will know how to respond to everyone rightly.
COLOSSIANS 4:5–6 VOICE

In an increasingly sinful world, it may sometimes feel like our Christian lights can't make a difference in the oppressive darkness. Our beliefs and hearts are often at odds with what's happening around us, and it might be tempting to give in to a feeling of defeat.

Take heart, friend. God hasn't called you to save the world—that's His job. What He *has* called to you to is to take advantage of the opportunities around you to inject Jesus into your little corner of the world—*especially* with your non-Christian friends, family, coworkers, and acquaintances.

As with everything in God's kingdom, it starts with love. Get creative in ways to serve others while expecting nothing in return. Pray for the people you know who don't have a relationship with Jesus. If they come to you with questions, be open and willing to meet them where they are in their understanding—or lack thereof—of God, faith, and the Bible. Ask the Holy Spirit to give you the right words to say that will help them connect with Him.

Use me, Lord, to connect You with the people in my life who don't know You. . .yet.

TUESDAY, OCTOBER 20

Jeremiah 26–27 / 1 Thessalonians 1:1–2:8 / Proverbs 11:12–21

Borrowers and Cosigners

*There's danger in putting up security for a stranger's debt;
it's safer not to guarantee another person's debt.*
PROVERBS 11:15 NLT

This nugget of wisdom in Proverbs 11:15 is important enough that it's mentioned six times throughout the thirty-one chapters of Proverbs. Essentially, the proverb says it's a bad idea to cosign for someone else's debt (see also 6:1–5; 17:18; 20:16; 22:26; 27:13).

At face value, being a cosigner seems like it would be a kind and loving thing to do—to back up someone who doesn't have enough credit to qualify for a loan. But as soon as you are the backup source of payment if/when that person defaults on the loan, that relationship changes. First, whatever your ties to that person are (friend, family), your finances are now legally tied. Outside of a marriage, it's not wise to be personally financially entangled with anyone in this way. Second, there's a real chance that any financial misstep by the borrower will severely damage or break your relationship. Cosign a loan, and you're playing with relational and fiscal fire.

Of course, there are situations where you may really want to help. If you are financially able, consider simply giving that person the money—no repayment plan, no strings attached. It's a beautiful metaphor of the love and grace that God offers everyone, and it may open an opportunity for not only your faith but also the other person's faith to blossom.

*God, please give me the wisdom to know
how to handle my finances wisely.*

WEDNESDAY, OCTOBER 21

Jeremiah 28–29 / 1 Thessalonians 2:9–3:13 / Proverbs 11:22–26

His Plans Are Good

"For I know the plans I have for you," says the Lord.
"They are plans for good and not for disaster,
to give you a future and a hope."
JEREMIAH 29:11 NLT

Jeremiah 29:11 is often quoted around graduation time—when we send our young, eager-eyed youths on to their next great adventure. While God certainly has plans for good for His children in that season, the context for this verse is very different from that.

Jeremiah 29:11 is part of a prophecy spoken to the nation of Judah after they were defeated in battle and taken to Babylon. There they will remain—in captivity as slaves—for seventy years. As a people, they're lost and not sure how to act in a foreign land. So through Jeremiah, God sent some instructions telling them that while they are in Babylon they should build homes, plant gardens, marry, and have children—dig in and seek peace and prosperity where they are. All of this, verse 11 says, is part of God's plan for ultimate good. Judah's future is safe in the hands of their Almighty God and Father.

Jeremiah chapter 29 reminds us that even in difficult situations, sometimes we are called to put one foot in front of the other, keep going, and be resilient. Blessings can blossom anywhere His path leads us.

God, when I'm struggling in a difficult season, remind me that You have not forgotten me. I trust You with my future, Father!

THURSDAY, OCTOBER 22

Jeremiah 30:1–31:22 / 1 Thessalonians 4:1–5:11 / Proverbs 11:27–31

Get Ready

But since we belong to the day, let us be sober, having put on the breastplate of faith and love, and for a helmet the hope of salvation. . . . Therefore encourage one another and build one another up, just as you are doing.

1 Thessalonians 5:8, 11 esv

Some full-time firefighters who work twenty-four-hour shifts choose to sleep in their uniforms. That way they are prepared to jump into action when the bell goes off with an emergency call for their station and crew.

Paul, in 1 Thessalonians 5:8, urges Christians—both in the first century and today—to stay alert and prepare ourselves for Christ's return by dressing ourselves in the armor of God (see Ephesians 6:10–18). The Bible tells us that nobody knows when Jesus will return (Matthew 24:36, 42), and for someone who isn't prepared for Jesus' second coming, this is a frightening prospect. But for Christians—those of us saved by grace through faith for the forgiveness of our sins—we can be assured that our eternal home is in heaven in the presence of God. We don't need to live in fear of the future!

We should build up our fellow Christians by living in this confident hope of heaven. Today and every day, suit up in the armor of God, keep your eyes on the clouds, and encourage others to do the same.

Come quickly, Lord Jesus! This world needs redemption, and I will stay focused, prepared for You to make all things new.

FRIDAY, OCTOBER 23

Jeremiah 31:23–32:35 / 1 Thessalonians 5:12–28 / Proverbs 12:1–14

A Daily Choice

Wickedness never brings stability, but the godly have deep roots. . . . The wicked die and disappear, but the family of the godly stands firm. . . . Wise words bring many benefits, and hard work brings rewards.
Proverbs 12:3, 7, 14 nlt

Every day you have a choice of what to put your trust in. Maybe you choose to rely on your bank account and investments in the stock market; your career and current position at work; or your reputation, friends, family, or circle of influence. While any of these can be blessings from God, none are firm foundations to build a life upon—just ask Job!

Instead, if you want stability (and who in their right mind doesn't?), choose to root down into your relationship with God and build your life on Him. Create connections and lasting bonds with other believers through His church—Jesus' beacon of hope and steadfast anchor in this dark world. Work hard in whatever you do, as if you're working for the Savior Himself—because working for His glory brings lasting blessings both now and for eternity.

When life feels chaotic, check your footing. His way is the only way to hope, confidence, and lasting peace.

Lord, I will stand on and for Your truth in this world. With the help of the Holy Spirit, I will walk with confident steps on Your path. Please lead me in a life of integrity. Help me to trust in You more each day.

SATURDAY, OCTOBER 24

Jeremiah 32:36–34:7 / 2 Thessalonians 1–2 / Proverbs 12:15–20

Hold Tight

So then, brothers and sisters, stand firm and hold fast to the teachings we passed on to you, whether by word of mouth or by letter.
2 Thessalonians 2:15 niv

The tightest grip strength in the universe is a mom holding hands with a "runner" toddler in a busy parking lot. The very life of her little one depends on her ability to keep a firm hold on a tiny, wriggling, often-sticky hand. She loves her little runner more than she loves her own life, and she'd do anything to keep her child safe.

That's the kind of intention and devotion that the apostle Paul encourages us to have when it comes to holding on to the godly teaching we learn. Whether that's through scriptural wisdom passed down from parents and grandparents, Sunday school or vacation Bible school lessons, biblical teaching through sermons, or our personal Bible study, all of these are precious to our faith and should be guarded at all costs.

Keeping a firm grip on our biblical knowledge is easiest when we are regularly in His Word. Devotional books like this one—resources that rely on God's Word as the source of its inspiration and encouragement—are fantastic tools for doing just that. Ask the Lord to give you a renewed hunger for His wisdom and teachings today!

Lord, I will hold tight to Your wisdom and knowledge I have learned in the past, and I look forward to deepening my understanding now and in the future.

SUNDAY, OCTOBER 25

Jeremiah 34:8–36:10 / 2 Thessalonians 3 / Proverbs 12:21–28

Humble Wisdom

*The wise don't make a show of their knowledge,
but fools broadcast their foolishness.*
PROVERBS 12:23 NLT

There are those among us who just *have* to be right...those whose favorite response is "I told you so." This sort of personality can often be described with words that start with a *b*: braggart, boaster, blustering...blowhard. These know-it-alls are often insufferable and arrogant, and they can't be reasoned with. And forget having a civil debate on any topic...because they're often unable to see or even open themselves up to another opinion or perspective.

God's Word tells us this is an unwise way to live. "Fools have no interest in understanding," Proverbs 18:2 (NLT) says, "they only want to air their own opinions."

So if you catch a glimpse of yourself in any of the descriptors above, search your heart and your motives. What's causing you to feel like you must have all the answers and always be right? Free yourself from that burden by admitting that you don't know it all—only God does. Submit to the Father's radical teaching that calls you to lay down your pride and find true wisdom and peace in humility (Proverbs 11:2).

When I admit I don't know it all, Lord, I feel adrift and vulnerable. Help me to rest in the fact that it's not my job to have all knowledge—that's Your job. Give me peace to know that You have everything under control.

MONDAY, OCTOBER 26

Jeremiah 36:11–38:13 / 1 Timothy 1:1–17 / Proverbs 13:1–4

Your Jesus Story

Here is a trustworthy saying that deserves full acceptance: Christ Jesus came into the world to save sinners—of whom I am the worst. But for that very reason I was shown mercy so that in me, the worst of sinners, Christ Jesus might display his immense patience as an example for those who would believe in him and receive eternal life.

1 TIMOTHY 1:15–16 NIV

You have a Jesus story to tell. It doesn't matter if you were born into a family that lavished you in God's love from the moment you took your first breath. . .or if the Father's love found you in another way and through people who may not be blood related to you. Your path to salvation and your journey in faith are important and unique and influential—not because of what you have done but because of everything Jesus has done.

The apostle Paul used his story to reach out to others and to connect them to their salvation and Savior. He was real, open, and honest about his shameful past, joyful present, and hopeful future. We too have stories and struggles that are so important to share with others—to encourage them in the fact that no one is beyond God's reach and love.

Who needs to hear your story today?

You have written Your good news all over my life, Jesus. Forgive me when I've kept Your story to myself. Show me opportunities to share our story today.

TUESDAY, OCTOBER 27

Jeremiah 38:14–40:6 / 1 Timothy 1:18–3:13 / Proverbs 13:5–13

Pray for All People

I urge God's people to pray. They should make their requests, petitions, and thanksgivings on behalf of all humanity. Teach them to pray for kings (or anyone in high places for that matter) so that we can lead quiet, peaceful lives—reverent, godly, and holy—all of which is good and acceptable before the eyes of God our Savior.

1 TIMOTHY 2:1–3 VOICE

The apostle Paul wrote this letter to Timothy, who was combating false teaching in the church at Ephesus. These teachers may have been telling believers to pray only for certain people. But Paul reminds Timothy and us that God's plan, God's love, and God's mercy are for everyone—so we should pray for *all people*. That includes praying for our enemies and those who mean to do us harm (Matthew 5:44), those who aren't yet saved (1 Timothy 2:4), and even those in authority over us—employers, officials, those in the government. . .whether we voted for them or not. This takes *immense* humility, especially today. But even when our leaders and elected officials are not who we would choose to hold the power, we must acknowledge that God's plan includes them being in that position. And His plan is always good.

How many people are on your prayer list? When you pray for all people, you are praying in harmony with the heart of God.

You are the Lord of all humanity, Father, and I will be faithful to pray for all!

WEDNESDAY, OCTOBER 28

Jeremiah 40:7–42:22 / 1 Timothy 3:14–4:10 / Proverbs 13:14–21

Shouting into the Void

Do not waste time arguing over godless ideas and old wives' tales. Instead, train yourself to be godly. "Physical training is good, but training for godliness is much better. . . ." This is a trustworthy saying, and everyone should accept it.

1 TIMOTHY 4:7–9 NLT

This world is full of meaningless arguments. Misunderstandings, popular opinion, politics, child-rearing tactics, interior design, health and fitness strategies. . .the list is endless. Whether the arguments take place on the internet or face-to-face, these fights leave us frustrated and accomplish nothing.

The apostle Paul knew that Christians would be tempted by these meaningless traps, so he wrote in 1 Timothy 6:20 (NLT) to "avoid godless, foolish discussions with those who oppose you with their so-called knowledge." Even the first-century Christians had to deal with a world that was shouting into the void. . .without the help of social media!

Instead of engaging in meaningless debate, Paul writes, pursue becoming godly in your thoughts, actions, and words. What's the best way to do that? Seek wisdom in His Word and let it soak into your heart and mind. Ask God to grant you wisdom. Find biblical teaching in a fellowship of believers. Then put into practice what you have learned by working hard to avoid meaningless conversations and, if you do get pulled into a godless debate, always respond wisely with God's love.

Keep me away from the trap of meaningless arguments, Father.

THURSDAY, OCTOBER 29

Jeremiah 43–44 / 1 Timothy 4:11–5:16 / Proverbs 13:22–25

Church Relationships

Respect an elderly man. Don't speak to him sharply; appeal to him as you would a father. Treat younger men as brothers, elderly women as mothers, and younger women as sisters in all purity.
1 TIMOTHY 5:1–2 VOICE

While Paul is writing to a pastor, Timothy, in the above verses, the apostle's instructions here are important for all Christians in the church. We are to treat our people in the church as we would our own family members. Those older than us deserve our respect in the same way our parents deserve our respect. Treat men and women who are our peers and younger than us as brothers and sisters in Christ. Church members, particularly those who hold leadership positions, can avoid certain sins—especially sexual sins—by seeing others as children of God rather than objects of temptation or manipulation. Paul's letter to Timothy builds on the metaphor of the church as the body of Christ—a body that cares for and protects each other.

If you are part of a loving and caring church—praise God for that blessing! If your church lacks in this area, prayerfully consider ways you could grow these kinds of relationships. We can and should honor God in all our relationships—especially within the church!

Father, thank You for the gift of Your church. We are imperfect and struggle in so many ways, but we ask You to be the Lord of our relationships. Bind us together in Your unity!

FRIDAY, OCTOBER 30

Jeremiah 45–47 / 1 Timothy 5:17–6:21 / Proverbs 14:1–6

Learning to be Content

*True godliness with contentment is itself great wealth. . . .
Teach those who are rich in this world not to be proud and
not to trust in their money, which is so unreliable. Their
trust should be in God, who richly gives us all we need for
our enjoyment. Tell them to use their money to do good.
They should be rich in good works and generous to those
in need, always being ready to share with others.*
1 Timothy 6:6, 17–18 nlt

Contentment is a choice, pure and simple.

But Satan whispers, *"You can't possibly be content. . .yet. You need more! When you have as much as your neighbor has. . .then you'll be content."* But "enough" is never truly enough, and our sinful selves crave more and more.

Instead, like the apostle Paul, we can *choose* to be content regardless of how much or how little we have. We can *choose* to be content no matter what difficult situation we find ourselves in. We can *choose* to trust in our loving Father rather than trust in wealth. We can live in confidence that God will provide what we need and help us curb our ravenous appetite for more. We can *choose* to use our money for good—in a way that honors God. We can *choose* the peace of a contented heart, mind, and spirit.

*Lord, show me how to contentedly rest in
Your goodness, no matter what.*

Halloween   SATURDAY, OCTOBER 31

Jeremiah 48:1–49:6 / 2 Timothy 1 / Proverbs 14:7–22

Wholesomeness

Hold fast and follow the pattern of wholesome and sound teaching which you have heard from me, in [all] the faith and love which are [for us] in Christ Jesus. Guard and keep [with the greatest care] the precious and excellently adapted [Truth] which has been entrusted [to you], by the [help of the] Holy Spirit Who makes His home in us.

2 TIMOTHY 1:13–14 AMPC

The apostle Paul uses the word *wholesome* to describe the biblical teaching he provided to his young protégé, Timothy. This word may seem too old-fashioned to be relevant to us today, but let's dig into what that word really means.

Something that's described as *wholesome* can mean that it promotes overall physical, mental, or spiritual health. *Wholesome* may indicate upright morality, purity, goodness, completeness, and wisdom.

Does that sound countercultural? You bet it is! But it's also part of what makes Christianity so appealingly different from the world's manipulation, cruelty, evil, and darkness. And it's also why it's so important to ask the Holy Spirit to help you stand firm on the unerring truth of God's Word and resist the temptation to conform to the world's faulty definition of truth.

Father, teach me and mold me with the wisdom of Your righteously wholesome truth. Give me discernment to know when Your Word is being taught to me faithfully and well. Create in me a pure heart that is ready and willing to do Your will and hold fast to what is right, Lord.

NOVEMBER 2026

SUNDAY	MONDAY	TUESDAY	WEDNESDAY	THURSDAY	FRIDAY	SATURDAY
1 Daylight Saving Time Ends	2	3 Election Day	4	5	6	7
8	9	10	11 Veterans Day	12	13	14
15	16	17	18	19	20	21
22	23	24	25	26 Thanksgiving	27	28
29	30					

Daylight Saving Time Ends   SUNDAY, NOVEMBER 1

Jeremiah 49:7–50:16 / 2 Timothy 2 / Proverbs 14:23–27

Living Differently

God's servant must not be argumentative, but a gentle listener and a teacher who keeps cool, working firmly but patiently with those who refuse to obey. You never know how or when God might sober them up with a change of heart and a turning to the truth, enabling them to escape the Devil's trap, where they are caught and held captive, forced to run his errands.

2 Timothy 2:24–26 MSG

As believers, we should have lives that look different from those who don't (yet) follow God. We should conduct ourselves with an uncommon set of guidelines found in the Bible, telling us how to act and how to speak. Why? Because our life preaches, and we'd never want to be a barrier to someone coming into a saving faith in Christ.

The reality is that it's not always easy to be a gentle listener, because emotions often quickly get stirred up. Keeping our cool is so much easier said than done, especially when met with staunch resistance to what is good and right. Striking that perfect balance between persuasion and patience takes intentionality. Yet, we're called to live in such ways.

When we're confidently secure in Christ, knowing we're equipped for every situation, we'll find the courage to walk by faith as we interact with others. God will enable us to live with pure motives and a tender heart. And we will find the ability to glorify Him with our actions and words.

Lord, empower me to live differently.

MONDAY, NOVEMBER 2

Jeremiah 50:17–51:14 / 2 Timothy 3 / Proverbs 14:28–35

The Beauty of the Bible

All of Scripture is God-breathed; in its inspired voice, we hear useful teaching, rebuke, correction, instruction, and training for a life that is right so that God's people may be up to the task ahead and have all they need to accomplish every good work.

2 Timothy 3:16–17 voice

For the believer, the Bible is everything. Not only is it how God reveals Himself to those who love Him, it's also filled with relevant and timely teaching on how to live a life that pleases the Lord. Some say it's a man-made document and therefore tainted. They say it's lacking. But the truth is that every word is God-breathed. Men may have penned it, but they were divinely inspired to do so. We can trust the Word without fail.

Make reading the Bible part of your every day. It's how the Lord speaks to us. And if we read with a ready heart, He'll use it to rebuke and correct so we stay on the righteous path. God will let the scriptures provide training, showing us how to live so His name is glorified and our lives are blessed. And it will empower us to embrace the calling and purpose He placed on our one and only life here on earth.

Because your identity is now secured in Christ through a saving faith, spending time in the Word is essential to deepening your faith.

Lord, give me a supernatural love of Your holy Word.

Election Day   TUESDAY, NOVEMBER 3

Jeremiah 51:15–64 / 2 Timothy 4 / Proverbs 15:1–9

Pursuing Righteousness

*The way of the wicked is an abomination,
extremely disgusting and shamefully vile to the Lord,
but He loves him who pursues righteousness (moral
and spiritual rectitude in every area and relation).*

PROVERBS 15:9 AMPC

It doesn't take much to see wickedness in the world. In 2 Timothy 3:2–3 (VOICE), we're told what it looks like: "You see, the world will be filled with narcissistic, money-grubbing, pretentious, arrogant, and abusive people. They will rebel against their parents and will be ungrateful, unholy, uncaring, coldhearted, accusing, without restraint, savage, and haters of anything good." This is the way of the wicked, and it disgusts God.

But when we follow His recipe for righteous living found throughout the pages of His Word, the Lord is pleased. He's not expecting perfection. God fully and completely understands our limitations as humans. But He is looking for purposeful living where we pursue it daily. And unless we dig into scripture, we won't know how to love the Lord in all we do.

As we remember who we are and whose we are, our heart will ache for a deeper relationship with our Father. And accepting the fact that as believers we're in Christ will drive us toward moral and spiritual goodness. This way of walking through each day will please God and bless us.

*Lord, I confess my evil ways and thank You for the
gift of forgiveness. Help me desire righteousness
more and chase after it in every area of my life.*

WEDNESDAY, NOVEMBER 4

Jeremiah 52–Lamentations 1 / Titus 1:1–9 / Proverbs 15:10–17

It's a Certainty

We rest in this hope we've been given—the hope that we will live forever with our God—the hope that He proclaimed ages and ages ago (even before time began). And our God is no liar; He is not even capable of uttering lies. So we can be sure that it is in His exact right time that He released His word into the world—through the preaching that God our Savior has commanded into my care.

TITUS 1:2–3 VOICE

Let's remember that hope isn't wishful thinking. For believers, it's an assurance that God's promises will come to pass. Christian hope is a certainty. It's an inevitability for those whose identity is in Christ. Our God is trustworthy without failing. We can have a confident faith that the Lord is who He says He is and will do what He says He will do. If He declares it, nothing can stop our faithful God from following through. His will is perfect. His ways are perfect. And His timing is absolutely perfect.

Understanding this, how is your heart encouraged today? In what circumstances did you need this timely reminder? How does this strengthen your resolve and instill courage?

There are few things in this world we can count on, but our heavenly Father's love and promises are unwavering. Cling to Him now and be assured of eternity in His presence later.

> *Lord, I'm comforted knowing Your promises are unchanging and Your love for me is unshakable.*

THURSDAY, NOVEMBER 5

Lamentations 2:1–3:38 / Titus 1:10–2:15 / Proverbs 15:18–26

Not Out to Pasture

Guide older women into lives of reverence so they end up as neither gossips nor drunks, but models of goodness. By looking at them, the younger women will know how to love their husbands and children, be virtuous and pure, keep a good house, be good wives. We don't want anyone looking down on God's Message because of their behavior.

Titus 2:3–5 MSG

Paul is encouraging Titus in what to teach those living in Crete. And while these words were written so long ago, the truths found in these verses are still relevant for us today. Never forget that God's Word is alive and active and applicable for us even now.

The reality is that as we get older, we still have a divine purpose to walk out. We're not put out to pasture! Instead, the Lord calls us to represent righteous living for those who are younger and have less life experience to draw from. Scripture tells us to be "models of goodness" so they will know how to live and love according to God's plan.

Ask the Lord to open your eyes to see opportunities where you can humbly and graciously speak into the hearts of younger women. Let your life preach of His goodness in what you say and how you act. And be available. As daughters of the King, we are honored to be His hands and feet in the world.

Lord, use me to encourage others!

FRIDAY, NOVEMBER 6

Lamentations 3:39–5:22 / Titus 3 / Proverbs 15:27–33

There Was a Time

Don't tear down another person with your words. Instead, keep the peace, and be considerate. Be truly humble toward everyone because there was a time when we, too, were foolish, rebellious, and deceived—we were slaves to sensual cravings and pleasures; and we spent our lives being spiteful, envious, hated by many, and hating one another. But then something happened: God our Savior and His overpowering love and kindness for humankind entered our world.

TITUS 3:2–4 VOICE

We may be faithful believers who pursue righteous living that pleases God, but there was a time when we were wretched. Amen? In Titus 3:2–4, Paul reminds us of this truth so we will have compassion for those still stuck in their unrepentant ways of living. There was a time we were walking that same path. Our sins may have looked different, but we were foolish, rebellious, and deceived. But then we found Jesus.

He changed our heart when He became our Savior. And it's His love and compassion for all of humanity that now flows through our veins. Rather than sit in judgment and condemnation, let's choose to be humble as we navigate this life in service to the Lord. Let's be grateful for our transformation and generous as we minister to others. And let's remember the kindness He showed us so we can extend that grace toward those we encounter every day.

Lord, give me a heart of humility rather than one of harshness.

SATURDAY, NOVEMBER 7

Ezekiel 1:1–3:21 / Philemon 1 / Proverbs 16:1–9

God Is in Control

A man's mind plans his way, but the Lord
directs his steps and makes them sure.
PROVERBS 16:9 AMPC

Proverbs 16:9 brings to light the relationship between man's devising and God's directing. Often, they are very different! Maybe you've experienced this firsthand in your life. And while there is great wisdom in us making plans for the future, we should do so prayerfully as we seek His leading, knowing that the Lord is the great course corrector and will intervene as needed.

We can trust that God is in control, designing each situation for our good and His glory. We can trust that He will guide our steps and make them sure. Whether we're working through how to proceed in a relationship or deciding how to approach a difficult conversation at work or plotting personal goals for the next year, we can find comfort in God's sovereignty. Ultimately and thankfully, He is in control.

So as we plan ahead, let's remember these beautiful truths. Let's allow them to bring comfort because we know from scripture that our Father has power over every outcome. He will lead us in all the right ways according to His perfect will because we are His beloved daughters.

Lord, I want my life to have Your fingerprints all over it.
I want to conduct each day knowing You are pleased.
Be quick to get me back on track if I'm heading in
the wrong direction. I trust that You will!

SUNDAY, NOVEMBER 8

Ezekiel 3:22–5:17 / Hebrews 1:1–2:4 / Proverbs 16:10–21

The Problem with Pride

Pride precedes destruction; an arrogant spirit gives way to a nasty fall. It is better to be humble and live among the poor, than to divide up stolen property with the proud. Those devoted to instruction will prosper in goodness; those who trust in the Eternal will experience His favor.
PROVERBS 16:18–20 VOICE

The truth is that having a prideful attitude often leads us to moments of shame and embarrassment. Choosing to be haughty toward others only sets us up for a nasty fall. And scripture tells us it's better to be humble and poor rather than proud and wealthy. God doesn't want us to live life on a pedestal, thinking we are better. . .because we are not. And this kind of thinking is dangerous for believers because it keeps us from a spirit of reverence before the Lord—a surrendering of our will to His.

Friend, as His beloved, we desperately need God in our life. We need His wisdom and discernment. We need His guidance. We need the peace and comfort only the Lord can offer. But a prideful heart says we can provide for ourselves and there's no need for God's intervention. It says we're our own savior. It's deeply flawed, misguided, and ugly.

Whenever you're at the crossroads, choose humility over arrogance. Seek His way over yours. Admit your lacking, and ask God to meet the needs you simply cannot.

Lord, help me humbly trust You in every way and for all things.

MONDAY, NOVEMBER 9

Ezekiel 6–7 / Hebrews 2:5–18 / Proverbs 16:22–33

God Isn't Unfeeling

In the nations where they have been taken as exiles, those who have been spared will remember Me—how I have been wounded by their promiscuous hearts that turned away from Me, how I have been hurt by their wandering eyes that desired lifeless idols. They will hate themselves for the evil they have done and for their detestable actions. Then they will know I am the Eternal One. They will understand I did not utter empty threats when I said I would bring disaster on them.

EZEKIEL 6:9–10 VOICE

When we turn our back on God, it hurts Him. When we continue to make selfish choices instead of obeying His commands, the Lord is wounded. Today's verses reveal that our Father isn't unfeeling. Our words and actions can bring either delight or discouragement to His heart. And while God is clear in the Bible regarding His expectations and commands for those who belong to Him, the choice is ours to make.

Remember that He doesn't expect us to live perfect lives without flaws and blunders. He completely understands our shortcomings, because the Lord knows this is a fallen world full of sinners. He knows the enemy is at work every day. But instead, God wants us to live purposeful lives, seeking Him daily for hope and help. And as we do, He is well pleased and promises to work every situation we face for our good.

Lord, help me choose You first and foremost!

TUESDAY, NOVEMBER 10

Ezekiel 8–10 / Hebrews 3:1–4:3 / Proverbs 17:1–5

Loving Others

Wrongdoers perk up when listening to gossip, and liars lean in close to hear talk of mischief. Anyone who makes fun of the poor disparages his Maker, and those who celebrate another's misfortune will not escape certain punishment.

PROVERBS 17:4–5 VOICE

Because we are daughters of the King, our hearts should break for what breaks His. We should love what He loves and hate what He hates. God's compassion for the lost and broken should course through our veins as we willingly serve them. Rather than participate in bad behaviors like lying, gossiping, and acting disparagingly, our love for the Lord should extend toward those He created. We shouldn't celebrate when others run into trouble but show them mercy and offer help. The truth is that our heart and actions reveal our faith.

Even though we know it displeases God, sometimes we choose to withhold kindness. We feel justified for not being generous with our time and treasure. We may even smirk when they get what we think they deserve from life. But as women of God, we know this goes against His command to love others. This isn't the way we've been told to treat people.

Is the Lord asking you to repent? Is there someone you need to ask for forgiveness? Has your heart been hardened toward someone? Let today's verses drive you to God as you seek to make things right.

Lord, please give me Your heart for others so I bless rather than curse.

Veterans Day WEDNESDAY, NOVEMBER 11

Ezekiel 11–12 / Hebrews 4:4–5:10 / Proverbs 17:6–12

The Word of God

The word of God, you see, is alive and moving; sharper than a double-edged sword; piercing the divide between soul and spirit, joints and marrow; able to judge the thoughts and will of the heart. No creature can hide from God: God sees all. Everyone and everything is exposed, opened for His inspection; and He's the One we will have to explain ourselves to.

HEBREWS 4:12–13 VOICE

There are so many blessings that we're thankful for as believers! We have forgiveness through Jesus' death on the cross. We have the Holy Spirit who lives within us, activating and growing our faith. We have God's steadfast love to cling to. We have the promise of eternity in heaven. And we have God's holy Word.

Hebrews 4:12–13 tells us that the Bible is alive and active. Within the heart of a believer, it has the power to convict, challenge, and celebrate. It allows us to see our desperate need for God in our life. It reveals His goodness in meaningful ways through the testimonies of those before us. It opens our eyes to sinful behavior and unpacks what righteous living looks like. And it helps to deepen our faith and connection to our Creator. The Word is a weighty tool in the hands of a Christ follower.

Lord, thank You for every blessing, including the Bible. Create in me a craving that drives me into its pages. Speak to me through it as I seek You in it.

THURSDAY, NOVEMBER 12

Ezekiel 13–14 / Hebrews 5:11–6:20 / Proverbs 17:13–22

The Blessing of Good Friendships

*A true friend loves regardless of the situation,
and a real brother exists to share the tough times.*
PROVERBS 17:17 VOICE

In this life, one of the greatest blessings we have here on earth are good friendships. If you really think about it, friends are often the ones who hold us up during difficult times, reminding us we are seen and valued. It's good friends who love us enough to call us out when we're at fault and link arms with us when we're facing attacks. And regardless of the situation at hand, they are our trusted battle buddies.

Who are the good friends in your life? Who are the ones who stand with you no matter what? Think of the women who've helped you navigate a divorce or prayed with you about a prodigal child. Who's supported you through infertility treatments or the loss of someone important? Who has talked you off the proverbial ledge more than once? Think of those who cleaned your house, cooked your family meals, or carted your kids back and forth when you were sick. Who are the ones you call when life punches you in the gut?

Take a minute and thank God for them, and then reach out and let them know how much you love and appreciate them.

Lord, thank You for the women You've put in my life. I appreciate how fully and completely You take care of those who are Yours.

FRIDAY, NOVEMBER 13

Ezekiel 15:1–16:43 / Hebrews 7:1–28 / Proverbs 17:23–28

Staying Silent

Those with knowledge know when to be quiet, and those with understanding know how to remain calm. Even a fool who keeps quiet is considered wise, for when he keeps his mouth shut, he appears clever.
PROVERBS 17:27–28 VOICE

Sometimes the best thing we can do is shut our mouth. There are moments when silence is golden. It's a smart move so we don't say the wrong thing. Keeping quiet allows us to maintain our composure, choosing not to say what may really be on our mind to share. But as believers, we can trust that God will always equip us to make the right choices at the right times. And because He understands us fully and completely, He knows when we need an extra dose of discernment.

Why are there moments when we should be quiet and remain calm? Because even while it may feel good to spew our thoughts and feelings on someone, chances are it's not how we truly feel. In the moment, yes. But it's foolish to show that lack of judgment.

When we placed our identity in Christ, the Holy Spirit took up residence in our heart to guide us and teach righteous living. We can trust Him to nudge us when headed down a dangerous path. And as we pray for God's help to not speak temporary feelings to wound or true feelings in the wrong way, He will.

Lord, help me know when to speak and when to stay quiet.

SATURDAY, NOVEMBER 14

Ezekiel 16:44–17:24 / Hebrews 8:1–9:10 / Proverbs 18:1–7

Our God of Order

In there they placed the golden incense altar and the golden ark of the covenant. Inside the ark were the golden urn that contained manna (the miraculous food God gave our ancestors in the desert), Aaron's rod that budded, and the tablets of the covenant that Moses brought down from the mountain. Above the ark were the golden images of heavenly beings of glory who shadowed the mercy seat.
HEBREWS 9:4–5 VOICE

Our God is not a God of confusion. He does not promote chaos for those who call on His name. While His thoughts are higher than our thoughts, the Lord doesn't think up ways to bring mayhem and turmoil into the lives of believers. Instead, He is a God of clarity and order.

Hebrews 9:4–5 revisits the detailed plans He gave to Moses for building His earthly sanctuary, setting up the rules and regulations for how to worship Him. He provided very specific blueprints, ensuring no misunderstanding.

Let this bring you great encouragement today, friend. We can trust God to speak to our heart calmly and in orderly fashion. The Holy Spirit will guide us with stability. And we can rest in His presence, knowing we are secure as His daughters. He deeply and perfectly loves us, and as we seek Him, God's voice will provide clear direction.

Lord, help me know Your plans for my life. Direct me in each step. Bring order to the chaos my heart is feeling right now.

SUNDAY, NOVEMBER 15

Ezekiel 18–19 / Hebrews 9:11–28 / Proverbs 18:8–17

The Promise of Eternity

Just as mortals are appointed to die once and then to experience a judgment, so the Anointed One, our Liberating King, was offered once in death to bear the sins of many and will appear a second time, not to deal again with sin, but to rescue those who eagerly await His return.
HEBREWS 9:27–28 VOICE

As a child of God, you have the assurance that He will return. Jesus came to earth to share the good news and eventually hang on a cross, paying for the sins of those who accept Him as Savior. He liberated us and bridged the gap our trespasses created between us and the Father! Believers now have the gift of the Holy Spirit to lead and guide life while here. And soon—be it through death or His return—we will see Him face-to-face and spend eternity in the Lord's presence. Can you even imagine?

Never forget the value you have in the eyes of God. Jesus' sacrifice has made you accepted, forgiven, and redeemed. Through Him, you're equipped for all good works and will find the courage and confidence to walk out the mighty purpose He created just for you. The Lord promises to protect you, keeping you safe in His arms. Trust, without a doubt, that you're deeply loved by a perfect God who knows every detail of your life. This is who you will spend eternity with!

Lord, You are my everything!

MONDAY, NOVEMBER 16

> Ezekiel 20 / Hebrews 10:1–25 / Proverbs 18:18–24

Choosing Togetherness

Let us hold strong to the confession of our hope, never wavering, since the One who promised it to us is faithful. Let us consider how to inspire each other to greater love and to righteous deeds, not forgetting to gather as a community, as some have forgotten, but encouraging each other, especially as the day of His return approaches.
HEBREWS 10:23–25 VOICE

The writer of Hebrews offers solid advice as we navigate the ups and downs of life. We're to cling to the hope of Jesus, find ways to encourage others to stand strong in faith, and gather in community regularly.

Which of these seems to be the hardest for you? Which one poses the biggest challenges? For many, it's intentionally choosing togetherness. Why? Because community is messy and offers countless reasons to shy away from it. Yet as our Father, God created us for it, and His command is that we connect in meaningful and significant ways. We need each other! We need to be around those who've also anchored their identity in Christ. And as life beats us up and the world gets crazier, we need the unity and cooperation that being together offers believers. The Lord knows what is best for those He loves. We can trust in that!

Lord, give me a heart for community and the grace for its imperfections. And use me in it to bless others, as they bless me.

TUESDAY, NOVEMBER 17

Ezekiel 21–22 / Hebrews 10:26–39 / Proverbs 19:1–8

Does It Sound Crazy?

Now as for you, son of man, groan as if your heart is breaking. Groan in front of people because of your bitter agony! When they see you, they will ask you, "Why all this loud and noisy groaning?" Answer them this way: "I am groaning because of the horrible news that is coming. Every heart will melt, every hand will fall limp, every spirit will grow faint, and every knee will become as weak as water. So pay attention. The time is near! It is going to happen soon."

Ezekiel 21:6–7 VOICE

The prophet Ezekial was a trooper. Throughout the book, you see how God wants him to act out His messages to the people, and most of Ezekiel's instructions from God are radical and seem crazy. But he obeys and trusts God and the ways He wants His messages to be delivered. Today's passage of scripture is one of those times. Ezekiel is physically demonstrating what it will be like when the bad news of what's happened in the city of Jerusalem reaches the people.

For us, it can sometimes feel like what God is asking is crazy too. We may feel incapable of obeying, physically or emotionally unable to do what's being asked. It may seem overwhelming to consider walking it out. But because we're women who love the Lord, our faith must win out. We must trust that His reasons are right.

Lord, give me the courage and confidence to obey, even when it sounds crazy.

WEDNESDAY, NOVEMBER 18

Ezekiel 23 / Hebrews 11:1–31 / Proverbs 19:9–14

Faith and Hope

Faith is the assurance of things you have hoped for, the absolute conviction that there are realities you've never seen. It was by faith that our forebears were approved. Through faith we understand that the universe was created by the word of God; everything we now see was fashioned from that which is invisible.

Hebrews 11:1–3 voice

The author follows these verses with powerful examples of men and women who demonstrated faith as "the assurance of things... hoped for." These pillars of the faith were still living in hope when they died. Abel, Enoch, Noah, Abraham, and Sarah all passed away without receiving the full promises in this life. They never gave up. Throughout the Bible, we read testimonies of the faithful who trusted God as they faced joy-draining and spine-weakening circumstances.

Hope is a powerful tool in the life of believers because it fuels our motivation to endure and drives us to obey. It did back in the day, and it still does now. It's why we can stand confidently in our faith and walk out the purposes God has for us. From serving the downtrodden to loving sacrificially to sharing the gospel, we are steadfast in our desire to please the one who created and called us. Let nothing stop you from running your race until you see Jesus face-to-face.

Lord, let my faith be what drives me to stand firm in my identity in Christ and all that comes with it.

THURSDAY, NOVEMBER 19

Ezekiel 24–26 / Hebrews 11:32–40 / Proverbs 19:15–21

The Command to Care

Whoever cares for the poor makes a loan to the Eternal; such kindness will be repaid in full and with interest.
PROVERBS 19:17 VOICE

The greatest commandment is to love God with all our heart, soul, mind, and strength, and the second is to love our neighbor as ourselves. Love is a big deal to the Lord, and the Bible is filled with charges to walk this out, especially as believers. We're to love what He loves. Our heart is to break for what breaks His. And when we turn our backs on others or refuse to show compassion and kindness, we're going against His plan.

God rewards those who care about the well-being of their neighbors. He delights when we show consideration to our enemies. He is pleased when we show generosity to those we don't even know. As His daughters, we're to be a light that shines into this dark world. And the Lord will equip us to love and care for others in meaningful and significant ways. He will give us the courage to be His hands and feet to the world.

We're able to love because He first loved us. Once we anchored our identity in Christ, we received the ability to show divine care and compassion through His empowerment. If you're struggling with this today and want your hardened heart tendered toward others, talk to God about it.

Lord, I know through You I'm capable of great things. Remind me.

FRIDAY, NOVEMBER 20

Ezekiel 27–28 / Hebrews 12:1–13 / Proverbs 19:22–29

Divine Discipline

Remember, when our human parents disciplined us, we respected them. If that was true, shouldn't we respect and live under the correction of the Father of all spirits even more? . . . When punishment is happening, it never seems pleasant, only painful. Later, though, it yields the peaceful fruit called righteousness to everyone who has been trained by it.
HEBREWS 12:9, 11 VOICE

No one enjoys being disciplined for a misstep. We don't like being called out for any wrongdoing, purposeful or accidental. And chances are this truth knits us together as women. It's not that we think we're perfect, but it can be embarrassing and discouraging to be corrected. We don't much appreciate our flaws being on display. But maybe we have the wrong perspective.

Being God's daughters brings with it the promise of His goodness. And part of that goodness is His divine discipline. It may seem painful in the moment, but when He brings correction, it's meant to keep us within the guardrails of righteousness. We may not even realize we've stepped outside of them. But we can rest knowing that our Father loves us enough to bring revelation and restoration. It's protection in the most loving way, and we can trust it.

If God didn't care about us, He wouldn't do all He could to bring us back into His will. We're not left to navigate life alone. And His discipline will always yield peaceful fruit.

Lord, I trust that Your discipline is part of Your love.

SATURDAY, NOVEMBER 21

Ezekiel 29–30 / Hebrews 12:14–29 / Proverbs 20:1–18

Unshakable

Do you see what we've got? An unshakable kingdom! And do you see how thankful we must be? Not only thankful, but brimming with worship, deeply reverent before God. For God is not an indifferent bystander. He's actively cleaning house, torching all that needs to burn, and he won't quit until it's all cleansed. God himself is Fire!

HEBREWS 12:28–29 MSG

What a relief to know that we are part of an unshakable kingdom. What does that mean? It means that our God is unchangeable. His love is unwavering. His will is unswerving. The Lord's promises are unmovable. His grace and mercy are unalterable. His compassion for those whose identity is in Christ is unyielding. God's forgiveness for our sins—past, present, and future—is unaffected by anything earthly or heavenly. He is unrelenting toward those He loves and calls His own. These are beautiful blessings we can count on.

While we're living in a world that shakes us constantly, let's choose to cling to the only one who can steady our heart. Relationships may be challenging and bring us angst. Our health may be a daily struggle. We may face unmentionable loss and grief, leaving us unable to find our footing. Finances may fail. And these may leave our faith shuddering at times. But we can choose to worship and praise a loving Father who cannot be shaken and will hold us securely in real time as we navigate each day.

Lord, thank You for being unshakable.

SUNDAY, NOVEMBER 22

Ezekiel 31–32 / Hebrews 13 / Proverbs 20:19–24

Is Your Love Misdirected?

Keep your lives free from the love of money, and be content with what you have because He has said, "I will never leave you; I will always be by your side." Because of this promise, we may boldly say, The Lord is my help—I won't be afraid of anything. How can anyone harm me?

HEBREWS 13:5–6 VOICE

Because we live in a world that worships everything of its own making, we can sometimes fall into the trap of materialism. We often unknowingly subscribe to what it says is good and right, pursuing all the things that promote selfishness. And at the root—at least most of the time—is the *love* of money. We want more. We want bigger and better. And we want to keep up with those around us. So, our daily pursuit becomes focused on the dollar rather than the divine.

But since we're believers, our love should be for God first and foremost and then toward others. Those are the two greatest commandments. When we misdirect that adoration to anything earthly, the love of it gets us in trouble.

Rather than crave treasures here, we should remember scripture's reminder that God is always with us. Our desire should be for more of Him. We should invest time and effort into deepening our relationship. And then we will truly grasp that the Father fully knows us and completely loves us, and the love of money will subside.

Lord, help me love You most.

MONDAY, NOVEMBER 23

Ezekiel 33:1–34:10 / James 1 / Proverbs 20:25–30

We Need Trials and Hardships

Don't run from tests and hardships, brothers and sisters. As difficult as they are, you will ultimately find joy in them; if you embrace them, your faith will blossom under pressure and teach you true patience as you endure. And true patience brought on by endurance will equip you to complete the long journey and cross the finish line—mature, complete, and wanting nothing.
JAMES 1:2–4 VOICE

It's hard to stand strong when life is beating you up. We may think that as believers, we'll be exempt from hardship, but that's wrong. We may think God will protect us from struggles, but that simply isn't how a life in Christ works. Instead, we will be tried by adversity. We can expect to be tested by fire. But the Bible says *we can do all things through Christ who strengthens us* (Philippians 4:13).

The truth is that we need these difficult moments to grow deeper in our faith. They produce in us the patience and endurance needed for this journey of faith. Unless we face hardship, how will we know how desperately we need God? How will we grow our faith muscle to withstand all the enemy throws our way? How will our dependence be moved from the earthly to the eternal? The truth is that we need tests and hardships because they have great purpose for those committed to following Jesus.

Lord, I trust You will use every trial for my good and Your glory.

TUESDAY, NOVEMBER 24

Ezekiel 34:11–36:15 / James 2 / Proverbs 21:1–8

Faith in Action

Just like our father in the faith, we are made right with God through good works, not simply by what we believe or think. Even Rahab the prostitute was made right with God by hiding the spies and aiding in their escape. Removing action from faith is like removing breath from a body. All you have left is a corpse.
JAMES 2:24–26 VOICE

The "father in the faith" referred to here is Abraham. He demonstrated his faith by willingly laying his son Isaac on the altar as God asked. For so many reasons, that was a big ask! But he fully trusted the Lord and proved it through obedience. Abraham's faith manifested in his behavior. And it earned him the title of "God's friend."

James says that removing action from faith just doesn't work. While salvation comes through faith alone, our life should reveal those deep beliefs in what we do and say. Salvation must show itself through works.

Let's be watchful to make sure our life is preaching in all the right ways. Do we love and forgive? Are we full of compassion for the broken? Do we make the hard choices that align with God's will? It's not performance driven but faith driven. It's simply an overflow of the heart, knowing we're perfectly and fully loved by the Father.

Lord, let my faith be naturally demonstrated in how I live and love each day. Let my life choices always point to You.

WEDNESDAY, NOVEMBER 25

Ezekiel 36:16–37:28 / James 3 / Proverbs 21:9–18

To Bless and Not Curse

Have you ever seen a massive ship sailing effortlessly across the water? Despite its immense size and the fact that it is propelled by mighty winds, a small rudder directs the ship in any direction the pilot chooses. It's just the same with our tongues! It's a small muscle, capable of marvelous undertakings.

JAMES 3:4–5 VOICE

The tongue may be a small muscle, but it's a mighty one. If not careful, it can do irreparable damage to those we love the most. It can also be used to bring encouragement and affirmation that's a game changer. And we get to decide.

The more time we spend in God's Word, the more manageable the tongue will become. The Bible is alive and active, and it trains believers in how to live righteously, blessing others and glorifying the Lord. It helps highlight the places we need Him to soften our words and tender our heart. And its transformative power will be demonstrated through our tongue.

When we put our identity in Christ through saving faith, we invited Him to make us more like Jesus. We surrendered our will to His. And we revealed the desire for divine changes to take place in our heart that would be displayed in our life. And with that comes the ability to tame the tongue to bless and not curse.

> *Lord, help me know when to speak and when to stay silent. Let my words only be used for good.*

THURSDAY, NOVEMBER 26 *Thanksgiving*

Ezekiel 38–39 / James 4:1–5:6 / Proverbs 21:19–24

Submit and Draw Close

So submit yourselves to the one true God and fight against the devil and his schemes. If you do, he will run away in failure. Come close to the one true God, and He will draw close to you. Wash your hands; you have dirtied them in sin. Cleanse your heart, because your mind is split down the middle, your love for God on one side and selfish pursuits on the other.

JAMES 4:7–8 VOICE

What a needed reminder that we're to submit and draw close to God when temptation comes our way. This is what enables us to stand strong in faith and not rely on our own strength, which always fails and fumbles. The moment we feel the battle begin, as believers we're invited to go right to God because He will draw us close and empower us in all the right ways.

Where is your battle today, weary one? Are you navigating loss in negative ways? Are you being tempted to step outside your unfulfilling marriage? Are you at a loss for how to parent a troubled teen? Are you being asked to compromise for your job? Do your finances feel overwhelming and unmanageable? Do you want to give up?

You are God's beloved. You are accepted, forgiven, redeemed, and valued. You have a great purpose and are equipped for it. As a believer, you are secure and protected in His arms. Don't let sin and selfishness derail you.

Lord, I surrender all.

FRIDAY, NOVEMBER 27

Ezekiel 40 / James 5:7–20 / Proverbs 21:25–31

Grace Over Grumble

Brothers and sisters, don't waste your breath complaining about one another. If you judge others, you will be judged yourself. Be very careful! You will face the one true Judge who is right outside the door.
JAMES 5:9 VOICE

Can you remember the last time you complained about someone? Maybe they frustrated you in a business meeting or they acted selfishly. Maybe they severed your friendship over a petty issue or betrayed your confidence. Or maybe they're haughty, thinking themselves better than everyone else. And out of your wounding, you sat in judgment and gossiped about them to anyone who would listen. We're all guilty of this. But because we are believers, God calls us higher and expects love to rule in our heart.

James 5:9 says complaining and judging are a waste of our time. And if we partake in them, we will face these in return. So let's choose to stand in faith, knowing how deeply loved we are and loving others with the same passion and purpose. If asked, God will equip us to do the hard things. He adds the *extra* to our *ordinary*, enabling great acts of faith from those who are His.

What is the Holy Spirit speaking to you today? Where is He challenging and convicting you? Where do you need to repent? Let the Lord soften your spirit and tender your heart for grace over grumble.

Lord, help me see others through Your eyes, loving even when it's not easy.

SATURDAY, NOVEMBER 28

Ezekiel 41:1–43:12 / 1 Peter 1:1–12 / Proverbs 22:1–9

Enduring the Trials

So be truly glad. There is wonderful joy ahead, even though you must endure many trials for a little while. These trials will show that your faith is genuine. It is being tested as fire tests and purifies gold—though your faith is far more precious than mere gold. So when your faith remains strong through many trials, it will bring you much praise and glory and honor on the day when Jesus Christ is revealed to the whole world.

1 PETER 1:6–7 NLT

This is one of those passages of scripture that clearly tells us that as believers, we will endure hardship. We can expect there to be discouraging and frustrating trials of every kind that will often feel overwhelming. They may be but a moment or an exhausting season, but they will come. We can also expect, however, that God will use them to prove our faith authentic. And that is golden.

It may be a broken marriage or an epic failure as a parent. It may be a financial crisis or an unexpected loss. You may be struggling to get pregnant or tired of being single. Maybe all your best efforts for reconciliation fell short once again. It's times like this when the rubber meets the road of your faith. Will you stand strong in the Lord or fall flat in hopelessness?

Lord, I'm Your child, equipped and capable of great things. Help me lean into my identity in Christ when the trials come.

SUNDAY, NOVEMBER 29

Ezekiel 43:13–44:31 / 1 Peter 1:13–2:3 / Proverbs 22:10–23

Earthly or Eternal

You have been reborn—not from seed that eventually dies but from seed that is eternal—through the word of God that lives and endures forever. For as Isaiah said, All life is like the grass, and its glory like a flower; the grass will wither and die, and the flower falls, but the word of the Lord will endure forever. This is the word that has been preached to you.

1 PETER 1:23–25 VOICE

Everything earthly stays earthly, and eventually withers and dies. But what is eternal rests there, never ending and always enduring. As believers, we should keep this in mind as we navigate this life.

The problem is that too often we invest our time and treasure in the here and now. We overspend to keep up and focus on satisfying our fleshy needs and desires. Do you see this happening in your own life? Are you more concerned with what the world offers, working hard to create something perfect and comfortable here? Do you crave the treasures this life provides first and foremost? Or are your eyes trained on deepening your relationship with God and walking out His commands each day? Are you committed to storing up your treasures in heaven?

Today, spend time unpacking this with the Lord, taking an honest inventory and making changes where necessary.

Lord, give me keen discernment to know when my focus turns from eternal to earthly. Let my eyes stay trained on what endures forever.

MONDAY, NOVEMBER 30

Ezekiel 45–46 / 1 Peter 2:4–17 / Proverbs 22:24–29

Your True Identity

But you are the ones chosen by God, chosen for the high calling of priestly work, chosen to be a holy people, God's instruments to do his work and speak out for him, to tell others of the night-and-day difference he made for you—from nothing to something, from rejected to accepted.

1 PETER 2:9–10 MSG

This world may beat you up and call you names. They may try to steal your joy and upend your peace. You may be slandered, labeled, and judged harshly simply for being yourself. But that doesn't take anything away from who you are in Christ Jesus. Be encouraged today to stand strong in that identity, no matter what anyone has to say.

Never forget you are accepted, forgiven, and redeemed through the cross. You're celebrated and deeply loved. You hold immeasurable value in your Father's eyes, regardless of those pesky imperfections. You're chosen for a high calling and capable through God's equipping. Through the blood of Jesus, you're holy. You were designed for a purpose that He personalized just for you. And God knows you fully and completely, delighting in His creation.

Be courageous. Keep your eyes turned toward the Lord every day. For He will hold you securely in His arms and empower you to withstand anything the world throws at you.

Lord, thank You for creating me to have great value and making me for a purpose. Help me stand firm in faith no matter what.

DECEMBER 2026

SUNDAY	MONDAY	TUESDAY	WEDNESDAY	THURSDAY	FRIDAY	SATURDAY
		1	2	3	4 Hanukkah Begins at Sundown	5
6	7	8	9	10	11	12
13	14	15	16	17	18	19
20	21 First Day of Winter	22	23	24 Christmas Eve	25 Christmas Day	26
27	28	29	30	31 New Year's Eve		

TUESDAY, DECEMBER 1

Ezekiel 47–48 / 1 Peter 2:18–3:7 / Proverbs 23:1–9

Unfading Beauty

Wives, in the same way submit yourselves to your own husbands so that, if any of them do not believe the word, they may be won over without words by the behavior of their wives, when they see the purity and reverence of your lives. Your beauty should not come from outward adornment, such as elaborate hairstyles and the wearing of gold jewelry or fine clothes. Rather, it should be that of your inner self, the unfading beauty of a gentle and quiet spirit, which is of great worth in God's sight. For this is the way the holy women of the past who put their hope in God used to adorn themselves.

1 PETER 3:1–5 NIV

In a world so focused on appearances, we need to keep a good perspective. Does real, unfading beauty and a person's value come from outer appearance? Of course not. We all know people who follow the fashion and beauty trends and have horrible character. And we all know people who never follow fashion and beauty trends, but they seem to overflow with kindness and love for God and others—and that's truly beautiful. God focuses on the inner selves and hearts of people, not outward appearance, and we are called to do so as well—for both ourselves and others.

Heavenly Father, please help me not to care too much about outward appearances. I want to be known for unfading beauty that comes from my heart because I truly love You and others.

WEDNESDAY, DECEMBER 2

Daniel 1:1–2:23 / 1 Peter 3:8–4:19 / Proverbs 23:10–16

Bold, Brave Faith

The king assigned them a daily portion of the food that the king ate, and of the wine that he drank. They were to be educated for three years, and at the end of that time they were to stand before the king. Among these were Daniel, Hananiah, Mishael, and Azariah of the tribe of Judah. . . . But Daniel resolved that he would not defile himself with the king's food, or with the wine that he drank. Therefore he asked the chief of the eunuchs to allow him not to defile himself. And God gave Daniel favor and compassion.
Daniel 1:5–6, 8–9 esv

The book of Daniel holds several of the most incredible and well-known Bible stories—like the account of Daniel being thrown into the lions' den because he refused to stop praying to God. And the account of Daniel's friends Shadrach, Meshach, and Abednego, who were thrown into a furnace because they would not bow down to a false god. These stories and others about bold, brave faithfulness to God, even in the worst of situations, help us to be strong and courageous in our faith as well.

Heavenly Father, thank You for the examples in Your Word of unwavering faith and the miracles that You worked because of that kind of steadfast faith. Let the accounts in the book of Daniel inspire and motivate me and keep me brave and bold.

THURSDAY, DECEMBER 3

Daniel 2:24–3:30 / 1 Peter 5 / Proverbs 23:17–25

Give God All Your Worries and Cares

Humble yourselves under the mighty power of God, and at the right time he will lift you up in honor. Give all your worries and cares to God, for he cares about you.

1 PETER 5:6–7 NLT

When we're feeling exhausted, stressed out, and struggling and someone comes along and says, "Let me help you with that"—it's such a blessing! And that's what Jesus says to us about our every worry and care. He wants to take them from us and give us peace and rest instead. He says, "Come to Me, all of you who work and have heavy loads. I will give you rest. Follow My teachings and learn from Me. I am gentle and do not have pride. You will have rest for your souls. For My way of carrying a load is easy and My load is not heavy" (Matthew 11:28–30 NLV). We can talk to Him about our problems. He cares about each and every one. As we tell Him our needs and confess any sins and follow His ways and learn from Him, we will have all the peace, rest, and care we truly need.

Dear Jesus, thank You for wanting to take away all my worries and cares. I crave the peace and rest that only You can provide as I love You, learn from You, and live for You.

Hanukkah Begins at Sundown   FRIDAY, DECEMBER 4

Daniel 4 / 2 Peter 1 / Proverbs 23:26–35

Make Every Effort

For this very reason, make every effort to supplement your faith with virtue, and virtue with knowledge, and knowledge with self-control, and self-control with steadfastness, and steadfastness with godliness, and godliness with brotherly affection, and brotherly affection with love. For if these qualities are yours and are increasing, they keep you from being ineffective or unfruitful in the knowledge of our Lord Jesus Christ.

2 PETER 1:5–8 ESV

All kinds of tests and surveys will try to tell us about personality—what number we are or what letter combination we are and a whole bunch of info about our strengths and weaknesses and interactions with others. Those are interesting to evaluate ourselves, for sure, but the bottom line is that we all have very unique personality traits from an infinitely creative, good God! What matters most is that we're aware of how He designed us and that we ask Him to use the personality and the gifts He's given to serve Him in the ways He wants for us. Our heavenly Father can continually grow and develop us with new traits, gifts, and skills according to His will—if we make every effort to let Him! We need to stay in constant good relationship and communication with Him. We need to never stop praying to Him, learning from Him, and serving Him.

Heavenly Father, help me to learn more about myself and how You designed me as I keep in close relationship with You.

SATURDAY, DECEMBER 5

Daniel 5 / 2 Peter 2 / Proverbs 24:1–18

There Will Be False Teachers

But there were also false prophets in Israel, just as there will be false teachers among you. They will cleverly teach destructive heresies and even deny the Master who bought them. In this way, they will bring sudden destruction on themselves. Many will follow their evil teaching and shameful immorality. And because of these teachers, the way of truth will be slandered. . . . But God condemned them long ago, and their destruction will not be delayed.

2 PETER 2:1–3 NLT

Believers throughout history had to beware of false teachers, and so do we today. They look harmless like sheep, but in reality they are dangerous like wolves. But the Holy Spirit within us will help recognize and protect against them. Jesus taught us,

> *"You can identify them by their fruit, that is, by the way they act. Can you pick grapes from thornbushes, or figs from thistles? A good tree produces good fruit, and a bad tree produces bad fruit. A good tree can't produce bad fruit, and a bad tree can't produce good fruit. So every tree that does not produce good fruit is chopped down and thrown into the fire. Yes, just as you can identify a tree by its fruit, so you can identify people by their actions." (Matthew 7:16–20 NLT)*

Lord Jesus, please help me to beware of false teachers who want to draw people away from true saving relationship with You. Help me to recognize them and protect myself and others from them.

SUNDAY, DECEMBER 6

Daniel 6:1–7:14 / 2 Peter 3 / Proverbs 24:19–27

Our Lord's Patience

A day is like a thousand years to the Lord, and a thousand years is like a day. The Lord isn't really being slow about his promise, as some people think. No, he is being patient for your sake. He does not want anyone to be destroyed, but wants everyone to repent. But the day of the Lord will come as unexpectedly as a thief. Then the heavens will pass away with a terrible noise, and the very elements themselves will disappear in fire, and the earth and everything on it will be found to deserve judgment. . . . But we are looking forward to the new heavens and new earth he has promised, a world filled with God's righteousness. And so, dear friends, while you are waiting for these things to happen, make every effort to be found living peaceful lives that are pure and blameless in his sight. And remember, our Lord's patience gives people time to be saved.

2 PETER 3:8–10, 13–15 NLT

We sometimes grow discouraged wondering how long this crazy world can go on and when exactly Jesus will return like He promised. But this passage reminds us to peacefully have hope. The Lord knows exactly what He's doing in His perfect timing. He's so loving that He's giving every possible chance for people to be saved.

> *Lord Jesus, I'm so impatient sometimes,*
> *but it's so good that You are not. I trust in Your*
> *timing. Thank You for Your merciful, saving love.*

MONDAY, DECEMBER 7

> Daniel 7:15–8:27 / 1 John 1:1–2:17 / Proverbs 24:28–34

If We Confess Our Sins

If we walk in the light, as he is in the light, we have fellowship with one another, and the blood of Jesus his Son cleanses us from all sin. If we say we have no sin, we deceive ourselves, and the truth is not in us. If we confess our sins, he is faithful and just to forgive us our sins and to cleanse us from all unrighteousness. If we say we have not sinned, we make him a liar, and his word is not in us.

1 John 1:7–10 ESV

We all have sins to admit, and we need to bring them out of darkness and into the light as we confess them to God. To pretend like we don't sin sometimes is just ridiculous because God knows anyway. He is aware of everything about us, even every single thought we have (Psalm 139:1–6). So we must take time to pray and repent and ask forgiveness from our sins rather than try to hide them or act like they're harmless. We can have such gratitude and peace as we confess and then remember that Psalm 103:12 (NLV) promises, "He has taken our sins from us as far as the east is from the west."

Heavenly Father, I confess these sins to you today: _____. I ask for Your forgiveness. Thank You for being such a merciful God who removes my sin and gives endless grace and love!

TUESDAY, DECEMBER 8

Daniel 9–10 / 1 John 2:18–29 / Proverbs 25:1–12

When Jesus Returns

You have received the Holy Spirit, and he lives within you, so you don't need anyone to teach you what is true. For the Spirit teaches you everything you need to know, and what he teaches is true—it is not a lie. So just as he has taught you, remain in fellowship with Christ. And now, dear children, remain in fellowship with Christ so that when he returns, you will be full of courage and not shrink back from him in shame.

1 John 2:27–28 NLT

The Bible assures us that Jesus could return to earth at any moment, and no person knows exactly when that will be (see Matthew 24:36–44 and Luke 12:35–40, for example). As believers, we're supposed to be watchful and ready. That might make some people anxious or scared, but for those of us who stay close to Jesus, it should be exciting and should fill us with joy and hope! If we keep good fellowship, staying in close connection with Jesus, then we will be confident and full of courage when Jesus returns to earth.

Lord Jesus, I want to watch and wait for You with no fear, only joy and hope and excitement! Please cover my sins with Your mercy and grace, and keep me in close fellowship with You.

WEDNESDAY, DECEMBER 9

Daniel 11–12 / 1 John 3:1–12 / Proverbs 25:13–17

God's Children

See how very much our Father loves us, for he calls us his children, and that is what we are! But the people who belong to this world don't recognize that we are God's children because they don't know him. Dear friends, we are already God's children, but he has not yet shown us what we will be like when Christ appears. But we do know that we will be like him, for we will see him as he really is. And all who have this eager expectation will keep themselves pure, just as he is pure.

1 JOHN 3:1–3 NLT

"We're all God's children," we sometimes hear well-meaning people say. And in a sense it's true because God is the Creator of all. But to be truly called His child means we have come to Him in repentance of our sin, asking Jesus to be our Savior. That is what brings us into right relationship with our perfect heavenly Father. And while we who love Jesus are God's children right this very moment, we also have so much more to look forward to when Jesus returns again!

Heavenly Father, I'm so grateful that I am truly Your child because Jesus is my one and only Savior from sin. Please help me to understand and share this truth with others so that they also will choose Jesus and truly become Your children too.

THURSDAY, DECEMBER 10

Hosea 1–3 / 1 John 3:13–4:16 / Proverbs 25:18–28

He Who Is in Us Is Greater

You are from God and have overcome them,
for he who is in you is greater than he who is in the world.
1 JOHN 4:4 ESV

This is such a simple yet powerful scripture to memorize and repeat when we're worried about anything at all. Our enemy, the devil, is instigating all kinds of evil in this world. And we unfortunately will be under attack from him sometimes, in all sorts of different ways—through anxiety attacks, through someone else's cruel words or actions, through injustice and terrible times for our families and friends, through loss and sickness, and on and on. But no matter how strong the enemy and his evil seem against us and our loved ones, they are never stronger than the power of God within us through the Holy Spirit. We can't ever forget that. We can call on God to help us be strong, peaceful, and patient and to help us see how He is working and taking care of us through it all.

Almighty God, deep down I know You are stronger than anything that comes against me and my loved ones. But I do forget that truth sometimes and become overwhelmed with worry, and I'm sorry. Please remind me, fill me with Your power and peace, and do the fighting for me.

FRIDAY, DECEMBER 11

> Hosea 4–6 / 1 John 4:17–5:21 / Proverbs 26:1–16

Hosea Means "Salvation"

"Come, let us return to the LORD. He has torn us to pieces; now he will heal us. He has injured us; now he will bandage our wounds. In just a short time he will restore us, so that we may live in his presence. Oh, that we might know the LORD! Let us press on to know him. He will respond to us as surely as the arrival of dawn or the coming of rains in early spring."

HOSEA 6:1–3 NLT

The book of Hosea tells how the prophet Hosea obeyed God's instructions to marry a woman named Gomer, who was unfaithful to him. But when Gomer ran away, God told Hosea to pursue her and win her back. God used this as an example to show how even while the people of Israel were unfaithful to God, He still loved them and wanted to win them back to Him. How fitting that the prophet Hosea's name means "salvation." We have a God who loves and pursues us and wants people to be saved from their sin.

Father, teach me and draw me closer to You as I read and learn from the book of Hosea. Remind me that You want salvation and eternal life for Your people, and no sin is too great for You to forgive—because Your Son, Jesus, paid the price for it on the cross.

SATURDAY, DECEMBER 12

Hosea 7–10 / 2 John / Proverbs 26:17–21

This Is Love

I ask that we love one another. And this is love: that we walk in obedience to his commands. As you have heard from the beginning, his command is that you walk in love. I say this because many deceivers, who do not acknowledge Jesus Christ as coming in the flesh, have gone out into the world. Any such person is the deceiver and the antichrist. Watch out that you do not lose what we have worked for, but that you may be rewarded fully. Anyone who runs ahead and does not continue in the teaching of Christ does not have God; whoever continues in the teaching has both the Father and the Son. If anyone comes to you and does not bring this teaching, do not take them into your house or welcome them. Anyone who welcomes them shares in their wicked work.

2 JOHN 5–11 NIV

Our world tries to tell us all kinds of ideas about what love means, but they are dishonest and meaningless unless they match up with God's Word. We can't truly love others as our Creator God intended unless we obey His commands and continue in His teachings. And we're given firm warnings to keep strong boundaries to avoid and guard against the wicked work of false teachers who lead us away from God's truth about real love.

Heavenly Father, help me to know what real love is and to continue in Your teaching every day of my life. Give me wisdom and discernment to recognize and demolish false teaching.

SUNDAY, DECEMBER 13

Hosea 11–14 / 3 John / Proverbs 26:22–27:9

Follow Only What Is Good

I wrote to the church about this, but Diotrephes, who loves to be the leader, refuses to have anything to do with us. When I come, I will report some of the things he is doing and the evil accusations he is making against us. Not only does he refuse to welcome the traveling teachers, he also tells others not to help them. And when they do help, he puts them out of the church. Dear friend, don't let this bad example influence you. Follow only what is good. Remember that those who do good prove that they are God's children, and those who do evil prove that they do not know God.

3 JOHN 9–11 NLT

It's nothing new that there are leaders in some churches who have no business being Christian leaders at all. That's sad and frustrating, for sure, but John writes instruction and encouragement to us here to not let bad examples influence us. Through their actions, God will show us the proof regarding who are truly His children and His chosen leaders. As we stay close to our heavenly Father and ask Him for wisdom and discernment, He will guide us well to "follow only what is good."

Heavenly Father, help me not to grow too discouraged by so-called Christians who are setting bad examples. Help me to recognize them, call them out, and avoid them. Lead me to fellowship with and learn from Your humble, sincere followers and the ones You have truly called and equipped to be leaders and teachers.

MONDAY, DECEMBER 14

Joel 1:1–2:17 / Jude / Proverbs 27:10–17

Build to Stand Strong

You, dear friends, must build each other up in your most holy faith, pray in the power of the Holy Spirit, and await the mercy of our Lord Jesus Christ, who will bring you eternal life. In this way, you will keep yourselves safe in God's love. And you must show mercy to those whose faith is wavering. Rescue others by snatching them from the flames of judgment. Show mercy to still others, but do so with great caution, hating the sins that contaminate their lives. Now all glory to God, who is able to keep you from falling away and will bring you with great joy into his glorious presence without a single fault.

JUDE 20–24 NLT

No building can stand for long unless it has a strong foundation. And in the same kind of way, our lives need a strong foundation of faith in the one true God. Otherwise, we can easily be overwhelmed and destroyed by sin and stress and anxiety and all the hard things of this broken world. Prayer is a major source of support as we build lives of faith with strong foundations as followers of Jesus. Spending time in God's Word, learning at a whole-Bible-teaching church, serving God by serving others, and having fellowship with other Christians are all major sources of strength and support too.

Heavenly Father, I want to build intentionally so that I can always stand strong in my faith in You. Help me to pray to and learn from and serve You every day of my life.

TUESDAY, DECEMBER 15

Joel 2:18–3:21 / Revelation 1:1–2:11 / Proverbs 27:18–27

Revelation from Jesus Christ

The revelation of Jesus Christ, which God gave him to show to his servants the things that must soon take place. He made it known by sending his angel to his servant John, who bore witness to the word of God and to the testimony of Jesus Christ, even to all that he saw. Blessed is the one who reads aloud the words of this prophecy, and blessed are those who hear, and who keep what is written in it, for the time is near.
REVELATION 1:1–3 ESV

The book of Revelation can be intimidating, but a super-quick summary is this: God sent an angel to John, one of Jesus' original twelve disciples, to give him visions to record. These visions were full of prophecy, imagery, and symbols of what will happen in the last days of this world. And all of that can often seem very confusing and scary. But the main point of Revelation is that Jesus is coming soon to gather those of us who love and trust in Him to take us to a new home to live peacefully and perfectly forever.

> *Heavenly Father, please help me not to feel intimidated by reading Revelation. Please give me understanding and wisdom and blessings as I read it. Teach me how to apply its truth to my life and to share it with others.*

WEDNESDAY, DECEMBER 16

Amos 1:1–4:5 / Revelation 2:12–29 / Proverbs 28:1–8

God's Message Through Amos

This message was given to Amos, a shepherd from the town of Tekoa in Judah. He received this message in visions two years before the earthquake, when Uzziah was king of Judah and Jeroboam II, the son of Jehoash, was king of Israel. This is what he saw and heard: "The Lord's voice will roar from Zion and thunder from Jerusalem!"

Amos 1:1–2 nlt

In the book of Amos we learn from a shepherd and a fruit picker, just an ordinary guy who became a prophet for God. This shows us that God can use anyone He chooses, no matter their background, to do His good works. Amos warned God's people that even though things were going well for them overall, they would soon be judged for the sin they were holding on to. The message from Amos reminds us as well that we should look for any sin we're holding on to in our lives and confess it to God and ask for forgiveness. God loves to give mercy and blessing when we repent from wrongdoing and come close to Him again.

Heavenly Father, thank You that You use regular people to accomplish Your will and share Your truth. Please use me as You see fit. Please help me as I learn from the message of Amos to turn away from sin and keep close to You.

THURSDAY, DECEMBER 17

Amos 4:6–6:14 / Revelation 3 / Proverbs 28:9–16

Come to the Lord and Live!

"Come back to me and live! Don't worship at the pagan altars at Bethel...." Come back to the Lord and live! Otherwise, he will roar through Israel like a fire, devouring you completely.... It is the Lord who created the stars, the Pleiades and Orion. He turns darkness into morning and day into night. He draws up water from the oceans and pours it down as rain on the land. The Lord is his name!

Amos 5:4–6, 8 NLT

"Come back to the Lord and live!" Our hearts might be aching for loved ones we know today who we wish would also heed the pleadings and warnings of the prophet Amos. As we pray for them, we should also examine our own hearts and lives to search out any sins we need to run and repent from so we can come back to the Lord for cleansing and refreshing. We rejoice in the fact that we know the one true almighty Creator God, and the Lord is His name! What an incredible blessing that He knows our names and loves us so much!

> *Almighty God, I love and praise You! I come to You and live! I pray for all of those who need to come back to You and live as well. Soften their hearts and humble them. Let them listen to Your Holy Spirit calling. Help me to do whatever I can to lovingly point them to salvation in You.*

FRIDAY, DECEMBER 18

Amos 7–9 / Revelation 4:1–5:5 / Proverbs 28:17–24

Holy, Holy, Holy

*The one sitting on the throne was as brilliant as gemstones. . . .
In the center and around the throne were four living beings. . . .
Each of these living beings had six wings, and their wings were
covered all over with eyes, inside and out. Day after day and night
after night they keep on saying, "Holy, holy, holy is the Lord God,
the Almighty—the one who always was, who is, and who is still
to come." Whenever the living beings give glory and honor and
thanks to the one sitting on the throne (the one who lives forever
and ever), the twenty-four elders fall down and worship the one
sitting on the throne (the one who lives forever and ever). And they
lay their crowns before the throne and say, "You are worthy, O Lord
our God, to receive glory and honor and power. For you created all
things, and they exist because you created what you pleased."*

REVELATION 4:3, 6, 8–11 NLT

The descriptions in Revelation just give us a small glimpse of what worship in heaven is like—obviously unlike anything we've ever experienced here on earth. It's hard for our earthly minds to fully comprehend the Bible's pictures of heaven, but it will be beyond amazing to be in the presence of the one true holy God who deserves all honor and praise!

*Father God, You are holy, holy, holy! You are worthy of
all honor and glory and power, and I'm so grateful for
my confident hope of heaven forever with You!*

SATURDAY, DECEMBER 19

Obadiah–Jonah / Revelation 5:6–14 / Proverbs 28:25–28

Lessons We Learn from Jonah

Now the word of the LORD came to Jonah the son of Amittai, saying, "Arise, go to Nineveh, that great city, and call out against it, for their evil has come up before me." But Jonah rose to flee to Tarshish from the presence of the LORD. He went down to Joppa and found a ship going to Tarshish. So he paid the fare and went down into it, to go with them to Tarshish, away from the presence of the LORD.

JONAH 1:1–3 ESV

Jonah being swallowed by a big fish is one of the most well-known stories in the Bible, and it's good for us to regularly remember and reflect on why he found himself in such a bizarre predicament. Jonah ended up inside that fish belly because he didn't want to be God's prophet to Nineveh, and so he disobeyed. We disobey God sometimes too, and we can learn much wisdom and warning from Jonah's story—especially that even if He must take extreme and strange measures, God will show us how we've sinned and disobeyed and help us to get back on the path He has planned for us.

Heavenly Father, please help me to heed the lessons and warnings from the account of Jonah. Remind me that disobedience to You results in negative consequences. And while following Your good directions might not always be easy, it will always ultimately result in the best kind of peace and blessing.

SUNDAY, DECEMBER 20

Micah 1:1–4:5 / Revelation 6:1–7:8 / Proverbs 29:1–8

Micah's Message from God

The word of the LORD that came to Micah of Moresheth in the days of Jotham, Ahaz, and Hezekiah, kings of Judah, which he saw concerning Samaria and Jerusalem. Hear, you peoples, all of you; pay attention, O earth, and all that is in it, and let the Lord GOD be a witness against you, the Lord from his holy temple. For behold, the LORD is coming out of his place, and will come down and tread upon the high places of the earth. And the mountains will melt under him, and the valleys will split open, like wax before the fire, like waters poured down a steep place.

MICAH 1:1–4 ESV

When the nations of Judah and Israel were worshipping idols instead of God and mistreating and abusing poor and needy people, God warned them through the prophet Micah that they would be destroyed for loving idols and cruelty. Micah gave a message from God of both judgment and mercy, showing that God hates sin but never hates the people who sin. He wants each person to confess their sin and come back close to Him for forgiveness and love. He wants us to honor Him with the ways we act fairly and kindly and humbly in our lives.

Heavenly Father, thank You for loving people so much and for being so generous with mercy and forgiveness in spite of our sin. Please help me to share Your compassion and grace with others.

MONDAY, DECEMBER 21   *First Day of Winter*

Micah 4:6–7:20 / Revelation 7:9–8:13 / Proverbs 29:9–14

Micah's Confidence

As for me, I look to the LORD for help. I wait confidently for God to save me, and my God will certainly hear me. Do not gloat over me, my enemies! For though I fall, I will rise again. Though I sit in darkness, the LORD will be my light. I will be patient as the LORD punishes me, for I have sinned against him. But after that, he will take up my case and give me justice for all I have suffered from my enemies. The LORD will bring me into the light, and I will see his righteousness.

MICAH 7:7–9 NLT

The prophet Micah knew he would sometimes have to wait on God. But he was sure our Lord would always help him triumph with justice over enemies. In times of darkness, Micah believed that the Lord would be his light. And even in times of punishment, Micah never stopped trusting God, and he took ownership of his sin that caused negative consequences. Through it all Micah was certain that ultimately our Lord would save him and make him righteous. Micah clearly had great confidence in God—and it's exactly the kind of confidence that we should imitate.

Heavenly Father, thank You for Micah's example of strong, bold, confident faith in You. Keep me coming back to Your Word to be inspired and taught by Your prophets.

TUESDAY, DECEMBER 22

Nahum 1–3 / Revelation 9–10 / Proverbs 29:15–23

Nahum's Warnings

This message concerning Nineveh came as a vision to Nahum, who lived in Elkosh. The Lord is a jealous God, filled with vengeance and rage. He takes revenge on all who oppose him and continues to rage against his enemies! The Lord is slow to get angry, but his power is great, and he never lets the guilty go unpunished.
NAHUM 1:1–3 NLT

God had sent Jonah to preach to the people of Nineveh, and the people of Nineveh did repent and God had mercy on them. But one hundred years later, they were back to sinning again in all the ways that caused all the trouble for them the first time. So God sent a message through the prophet Nahum that God was going to destroy Nineveh, and He did destroy it about fifty years after Nahum's warning. Through Nahum's message, we must learn and remember that God is good and is a refuge for all who trust and follow Him. But He will destroy those who hate Him.

Heavenly Father, You have so much patience and give so much warning for people to turn away from sin. Help us all to heed Your warnings well and not take them for granted. Help us not to forget that while You are patient and compassionate, You are also good and just, and there will be terrible consequences for not turning to You for forgiveness and salvation.

WEDNESDAY, DECEMBER 23

Habakkuk 1–3 / Revelation 11 / Proverbs 29:24–27

Confusion and Questions

Though the fig tree should not blossom, nor fruit be on the vines, the produce of the olive fail and the fields yield no food, the flock be cut off from the fold and there be no herd in the stalls, yet I will rejoice in the LORD; I will take joy in the God of my salvation. GOD, the Lord, is my strength.
HABAKKUK 3:17–19 ESV

We can all relate to asking God questions, so we can all relate to Habakkuk, as he was a prophet of God who had lots of questions. He started out writing, "O Lord, how long must I call for help before You will hear?" (1:2 NLV).

We also sometimes wonder why we must wait so long on God or why He doesn't answer our prayers the way we want. And so we can learn from Habakkuk that even though this prophet never got the exact answers he was hoping for from God, he got answers that reminded him of this: God is all-powerful and always good. He will work out His perfect plans in His perfect timing. In our own lives today, we must choose to keep trusting what Habakkuk learned and the message he shared.

Heavenly Father, I admit I grow so impatient and confused sometimes as I wait on You. Please fill me with peace and hope and patience as I choose to keep trusting in Your greatness and goodness and perfect timing.

Christmas Eve   THURSDAY, DECEMBER 24

Zephaniah 1–3 / Revelation 12 / Proverbs 30:1–6

A Mighty One Who Will Save

The LORD has taken away the judgments against you; he has cleared away your enemies. The King of Israel, the LORD, is in your midst; you shall never again fear evil. On that day it shall be said to Jerusalem: "Fear not, O Zion; let not your hands grow weak. The LORD your God is in your midst, a mighty one who will save; he will rejoice over you with gladness; he will quiet you by his love; he will exult over you with loud singing."

ZEPHANIAH 3:15–17 ESV

In the first chapter of the book of Zephaniah, this prophet preached a sobering message from God about awful suffering and judgment for the nation of Judah and all nations who turn away from God. Then he begged the people to turn to God before it was too late. And in the last chapter, Zephaniah preached that despite all the bad things that will happen to those who reject God, there is great hope in God's promises for all who turn to Him to love and trust and obey Him. Our world certainly needs these warnings and also this hope today, and we need to keep asking God for the wise ways He wants us to share His messages with others who don't yet know and love Him.

> *Heavenly Father, Your messages through Your prophets are not always easy messages to hear and learn from, but please help me to heed them well and share them with others according to Your will.*

FRIDAY, DECEMBER 25

Christmas Day

Haggai 1–2 / Revelation 13:1–14:13 / Proverbs 30:7–16

Get Back to Work

"'Be strong, all you people of the land,' declares the Lord, 'and work. For I am with you,' declares the Lord Almighty. 'This is what I covenanted with you when you came out of Egypt. And my Spirit remains among you. Do not fear.'"

HAGGAI 2:4–5 NIV

The prophet Haggai had a message for God's people to get back to work rebuilding the temple in Jerusalem. They'd had a good strong start, but then they got distracted and let the project sit—for *years*. We all can probably relate to that kind of thing. Sometimes we get excited about good things God has asked us to do, and we enjoy them for a while, and then we get off track to do our own thing instead. So the book of Haggai can be a great reminder to us to keep asking God what His will is and then never give up on His good plans for us. And if we do get off track, we can turn to God for help once again.

Heavenly Father, I've strayed away from Your will and the good works You have planned for me. Please forgive me. I want to get back on Your perfect paths. Please lead me and help me to follow You faithfully step-by-step, day by day.

SATURDAY, DECEMBER 26

Zechariah 1–4 / Revelation 14:14–16:3 / Proverbs 30:17–20

Return to the Lord

The word of the Lord came to the prophet Zechariah son of Berekiah, the son of Iddo: "The Lord was very angry with your ancestors. Therefore tell the people: This is what the Lord Almighty says: 'Return to me,' declares the Lord Almighty, 'and I will return to you,' says the Lord Almighty. Do not be like your ancestors, to whom the earlier prophets proclaimed: This is what the Lord Almighty says: 'Turn from your evil ways and your evil practices.' But they would not listen or pay attention to me, declares the Lord."

ZECHARIAH 1:1–4 NIV

Like Haggai, the prophet Zechariah preached to God's people to encourage them to finish the good work they had started of rebuilding the temple in Jerusalem. He told them it would one day be the home of the Messiah Himself—the Savior they were hoping for, who we know is Jesus Christ. Zechariah told the people about all the blessings that would come to the Jewish people once they had obeyed and finished their good work. Zechariah's message can motivate us to do the good work God has for us too. When we do, we will be blessed, and we have already been so very blessed by the gift of Jesus Christ as our Savior from sin.

Heavenly Father, thank You for Zechariah's message. Let it remind me to return to You so quickly if I ever start to stray away.

SUNDAY, DECEMBER 27

Zechariah 5–8 / Revelation 16:4–21 / Proverbs 30:21–28

Learning from God's Creation

There are four things that are small on the earth, but they are very wise: The ants are not a strong people, but they store up their food in the summer. The badgers are not a strong people, but they make their houses in the rocks. The locusts have no king, but they go as an army. You can take the lizard in your hands, but it is found in kings' houses.

PROVERBS 30:24–28 NLV

We can learn so much from the incredible designs and behaviors in nature and creatures in the world around us. Proverbs 30 gives us just a few examples: Ants teach us about being prepared. Badgers know how to build wisely. Locusts are great at orderly cooperation. And lizards are bold and brave. When we acknowledge our heavenly Father as one true Creator God and praise Him for His amazing creation and ask Him to teach us through it, He is happy to oblige! Job 12:7, 9–10 (ESV) says, "Ask the beasts, and they will teach you; the birds of the heavens, and they will tell you. . . . Who among all these does not know that the hand of the LORD has done this? In his hand is the life of every living thing and the breath of all mankind."

Almighty God, Your designs in nature are incredible! I'm in awe of You and I praise You! Please let me learn from creation and grow closer to You as I do!

MONDAY, DECEMBER 28

Zechariah 9–11 / Revelation 17:1–18:8 / Proverbs 30:29–33

God Pursues and Strengthens His People

"I will strengthen Judah and save Israel; I will restore them because of my compassion. It will be as though I had never rejected them, for I am the LORD their God, who will hear their cries. The people of Israel will become like mighty warriors, and their hearts will be made happy as if by wine. Their children, too, will see it and be glad; their hearts will rejoice in the LORD. When I whistle to them, they will come running, for I have redeemed them. From the few who are left, they will grow as numerous as they were before. Though I have scattered them like seeds among the nations, they will still remember me in distant lands. . . . By my power I will make my people strong, and by my authority they will go wherever they wish. I, the LORD, have spoken!"

ZECHARIAH 10:6–9, 12 NLT

God will never forget His people, and that includes those of us today who have become His children because we believe in Jesus as Lord and Savior. He knows where we are and what we're doing at all times. He pursues us and restores and strengthens us exactly when and how we need.

Heavenly Father, thank You for Your compassion and care of Your people throughout all of history and right now and in the future. I'm so grateful to be Your child forever.

TUESDAY, DECEMBER 29

Zechariah 12–14 / Revelation 18:9–24 / Proverbs 31:1–9

Day of the Lord

A day of the Lord is coming when the things of much worth taken from you will be divided among you. For I will gather all the nations against Jerusalem to battle. The city will be taken. The houses will be robbed. The women will be taken against their will. And half of the city will be taken away to a strange land. But the rest of the people will not be taken away from the city. Then the Lord will go out and fight against those nations, as when He fights on a day of battle. . . . The Lord will be King over all the earth. On that day the Lord will be the only one, and His name the only one.

ZECHARIAH 14:1–3, 9 NLV

The final chapter of Zechariah describes the eventual total victory of our Lord. He will be King over all the earth. He has the day planned, and only His people will be safe and cared for. We don't know God's timeline, so it's simply our job now to be watching and waiting and serving and loving others in Jesus' name—and hopefully helping many more to be saved alongside us on the day of the Lord.

Lord Jesus, I believe Your day is coming, and I'm ready. Please help me to share Your truth and love in the ways You want—to help more people be ready too.

WEDNESDAY, DECEMBER 30

Malachi 1–2 / Revelation 19–20 / Proverbs 31:10–17

God's Message Through Malachi

This is the message that the Lord gave to Israel through the prophet Malachi. "I have always loved you," says the Lord. But you retort, "Really? How have you loved us?" And the Lord replies, "This is how I showed my love for you: I loved your ancestor Jacob, but I rejected his brother, Esau, and devastated his hill country. I turned Esau's inheritance into a desert for jackals." Esau's descendants in Edom may say, "We have been shattered, but we will rebuild the ruins." But the Lord of Heaven's Armies replies, "They may try to rebuild, but I will demolish them again. Their country will be known as 'The Land of Wickedness,' and their people will be called 'The People with Whom the Lord Is Forever Angry.' When you see the destruction for yourselves, you will say, 'Truly, the Lord's greatness reaches far beyond Israel's borders!'"

MALACHI 1:1–5 NLT

Malachi was a prophet of God who spoke a message to help bring God's dearly loved people back into close relationship with Him. God wants that for us too. He loves us dearly and is upset when we choose sin that puts distance between Him and us and hurts our relationship with Him. He wants us to confess and turn away from sin so that we can be close and in good communication with Him again.

Heavenly Father, please teach me and mature me and bring me into closer relationship with You as I learn from the message of Malachi in Your Word.

THURSDAY, DECEMBER 31

New Year's Eve

Malachi 3–4 / Revelation 21–22 / Proverbs 31:18–31

Everything New

I heard a loud voice from the throne saying, "Look! God's dwelling place is now among the people, and he will dwell with them. They will be his people, and God himself will be with them and be their God. 'He will wipe every tear from their eyes. There will be no more death' or mourning or crying or pain, for the old order of things has passed away." He who was seated on the throne said, "I am making everything new!"
REVELATION 21:3–5 NIV

What will our forever life be like? The Bible tells us some detail but not a whole lot about the new heaven and earth. Maybe our earthly minds can't possibly understand how awesome it will be! First Corinthians 2:9 (NLT) says, "No eye has seen, no ear has heard, and no mind has imagined what God has prepared for those who love him." And God's Word also tells us that everything will be new and magnificent in architecture and beauty. Even better, there will be no more death or sorrow or crying or pain. We will have peace and joy forever as God makes His home among us. What a blessing it is to be able to dream about the perfect future that God guarantees us!

Heavenly Father, I believe in Your promises that the new heaven and earth will be fantastic beyond my best imagination. I thank You and praise You for the perfect paradise You promise to all who love You and trust Jesus as their one and only Savior.

Contributors

Annie Barkley made up her first story at the ripe old age of two when she asked her mom to write it down for her. Since then she has read and written many words as a student, newspaper reporter, author, and editor. She has a passion for making God's Word come to life for readers through devotions and Bible study. Annie loves snow (which is a good thing because she lives in Ohio), wearing scarves, eating sushi, playing Scrabble, and spending time with friends and family. Annie's devotions appear in February, June, and October.

Kelly McIntosh is a wife, twin mom, and editor from Ohio. She loves books, the beach, and everything about autumn (but mostly pumpkin spice lattes). Kelly's devotions appear in January, May, and September.

Carey Scott is an author, speaker, and certified Biblical Life Coach. With authenticity and humor, she challenges women to be real, not perfect, and reminds them to trust God as their source above all else. Carey is a single mom with two kids in college and lives in Colorado. You can find her at CareyScott.org. Carey's devotions appear in March, July, and November.

JoAnne Simmons is a writer and editor who's in awe of God's love and the ways He guides and provides. Her favorite things include coffee shops, libraries, the Bible, good grammar, being a wife and mom, dogs, music, Disney World, punctuation, church, the beach, and many dear family and friends—but not in that order. If her family weren't so loving and flexible, she'd be in big trouble; and if God's mercies weren't new every morning, she'd never get out of bed. JoAnne's devotions appear in April, August, and December.

Encouragement for Every (Busy) Day!

The Daily 5-Minute Bible Study for Women

In just 5 minutes, you will *Read* (minutes 1–2), *Understand* (minute 3), *Apply* (minute 4), and *Pray* (minute 5) God's Word through meaningful, focused Bible study. *The 5-Minute Bible Study for Women* includes 365 Bible studies that will speak to your heart in a powerful way.

Flexible Casebound / 978-1-63609-126-6

Find this and More from Barbour Publishing at Your Favorite Bookstore or www.barbourbooks.com

BARBOUR
PUBLISHING

Journal Your Way to a Stronger Prayer Life

A Year of God's Goodness:
A Prayer and Praise Tracker for Women

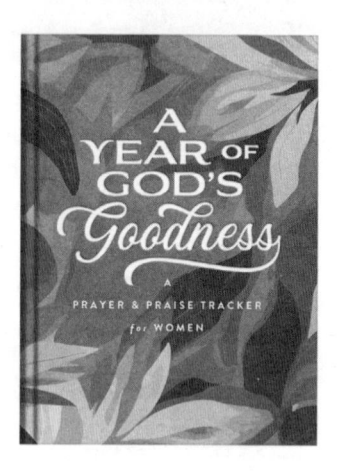

This unique prayer and praise tracker features scripture, faith-building quotes, and encouraging prayers alongside dedicated space to journal prayer requests, answers to prayers, and praise of God's goodness every day. At the end of the year, you will see just how your Father God worked in your life—in beautiful and sometimes unexpected ways!

Hardback / 979-8-89151-039-5

Find This and More from Barbour Publishing at Your Favorite Bookstore or www.barbourbooks.com

BARBOUR PUBLISHING